# Essays on Immigration

### EDITED BY
### BOB BLAISDELL

## DOVER PUBLICATIONS, INC.
### Mineola, New York

# DOVER THRIFT EDITIONS

GENERAL EDITOR: MARY CAROLYN WALDREP
EDITOR OF THIS VOLUME: JANET BAINE KOPITO

ACKNOWLEDGMENTS: SEE PAGES XI–XII.

## Copyright

## Bibliographical Note

*Essays on Immigration* is a new compilation, first published by Dover Publications, Inc., in 2013. Bob Blaisdell has selected and arranged the essays and provided all the introductory material. For the sake of authenticity, inconsistencies in spelling, capitalization, and punctuation have been retained in the texts, unless otherwise noted.

## Library of Congress Cataloging-in-Publication Data

Essays on immigration / edited by Bob Blaisdell.
     p. cm. — (Dover thrift editions)
   Summary: "The concept of immigration remains central to American culture, past and present. This original anthology surveys the experience from a wide range of cultural and historical viewpoints, ranging from the 17th to 21st centuries. Contributors include Hector St. John de Crevecoeur, Jacob Riis, Edwidge Danticat, Junot Díaz, and many others"—Provided by publisher.
   ISBN 13: 978-0-486-48902-5 (pbk.)
   ISBN 10: 0-486-48902-7 (pbk.)
    1. Immigrants—United States—History.  2. United States—Emigration and immigration—History.
3. Emigration and immigration—Social aspects.  I. Blaisdell, Robert.

JV6450.E77 2013
304.8'73—dc23

                                                                    2012030162

Manufactured in the United States by Courier Corporation
48902702     2014
www.doverpublications.com

# Note

EVEN IN THE best of circumstances, immigration is difficult. With money in hand, a job awaiting him, and a willing wife and enthusiastic children, the Englishman Horace J. Bridges describes his anxiety in *On Becoming an American: Some Meditations of a Newly Naturalized Immigrant* (1919):

> To our little ones the day was one of joyous adventure. They were faring forth into the unknown. The ship, with her marvels of science and ingenuity, was all a wonder and a wild desire. With the full flooding life of boyhood, they found the fleeting moment all-sufficient and all-entrancing. Yesterday was dead; today was so thrilling that tomorrow was unthought of. America was a magic name, like Atlantis or the Hesperides. They wondered at the grave faces of father and mother, for they recked nothing of the pain to their parents that had attended the ploughing up of the soil of heart and memory, and the plucking out of roots that had struck so much deeper than consciousness. Nor did they yet dream of the years of anxious pre-occupation which we already felt ahead,—the long labor of mental and spiritual adjustment to a new world of hearts and faces, a new physical environment, new manners and customs, ideals and standards, new life-values, a new social order. Fortunate were the youngsters, in that the change came for them at a time when their world was fluent and plastic, when they had not yet grappled other souls to theirs with the steel hoops of long love and firm-set will; when each new companion was welcome as the morning, and each older face no harder to part from than yesterday when it is gone!

While immigrant children understand America in ways their parents may not be able to and have experiences their parents won't understand, the parents themselves have experiences that their own parents won't sympathize with or understand: "Why does raising Delia create such a difficulty?" wonders Dympna Ugwu-Oju.

Because I sense that my success or failure as an individual ultimately rests on what becomes of my only daughter. Because each day, each activity, each decision concerning her is a tug-of-war between the old and the new, between my Ibo and American selves, between my mother and me. Because where and when I was growing up, children, especially daughters, accepted their parents' authority completely, without question or resentment. Therein lies my conflict, one that I'm sure is shared by millions of immigrant women who, like me, are raising American-born daughters. We are having to deal with situations that our mothers could not have anticipated.

Among the surprising situations are the challenges of one's very name being met with confusion: "All of us immigrants knew that moving to America would be fraught with challenges, but none of us thought that our names would be such an obstacle. How could our parents have ever imagined that someday we would end up in a country where monosyllabic names reign supreme, a land where 'William' is shortened to 'Bill,' where 'Susan' becomes 'Sue,' and 'Richard' somehow evolves into 'Dick'? America is a great country, but nobody without a mask and a cape has a $z$ in his name," muses Firoozeh Dumas, whose family emigrated from Iran.

A child's idea of "back home" is less a longing than a desire to reconnect with family history and culture. Returning "home" then, as an adult, can be an embarrassing and sometimes comical adventure as, for instance, Junot Díaz discovers when many years later he returns to the Dominican Republic, the country that he claims but which doesn't return the favor; the people in their native lands now consider them Americans: "What I wanted more than anything was to be recognized as the long-lost son I was, but that wasn't going to happen. Not after nearly twenty years. Nobody believed I was Dominican! You? one cabdriver said incredulously, and then turned and laughed. That's doubtful. Instead of being welcomed with open arms, I was overcharged for everything and called un americano."

All of the writers included here describe their experiences and thoughts on the transformation wrought from a new life in America, with its joys, agonies, and awakenings. Almost four hundred years ago, Richard Frethorne, an indentured servant from England, found himself in a strange and terrifying land—a settlement near Jamestown, Virginia—and begged his parents to buy him back out of service:

> Wherefore my humble request is that I may be freed out of this Egypt, or else that it would please you to send over some beef and some cheese and butter, or any eating victuals will be good trading and I will send you all that I make of it. Only I would entreat the gain to redeem me, or if you please to speak to the rest of the parishioners, that a small gathering may be made to send me these things or else to redeem me suddenly, for I am almost pined and I want clothes, for truly I have but one shirt, one ragged one and one pair of hose, one pair of shoes, one suit of clothes, so that I am like to perish for want of succor and relief.

Hundreds of thousands of other indentured servants from Europe and slaves from Africa soon came to America and necessarily suffered even more than those who had chosen to come.

Not all who came, but almost all, grew to love their new land. In the middle of the eighteenth century Gottlieb Mittelberger wrote a tract about the ploys of those in Pennsylvania trying to entice emigrants from Germany, a journey that he argued usually ended in death or indenture:

> When a husband or wife has died at sea, when the ship has made more than half of her trip, the survivor must pay or serve not only for himself or herself, but also for the deceased. When both parents have died over half-way at sea, their children, especially when they are young and have nothing to pawn or to pay, must stand for their own and their parents' passage, and serve till they are twenty-one years old.

The great writer Hector St. John Crevecoeur, on the other hand, was thrilled by the social and political experiment being conducted in eighteenth-century America—the marvelous mix of European cultures in a new geography:

Here the rewards of his industry follow with equal steps the progress of his labor; his labor is founded on the basis of nature, self-interest; can it want a stronger allurement? Wives and children, who before in vain demanded of him a morsel of bread, now, fat and frolicsome, gladly help their father to clear those fields whence exuberant crops are to arise to feed and to clothe them all; without any part being claimed, either by a despotic prince, a rich abbot, or a mighty lord. Here religion demands but little of him; a small voluntary salary to the minister, and gratitude to God; can he refuse these? The American is a new man, who acts upon new principles; he must therefore entertain new ideas, and form new opinions. From involuntary idleness, servile dependence, penury, and useless labor, he has passed to toils of a very different nature, rewarded by ample subsistence.—This is an American.

Fortunately, in these essays there is more joy than agony; there is accomplishment, achievement, a successful stretch across the sea and land to another place, a place that for almost all of the immigrants was fully, if incorrectly, imagined before the emigration. "Now and then," recalls Rocco Corresca, "I had heard things about America—that it was a far-off country where everybody was rich and that Italians went there and made plenty of money, so that they could return to Italy and live in pleasure ever after." But the American initiation into a new life, a world of new customs, can be incidentally humiliating. Language and social customs, of course, are stumbling blocks for many. Abraham Rihbany, an immigrant from Syria, explains that "my struggles with the technicalities of language were not the only pains of my second birth into the new environment. The social readjustments were even more difficult to effect. Coming into the house in Syria, a guest removes his shoes from his feet at the door, but keeps his fez or turban on. It was no easy matter, therefore, for me, on going into an American home, to realize instantly which extremity to uncover."

Immigration can also be purposefully brutal, from the hazing of children in school to the lack of community support.

Until very lately the immigrant in Chicago, unless he had waiting friends, found no gateway open to him except the saloon, the brothel, the cheap lodging house and finally the 'lock up.' The agencies which began the assimilative process were all anti-social, greedy for their prey and, worst of all, the police was in league with them and protected them. There was nothing left to do but walk up and down in impotent rage and inveigh against a city which permitted its newest and most potential human material to be polluted, if not corrupted, at the very entrance into its life

remembers Edward Steiner.

There has also been the legal intimidation effected by governmental policies. The first official United States act against immigration (sometimes referred to as the "Chinese Exclusion Act") was the Immigration Act of 1882. Ever since, immigration has been a political topic, with political aims, with prevailing prejudices too often excluding or limiting non-Europeans or non-Christians. For many adult immigrants, the culture shock is dispiriting and distressing. Carlos Bulosan, from the Philippines, describes the disorientation of his early years:

I had picked hops with some Indians under the towering shadow of Mt. Rainier. I had pruned apples with dispossessed Americans in the rich deltas of the Columbia River. I had cut and packed asparagus in California. I had weeded peas with Japanese in Arizona. I had picked tomatoes with Negroes in Utah. Yet I felt that I did not belong in America. My departure from the Philippines was actually the breaking of my ground, the tearing up of my roots. As I stayed longer and searched farther, this feeling of not belonging became more acute, until it distorted my early vision of America. I did not know what part of America was mine, and my awareness of not belonging made me desperate and terribly lonely.

But other immigrants find a shorter route, and the desperation and loneliness dissipate with the fulfillment of a calling. And we see, after all, how quickly most of the accounts in this collection (a select group, of course, of talented authors and storytellers) find their feet and make their way into American life: "Sometimes I felt discouraged, for what was I—a stranger—to do in this city, where no one was interested in me and my plans? On the other hand, I had two hands which, though empty, were willing, and the will which directed me to 'ride on over all obstacles and win the race,'" writes Anna Hilda Louise Walther.

These essays show that the vitality and spirit of America is continuously renewed not for, but *because of,* immigrants. America without immigration is a stagnant pond. The ingenuity and positive spirit of America is a creation of those who imagine it into reality and perpetuate it. The most truly patriotic Americans we meet are usually immigrants who see what we descendants of immigrants too often take for granted. They see the belief in democracy and justice, in tolerance and inclusiveness. They keep America an open society. "My notion of the United States then, and for a few years after," remembers Louis Adamic, "was that it was a grand, amazing, somewhat fantastic place—the Golden Country—a sort of Paradise—the Land of Promise in more ways than one—huge beyond conception, thousands of miles across the ocean, untellably exciting, explosive, quite incomparable to the tiny, quiet, lovely Carniola; a place full of movement and turmoil, wherein things that were unimaginable and impossible in Blato happened daily as a matter of course. . . . In America everything was possible. There even the common people were 'citizens,' not 'subjects,' as they were in Austria and in most other European countries. A citizen, or even a non-citizen foreigner, could walk up to the President of the United States and pump his hand. Indeed, that seemed to be a custom in America."

But the history of North America also includes the ugly truths that between 1619 and 1808, hundreds of thousands of Africans were brought here not as immigrants but as slaves, and that for two centuries at least half of the Europeans who came to America were brought here not as immigrants but as indentured servants who worked for years before being released. Finally, there's the grim truth that the aboriginal inhabitants of the Americas had no immigration policy; that Europeans helped themselves to the land and resources without so much as a how-do-you-do, too many with a shameless sense of entitlement. Those of us who have non-Native American ancestors have much to be grateful for and humble about. As proud as we are of our non-American ancestors, we need to have some humility when we recall the various indigenous groups whose hospitality we took advantage of.

So we're in this America together, we immigrants and descendants of immigrants. Professor Paul Spickard, author of *Almost All Aliens: Immigration, Race, and Colonialism in American History and Identity*, concludes his important and critical work on a hopeful note: "One of the things we have most in common is that we all came here from some other place. That makes us all guests in this land. Perhaps it will also help us see each other as something like family, for we are all in this together."*

★ ★ ★

In acknowledgment, I thank Elizabeth Stone, Professor of English, Media and Communication Studies at Fordham University, for her suggestions on contemporary authors and for sharing her course materials. There are many previous anthologies from which I learned about the authors and works I have collected here. Gordon Hutner's excellent *Immigrant Voices: Twenty-Four Narratives on Becoming an American* (New York: Signet, 1999) is the best. Others include Angela Jane Fountas's *Waking Up American: Coming of Age Biculturally* (Emeryville, California: Seal Press, 2005), Arthur Mann's *Immigrants in American Life* (Boston: Houghton Mifflin, 1974), Thomas Dublin's *Immigrant Voices: New Lives in America, 1773–1986* (Urbana: University of Illinois Press, 1993), Diane Yen-Mei Wong's *Making Waves: An Anthology of Writings by and about Asian American Women* (Boston: Beacon Press, 1989), Ilan Stavans's *Becoming Americans: Four Centuries of Immigrant Writing* (New York: The Library of America, 2009), Meri Nana-Ama Danquah's *Becoming American: Personal Essays by First Generation Immigrant Women* (New York: Hyperion, 2000), and Tim Prchal and Tony Trigilio's *Visions and Divisions: American Immigration Literature, 1870–1930* (New Brunswick: Rutgers University Press, 2008).

—*Bob Blaisdell*
*New York City*
*February 2012*

---

*Paul Spickard. *Almost All Aliens: Immigration, Race, and Colonialism in American History and Identity.* New York: Routledge. 2007. 464.

# Acknowledgments

Louis Adamic:"Amerikansi in Carniola," from *Laughing in the Jungle: The Autobiography of an Immigrant in America*. New York: Harper and Row. 1932.

Sooyan Pribichevich: "In an American Factory," *Harper's Magazine*. September 1938.

Andres Aragon:"After the Death of Spain," from *First Generation: In the Word of Twentieth-Century American Immigrants*. Copyright © 1978, 1992 by June Namias. Used with permisson of the University of Illinois Press.

Nicholas Gerros:"Greek Horatio Alger," from *First Generation: In the Word of Twentieth-Century American Immigrants*. Copyright © 1978, 1992 by June Namias. Used with permisson of the University of Illinois Press.

Carlos Bulosan:"My Education," from *On Becoming Filipino: Selected Writings of Carlos Bulosan*. University of Washington Press. 1973.

Edwidge Danticat: "A New World Full of Strangers," from *American Me: Teens Write About the Immigrant Experience*. Edited by Marie Glancy O'Shea. New York: New Youth Connections. 2010.

Vladimir Vernikov: "Taxi from Hell," from *Confessions of a Russian Hack*. New York: Soho Press. 1991. Translated from the Russian by Tamara Glenny.

Dympna Ugwu-Oju: "Raising Delia," from *What Will My Mother Say: A Tribal African Girl Comes of Age in America*. Chicago: Bonus Books. 1995.

# Contents

# Essays on Immigration

# RICHARD FRETHORNE

*Letters from an Indentured Servant*
(England; 1623)

*Frethorne's misery, shared by many indentured servants in America, is clearly communicated in these letters from Virginia, near Jamestown. The first is to a "Mr. Bateman"; the second is to his parents, back in England. His father indentured him, which Frethorne would argue was his father's terrible misunderstanding of the desperate conditions under which he, Richard, would have to work. With an eye for business, he pleads for goods that he can resell and thereby purchase his release from the indenture contract. (I have corrected the fitful spelling of the time and added punctuation.)*

## Letter of March 5, 1623, to Mr. Bateman

Right Worthy, this is to let you understand that I am in a most miserable and pitiful case both for want of meat and want of clothes, for we had meal and provision for twenty and there is ten dead and yet our provision will not last till the *Seaflower* come in. For those servants that were there before us were almost pined [wasted away] and then they fell to feeding so hard of our provision that it killed them that were old Virginians as fast as the scurvy & bloody flux did kill us new Virginians, for they were in such a case by reason of the murder done all over the land that they could not plant anything at all and at every Plantation all of them for the most part were slain and their houses and goods burnt. Some the Indians kept alive and took them away with them, and now these two Indians that have taken do tell us that the Indians have 15 alive with them. Thus through their roguery the land is ruinated and spoiled, and it will not be so strong again not this 12 years, for at our plantation, of seven-score, there was but 22 left alive, and of all their houses there is but 2 left, and a piece of a church and our master doth say that 3,000 pounds will not make good our plantation again. And the merchants lost by it the last year, and they can get little or nothing this year, for we must plant but a

1

little Tobago, but all corn for bread, and when we have done if the rogues come and cut it from us as they have sent all the plantations word that they will have a bout with them, and then we shall quite be starved, for is it not a poor case when a pint of meal must serve a man 3 days as I have seen it since I came. Wherefore my humble request is that I may be freed out of this Egypt, or else that it would please you to send over some beef and some cheese and butter, or any eating victuals will be good trading and I will send you all that I make of it.

Only I would entreat the gain to redeem me, or if you please to speak to the rest of the parishioners, that a small gathering may be made to send me these things or else to redeem me suddenly, for I am almost pined and I want clothes, for truly I have but one shirt, one ragged one and one pair of hose, one pair of shoes, one suit of clothes, so that I am like to perish for want of succor and relief.

Therefore I beseech you and most humbly entreat and entirely at your merciful hands (not with Pharaoh's butler to forget me, as he did forget Joseph in the prison), but I entreat you to use the words of God ( Jeremiah in his 31st chapter and the 10th verse) where he sayeth, "I have surely heard Ephraim bemoaning himself," even so you may see me bemoaning myself. Wherefore I entreat you to follow his words in the latter end of the 20th verse of the same chapter, that is, "I will surely have mercy upon him," sayeth the Lord, so I beseech you to have mercy upon me, remembering what Solomon sayeth in the 35th chapter of Ecclesiastes and the 20th verse, that mercy is seasonable in the time of affliction and "as clouds of rain in the time of drought," so now mercy is seasonable to me at this time. I need not set down the words of Solomon in the 37th Ecclesiastes and the 6th verse because the Lord hath endued your heart with many of those blessings. And thus I commit you into the hands of almighty God and entreat you to help me so suddenly as you can. So in Christ.

Your poor servant in command,
*Richard Frethorne*

★ ★ ★

## Letter of March 20, April 2 and 3, 1623,
## to His Father and Mother

Loving and kind father and mother, my most humble duty remembered to you hoping in God of your good health, as I myself am not at the making hereof, this is to let you understand that I, your child, am in a most heavy case by reason of the nature of the country is such that it causeth much sickness, as the scurvy and the blood flux and divers other diseases, which maketh the body very poor and weak, and when we are sick there is nothing to comfort us. For since I came out of the ship, I never ate anything but peas, and loblollie (that is, watery gruel). As for deer or venison, I never saw any since I came into this land. There is indeed some fowl, but we are not allowed to go and get it, but must work hard both early and late for a mess of watery gruel and a mouthful of bread and beef. A mouthful of bread for a penny loaf must serve for four men, which is most pitiful. If you did know as much as I, when people cry out day and night, Oh, that they were in England, without their limbs, and would not care to lose any limb to be in England again. Yes, though they beg from door to door, for we live in fear of the enemy every hour, yet we have had a combat with them on the Sunday before Shrovetide, and we took two alive and make slaves of them, but it was by policy, for we are in great danger, for our plantation is very weak by reason of the dearth and sickness of the company. For we are but twenty for the merchants and they are half dead just; and we look every hour when two more should go, yet there came for other men yet to live with us, of which there is but one alive, and our lieutenant is dead, and his father, and his brother, and there was some 5 or 6 of the last year's 20, of which there is but 3 left, so that we are fain to get other men to plant with us, and yet we are but 32 to fight against 3,000 if they should come, and the nighest help we have is ten miles of us, and when the rogues overcame this place last, they slew 80 persons.

How then shall we do, for we lie even in their teeth. They may easily take us but that God is merciful, and can save with few as well as with many, as he showed to Gilead and like Gilead, soldiers, if they lap water, we drink water which is but weak, and I have nothing to comfort me, nor there is nothing to be gotten here but sickness and death, except that one had money to lay out in some things for profit. But I have nothing at all. No, not a shirt to my back, but two rags nor no clothes but one poor suit, nor but one pair of shoes, but one pair of stockings, but one cap, but two bands, my cloak is stolen by one of my own fellows, and to his dying hour would not tell me what he did with it, but some of my fellows saw him have butter and beef out of a ship, which my cloak I doubt paid for, so that I have not a penny, nor a pennyworth, to help me to either spice or sugar or strong waters, without the which one cannot live here. For as strong beer in England doth fatten and strengthen them, so water here doth wash and weaken these here, only keep life and soul together. But am not half a quarter so strong as I was in England, and all is for want of victuals, for I do protest unto you that I have eaten more in a day at home than I have allowed me here for a week.

You have given more than my day's allowance to a beggar at the door; and if Mr. Jackson had not relieved me, I should be in a poor case, but he like a father and she, like a loving mother, doth still help me, for when we go up to Jamestown that is 10 miles of us, there lie all the ships that come to the land, and there they must deliver their goods, and when we went up to town as it may be on Monday, at noon, and come there by night, then load the next day by noon and go home in the afternoon, and unload, and then away again in the night, and be up about midnight, then if it rained or blowed never so hard, we must lie in the boat on the water and have nothing but a little bread, for whence we go into the boat we have a loaf allowed to two men, and it is all if we stayed there two days, which is hard, and must lie all that while in the boat, but that Goodman Jackson pitied me and made me a cabin to lie in always when I come up, and he would give me some poor jacks home with me, which comforted me more than peas, or watery gruel. Oh, they be very godly folks, and love me very well, and will do anything for me, and he much marveled that you would send me a servant to the company. He saith I had been better knocked on the head, and indeed so I find it now to my great grief and misery, and saith, that if you love me you will redeem me suddenly, for which I do entreat and beg, and if you cannot get the merchants to redeem me for some little money, then for God's sake get a gathering or entreat some good folk to lay out some little sum of money, in meal and cheese and butter and beef, any eating meat will yield great profit.

Oil and vinegar is very good, but, Father, there is great loss in leaking. But for God's sake, send beef and cheese and butter or the more of one sort and none of another, but if you send cheese it must be very old cheese, and at the cheesemonger's you may buy good cheese for twopence farthing or halfpenny that will be liked very well. But if you send cheese you must have care how you pack it in barrels, and you must put cooper's chips between every cheese, or else the heat of the hold will rot them, and look whatsoever you send me, be it never so much, look what I make of it. I will deal truly with you, I will send it over and beg the profit to redeem me, and if I die of it, who hath promised he will.

If you send you must direct your letters to Goodman Jackson, at Jamestown, a gunsmith. You must set down his freight, because there be more of his name there; good Father, do not forget me, but have mercy and pity my miserable case. I know if you did but see me you would weep to see me, for I have but one suit, but it is a strange one, it is very well guarded, wherefore for God's sake pity me. I pity you to remember my love to all my friends and kindred. I hope all my brothers and sisters are in good health, and as for my part I have set down my resolution that certainly will be, that is, that the answer of this letter will be life or death to me. Good Father, send as soon as you can, and if you send me anything, let this be the mark.

ROT,

Richard Frethorne,

Martyns Hundred.

SOURCE: American Memory. The Thomas Jefferson Papers. Series 8. Virginia Records Manuscripts, 1606–1737. Edited by Susan Myra Kingsbury. Records of the Virginia Company, 1606–1626. Volume IV: Miscellaneous. [loc.gov/loc.mss/mtj.mtjbib026606]

# GOTTLIEB MITTELBERGER

*Journey to Pennsylvania*
(Germany; 1754)

*Mittelberger arrived in America in 1750 with his organ, the first of its kind in America, and became a teacher and organist. He was so disappointed by the conditions and circumstances of his immigration, however, that when he returned to the Duchy of Wurttemberg, Germany, in 1754, he wrote a short book describing his experiences and discouraging emigrants, particularly those considering indenture, from following in his footsteps. (The complete title of his book is: "Journey to Pennsylvania in the Year 1750 and Return to Germany in the Year 1754, Containing: Not Only a Description of the Country According to Its Present Condition, but Also a Detailed Account of the Sad and Unfortunate Circumstances of Most of the Germans That Have Emigrated or Are Emigrating to That Country.")*

When the ships have for the last time weighed their anchors near the city of Kaupp [Cowes] in Old England, the real misery begins with the long voyage. For from there the ships, unless they have good wind, must often sail eight, nine, ten to twelve weeks before they reach Philadelphia. But even with the best wind the voyage lasts seven weeks.

But during the voyage there is on board these ships terrible misery, stench, fumes, horror, vomiting, many kinds of sea-sickness, fever, dysentery, headache, heat, constipation, boils, scurvy, cancer, mouth-rot, and the like, all of which come from old and sharply salted food and meat, also from very bad and foul water, so that many die miserably.

Add to this want of provisions, hunger, thirst, frost, heat, damp-ness, anxiety, want, afflictions and lamentations, together with other trouble, as *c. v.* the lice abound so frightfully, especially on sick people, that they can be scraped off the body. The misery reaches the climax when a gale rages for two or three nights and days, so that everyone believes that the ship will go to the bottom with all human beings on board. In such a visitation the people cry and pray most piteously.

When in such a gale the sea rages and surges, so that the waves rise often like high mountains one above the other, and often tumble over the ship, so that one fears to go down with the ship; when the ship is constantly tossed from side to side by the storm and waves, so that no one can either walk, or sit, or lie, and the closely packed people in the berths are thereby tumbled over each other, both the sick and the well—it will be readily understood that many of these people, none of whom had been prepared for hardships, suffer so terribly from them that they do not survive it.

I myself had to pass through a severe illness at sea, and I best know how I felt at the time. These poor people often long for consolation, and I often entertained and comforted them with singing, praying and exhorting; and whenever it was possible and the winds and waves permitted it, I kept daily prayer-meetings with them on deck. Besides, I baptized five children in distress, because we had no ordained minister on board. I also held divine service every Sunday by reading sermons to the people; and when the dead were sunk in the water, I commended them and our souls to the mercy of God.

Among the healthy, impatience sometimes grows so great and cruel that one curses the other, or himself and the day of his birth, and sometimes come near killing each other. Misery and malice join each other, so that they cheat and rob one another. One always reproaches the other with having persuaded him to undertake the journey. Frequently children cry out against their parents, husbands against their wives and wives against their husbands, brothers and sisters, friends and acquaintances against each other. But most against the soul-traffickers.

Many sigh and cry: "Oh, that I were at home again, and if I had to lie in my pig-sty!" Or they say: "O God, if I only had a piece of good bread, or a good fresh drop of water." Many people whimper, sigh and cry piteously for their homes; most of them get home-sick. Many hundred people necessarily die and perish in such misery, and must be cast into the sea, which drives their relatives, or those who persuaded them to undertake the journey, to such despair that it is almost impossible to pacify and console them. In a word, the sighing and crying and lamenting on board the ship continues night and day, so as to cause the hearts even of the most hardened to bleed when they hear it.

No one can have an idea of the sufferings which women in confinement have to bear with their innocent children on board these ships. Few of this class escape with their lives; many a mother is cast into the water with her child as soon as she is dead. One day, just as we had a heavy gale, a woman in our ship, who was to give birth and could not give birth under the circumstances, was pushed through a loop-hole [port-hole] in the ship and dropped into the sea, because she was far in the rear of the ship and could not be brought forward.

Children from 1 to 7 years rarely survive the voyage; and many a time parents are compelled to see their children miserably suffer and die from hunger, thirst and sickness, and then to see them cast into the water. I witnessed such misery in no less than 32 children in our ship, all of whom were thrown into the sea. The parents grieve all the more since their children find no resting-place in the earth, but are devoured by the monsters of the sea. It is a notable fact that children, who have not yet had the measles or small-pocks, generally get them on board the ship, and mostly die of them.

Often a father is separated by death from his wife and children, or mothers from their little children, or even both parents from their children; and sometimes whole families die in quick succession; so that often many dead persons lie in the berths beside the living ones, especially when contagious diseases have broken out on board the ship.

Many other accidents happen on board these ships, especially by falling, whereby people are often made cripples and can never be set right again. Some have also fallen into the ocean.

That most of the people get sick is not surprising, because, in addition to all other trials and hardships, warm food is served only three times a week, the rations being very poor and very little. Such meals can hardly be eaten, on account of being so unclean. The water which is served out on the ships is often very black, thick and full of worms, so that one cannot drink it without loathing, even with the greatest thirst. O surely, one would often give much money at sea for a piece of good bread, or a drink of good water, not to say a drink of good wine, if it were only to be had. I myself experienced that sufficiently, I am sorry to say. Toward the end we were compelled to eat the ship's biscuit which had been spoiled long ago; though in a whole biscuit there was scarcely a piece the size of a dollar that had not been full of red worms and spiders' nests. Great hunger and thirst force us to eat and drink everything; but many a one does so at the risk of his life. The sea-water cannot be drunk, because it is salt and bitter as gall. If this were not so, such a voyage could be made with less expense and without so many hardships.

At length, when, after a long and tedious voyage, the ships come in sight of land, so that the promontories can be seen, which the people were so eager and anxious to see, all creep from below on deck to see the land from afar, and they weep for joy, and pray and sing, thanking and praising God. The sight of the land makes the people on board the ship, especially the sick and the half dead, alive again, so that their hearts leap within them; they shout and rejoice, and are content to bear their misery in patience, in the hope that they may soon reach the land in safety. But alas!

When the ships have landed at Philadelphia after their long voyage, no one is permitted to leave them except those who pay for their passage or can give good security; the others, who cannot pay, must remain on board the ships till they are purchased, and are released from the ships by their purchasers. The sick always fare the worst, for the healthy are naturally preferred and purchased first; and so the sick and wretched must often remain on board in front of the city for two or three weeks, and frequently die, whereas many a one, if he could pay his debt and were permitted to leave the ship immediately, might recover and remain alive.

Before I describe how this traffic in human flesh is conducted, I must mention how much the journey to Philadelphia or Pennsylvania costs.

A person over 10 years pays for the passage from Rotterdam to Philadelphia 10 pounds, or 60 florins. Children from 5 to 10 years pay half price, 5 pounds or 30 florins. All children under 5 years are free. For these prices the passengers are conveyed to Philadelphia, and, as long as they are at sea, provided with food, though with very poor, as has been shown above.

But this is only the sea-passage; the other costs on land, from home to Rotterdam, including the passage on the Rhine, are at least 40 florins, no matter how economically one may live. No account is here taken of extraordinary contingencies. I may safely assert that, with the greatest economy, many passengers have spent 200 florins from home to Philadelphia.

The sale of human beings in the market on board the ship is carried on thus: Every day Englishmen, Dutchmen and High-German people come from the city of Philadelphia and other places, in part from a great distance, say 20, 30, or 40 hours away, and go on board the newly arrived ship that has brought and offers for sale passengers from Europe, and select among the healthy persons such as they deem suitable for their business, and bargain with them how long they will serve for their passage money, which most of them are still in debt for. When they have come to an agreement, it happens that adult persons bind themselves in writing to serve three, four, five or six years for the amount due by them, according to their age and strength. But very young people, from ten to fifteen years, must serve till they are twenty-one years old.

Many parents must sell and trade away their children like so many head of cattle; for if their children take the debt upon themselves, the parents can leave the ship free and unrestrained; but as the parents often do not know where and to what people their children are going, it often happens that such parents and children, after leaving the ship, do not see each other again for many years, perhaps no more in all their lives.

When people arrive who cannot make themselves free, but have children under five years, the parents cannot free themselves by them; for such children must be given to somebody without compensation to be brought up, and they must serve for their bringing up till they are twenty-one years old. Children from five to ten years, who pay half price for their passage, viz. thirty florins, must likewise serve for it till they are twenty-one years of age; they cannot, therefore, redeem their parents by taking the debt of the latter upon themselves. But children above ten years can take part of their parents' debt upon themselves.

A woman must stand for her husband if he arrives sick, and in like manner a man for his sick wife, and take the debt upon herself or himself, and thus serve five to six years not alone for his or her own debt, but also for that of the sick husband or wife. But if both are sick, such persons are sent from the ship to the sick-house, but not until it appears probable that they will find no purchasers. As soon as they are well again they must serve for their passage, or pay if they have means.

It often happens that whole families, husband, wife, and children, are separated by being sold to different purchasers, especially when they have not paid any part of their passage money.

When a husband or wife has died at sea, when the ship has made more than half of her trip, the survivor must pay or serve not only for himself or herself, but also for the deceased.

When both parents have died over half-way at sea, their children, especially when they are young and have nothing to pawn or to pay, must stand for their own and their parents' passage, and serve till they are twenty-one years old. When one has served his or her term, he or she is entitled to a new suit of clothes at parting; and if it has been so stipulated, a man gets in addition a horse, a woman, a cow.

When a serf has an opportunity to marry in this country, he or she must pay for each year which he or she would have yet to serve, 5 to 6 pounds. But many a one who has thus purchased and paid for his bride, has subsequently repented his bargain, so that he would gladly have returned his exorbitantly dear ware, and lost the money besides.

If someone in this country runs away from his master who has treated him harshly, he cannot get far. Good provision has been made for such cases, so that a runaway is soon recovered. He who detains or returns a deserter receives a good reward.

If such a runaway has been away from his master one day, he must serve for it as a punishment a week, for a week a month, and for a month half a year. But if the master will not keep the runaway after he has got him back, he may sell him for so many years as he would have to serve him yet.

Work and labor in this new and wild land are very hard and manifold, and many a one who came there in his old age must work very hard to his end for his bread. I will not speak of young people. Work mostly consists in cutting wood, felling oak-trees, rooting out, or as they say there, clearing large tracts of forest. Such forests, being cleared, are then laid out for fields and meadows. From the best hewn wood, fences are made around the new fields; for there all meadows, orchards and fruit-fields, are surrounded and fenced in with planks made of thickly split wood, laid one above the other, as in zigzag lines, and within such enclosures, horses, cattle, and sheep, are permitted to graze.

Our Europeans, who are purchased, must always work hard, for new fields are constantly laid out; and so they learn that stumps of oak-trees are in America certainly as hard as in Germany. In this hot land they fully experience in their own persons what God has imposed on man for his sin and disobedience; for in Genesis we read the words: In the sweat of thy brow shalt thou eat bread.

Who therefore wishes to earn his bread in a Christian and honest way, and cannot earn it in his fatherland otherwise than by the work of his hands, let him do so in his own country, and not in America; for he will not fare better in America. However hard he may be compelled to work in his fatherland, he will surely find it quite as hard, if not harder, in the new country. Besides, there is not only the long and arduous journey lasting half a year, during which he has to suffer, more than with the hardest work; he has also spent about 200 florins which no one will refund to him. If he has so much money, it will slip out of his hands; if he has it not, he must work his debt off as a slave and poor serf. Therefore let everyone stay in his own country and support himself and his family honestly. Besides I say that those who suffer themselves to be persuaded and enticed away by the man-thieves, are very foolish if they believe that roasted pigeons will fly into their mouths in America or Pennsylvania without their working for them.

How miserably and wretchedly so many thousand German families have fared, 1) since they lost all their cash means in consequence of the long and tedious journey; 2) because many of them died miserably and were thrown into the water; 3) because, on account of their great poverty, most of these families after reaching the land are separated from each other and sold far away from each other, the young and the old. And the saddest of all this is that parents must generally give away their minor children without receiving a compensation for them; inasmuch as such children never see or meet their fathers, mothers, brothers or sisters again, and as many of them are not raised in any Christian faith by the people to whom they are given.

[. . .]

Frequently many letters are entrusted in Pennsylvania and other English colonies to newlanders who return to the old country. When they get to Holland, they have these letters opened, or they open them themselves, and if anyone has written the truth, his letter is either rewritten so as to suit the purpose of these harpies, or simply destroyed. While in Pennsylvania, I myself heard such men-thieves say that there were [those] enough in Holland, ready to furnish them for a small consideration counterfeits of any seal, and who could perfectly forge any handwriting. They can imitate all characters, marks and tokens so admirably that even he whose handwriting they have imitated must acknowledge it to be his own. By means of such practices they deceive even people who are not credulous, thus playing their nefarious tricks in a covert manner. They say to their confidants that this is the best way to induce the people to emigrate. I myself came very near being deceived.

Some great merchants in Holland attempted not to let me continue my journey home, but to induce me by stratagem or force to return to England and America. For they not only told me verbally in Rotterdam, but even tried to prove to me by writing from Amsterdam, that my wife and child, together with my sister-in-law and many countrymen, had embarked for Philadelphia with the last transport last summer. They told me very accurately the names of my wife and child, how old and tall they were, and that my wife had said her husband had been an organist in Pennsylvania for four years; they also showed me my wife's name in a letter, and told me with what ship and captain had sailed from Amsterdam, and that my wife was lodged with four other women in berth No. 22, which circumstantial communication had the effect of making one exceedingly confused and irresolute. But I read to them letters from my wife in which she plainly said that she would never in all her life go there without me, on the contrary that she eagerly awaited my return. I said that I had written to her again that I had made up my mind to return, God willing, to Germany next year, wherefore I could not possibly believe all this. The merchants then produced witnesses, which made me so perplexed that I did not know what to believe or to do.

At length, however, after mature deliberation, and no doubt by divine direction, I came to the conclusion that, inasmuch as I had already the greater part of my arduous journey, viz. 1400 hours way, behind me, and had arrived at the borders of Germany, I would now in God's name continue and finish my journey, which I did, and thus, thanks to the Most High, I have escaped this great temptation. For I came to see that all that I had been told and shown in Holland with respect to my family had been untrue, as I found my wife and child safe at home. If I had believed those seducers of the people, and had returned to England and America, not only would this account of my journey not have been published so soon, but I should, perhaps, never have met my family again in this world. Those frequently mentioned men-thieves, as I subsequently learned, gave an accurate account of me and my wife to the merchants in Holland, and the newlanders tried a second time to persuade my wife to follow them. The merchants no doubt thought that, if I returned home, I should reveal their whole nefarious traffic and the deplorable condition of the numerous families that emigrated and rushed into their ruin, and that I should thereby cause great damage to their shipping interests and their traffic in human flesh.

I must state here something that I have forgotten above. As soon as the ships that bring passengers from Europe have cast their anchors in the port of Philadelphia, all male persons of fifteen years and upward are placed on the following morning into a boat and led two by two to the courthouse or town hall of the city. There they must take the oath of allegiance to the Crown of Great Britain. This being done, they are taken in the same manner back to the ships. Then the traffic in human souls begins, as related above. I only add that in purchasing these people no one asks for references as to good character or an honorable discharge. If anyone had escaped the gallows, and had the rope still dangling around his neck, or if he had left both his ears in Europe, nothing would be put in his way in Pennsylvania. But if he is again caught in wrong-doing, he is hopelessly lost. For gallows' birds and wheel candidates, Pennsylvania is, therefore, a desirable land.

SOURCE: *Journey to Pennsylvania in the Year 1750 and Return to Germany in the Year 1754.* Translated from the German by Carl Theo. Eben. Philadelphia: John Jos. McVey. 1898.

# HECTOR ST. JOHN DE CREVECOEUR

*What Is an American?*
(France; 1782)

*These excerpts are taken from Letter III of Crevecoeur's famous account,*
Letters from an American Farmer. *Crevecoeur (1735–1813) moved to
America in 1754, where he married and then cultivated his farm in New
York along the Hudson River. His book inspired many Americans, and in his
own time inspired many emigrants in his home country of France. Unfortunately, shortly after its publication, while he was traveling abroad, Crevecoeur's
farm was destroyed and his wife died. In 1790 he returned to France, where
he lived until his death.*

I wish I could be acquainted with the feelings and thoughts which
must agitate the heart and present themselves to the mind of an
enlightened Englishman, when he first lands on this continent. He
must greatly rejoice that he lived at a time to see this fair country discovered and settled; he must necessarily feel a share of national pride,
when he views the chain of settlements which embellishes these
extended shores. When he says to himself, this is the work of my
countrymen, who, when convulsed by factions, afflicted by a variety
of miseries and wants, restless and impatient, took refuge here. They
brought along with them their national genius, to which they principally owe what liberty they enjoy, and what substance they possess.
Here he sees the industry of his native country displayed in a new
manner, and traces in their works the embrios of all the arts, sciences,
and ingenuity which flourish in Europe. Here he beholds fair cities,
substantial villages, extensive fields, an immense country filled with
decent houses, good roads, orchards, meadows, and bridges, where
an hundred years ago all was wild, woody and uncultivated! What a
train of pleasing ideas this fair spectacle must suggest; it is a prospect
which must inspire a good citizen with the most heartfelt pleasure.

The difficulty consists in the manner of viewing so extensive a
scene. He is arrived on a new continent; a modern society offers itself

to his contemplation, different from what he had hitherto seen. It is not composed, as in Europe, of great lords who possess everything and of a herd of people who have nothing. Here are no aristocratical families, no courts, no kings, no bishops, no ecclesiastical dominion, no invisible power giving to a few a very visible one; no great manufacturers employing thousands, no great refinements of luxury. The rich and the poor are not so far removed from each other as they are in Europe. Some few towns excepted, we are all tillers of the earth, from Nova Scotia to West Florida. We are a people of cultivators, scattered over an immense territory communicating with each other by means of good roads and navigable rivers, united by the silken bands of mild government, all respecting the laws, without dreading their power, because they are equitable. We are all animated with the spirit of an industry which is unfettered and unrestrained, because each person works for himself. If he travels through our rural districts he views not the hostile castle, and the haughty mansion, contrasted with the clay-built hut and miserable cabin, where cattle and men help to keep each other warm, and dwell in meanness, smoke, and indigence. A pleasing uniformity of decent competence appears throughout our habitations. The meanest of our log-houses is a dry and comfortable habitation. Lawyer or merchant are the fairest titles our towns afford; that of a farmer is the only appellation of the rural inhabitants of our country.

It must take some time ere he can reconcile himself to our dictionary, which is but short in words of dignity, and names of honor. (There, on a Sunday, he sees a congregation of respectable farmers and their wives, all clad in neat homespun, well mounted, or riding in their own humble wagons. There is not among them an esquire, saving the unlettered magistrate. There he sees a parson as simple as his flock, a farmer who does not riot on the labor of others. We have no princes, for whom we toil, starve, and bleed: we are the most perfect society now existing in the world. Here man is free; as he ought to be; nor is this pleasing equality so transitory as many others are. Many ages will not see the shores of our great lakes replenished with inland nations, nor the unknown bounds of North America entirely peopled. Who can tell how far it extends? Who can tell the millions of men whom it will feed and contain? for no European foot has as yet traveled half the extent of this mighty continent!

The next wish of this traveler will be to know whence came all these people? They are mixture of English, Scotch, Irish, French,

Dutch, Germans, and Swedes. From this promiscuous breed, that race now called Americans have arisen. The eastern provinces must indeed be excepted, as being the unmixed descendants of Englishmen. I have heard many wish that they had been more intermixed also: for my part, I am no wisher, and think it much better as it has happened. They exhibit a most conspicuous figure in this great and variegated picture; they too enter for a great share in the pleasing perspective displayed in these thirteen provinces. I know it is fashionable to reflect on them, but I respect them for what they have done; for the accuracy and wisdom with which they have settled their territory; for the decency of their manners; for their early love of letters; their ancient college, the first in this hemisphere; for their industry; which to me who am but a farmer, is the criterion of everything. There never was a people, situated as they are, who with so ungrateful a soil have done more in so short a time. Do you think that the monarchical ingredients which are more prevalent in other governments, have purged them from all foul stains? Their histories assert the contrary.

In this great American asylum, the poor of Europe have by some means met together, and in consequence of various causes; to what purpose should they ask one another what countrymen they are? Alas, two thirds of them had no country. Can a wretch who wanders about, who works and starves, whose life is a continual scene of sore affliction or pinching penury; can that man call England or any other kingdom his country? A country that had no bread for him, whose fields procured him no harvest, who met with nothing but the frowns of the rich, the severity of the laws, with jails and punishments; who owned not a single foot of the extensive surface of this planet? No! urged by a variety of motives, here they came. Everything has tended to regenerate them; new laws, a new mode of living, a new social system; here they are become men: in Europe they were as so many useless plants, wanting vegetative mould, and refreshing showers; they withered, and were mowed down by want, hunger, and war; but now by the power of transplantation, like all other plants they have taken root and flourished! Formerly they were not numbered in any civil lists of their country, except in those of the poor; here they rank as citizens.

By what invisible power has this surprising metamorphosis been performed? By that of the laws and that of their industry. The laws, the indulgent laws, protect them as they arrive, stamping on them the symbol of adoption; they receive ample rewards for their labors; these accumulated rewards procure them lands; those lands confer on them the title of freemen, and to that title every benefit is affixed which men can possibly require. This is the great operation daily performed by our laws. From whence proceed these laws? From our government. Whence the government? It is derived from the original genius and strong desire of the people ratified and confirmed by the crown. This is the great chain which links us all, this is the picture which every province exhibits, Nova Scotia excepted. There the crown has done all; either there were no people who had genius, or it was not much attended to: the consequence is, that the province is very thinly inhabited indeed; the power of the crown in conjunction with the musketos has prevented men from settling there. Yet some parts of it flourished once, and it contained a mild harmless set of people. But for the fault of a few leaders, the whole were banished. The greatest political error the crown ever committed in America, was to cut off men from a country which wanted nothing but men!

What attachment can a poor European emigrant have for a country where he had nothing? The knowledge of the language, the love of a few kindred as poor as himself, were the only cords that tied him: his country is now that which gives him land, bread, protection, and consequence: *Ubi panis ibi patria,** is the motto of all emigrants. What then is the American, this new man? He is either an European, or the descendant of an European, hence that strange mixture of blood, which you will find in no other country. I could point out to you a family whose grandfather was an Englishman, whose wife was Dutch, whose son married a French woman, and whose present four sons have now four wives of different nations. He is an American, who leaving behind him all his ancient prejudices and manners, receives new ones from the new mode of life he has embraced, the new government he obeys, and the new rank he holds.

He becomes an American by being received in the broad lap of our great Alma Mater. Here individuals of all nations are melted into a new race of men, whose labors and posterity will one day cause great changes in the world. Americans are the western pilgrims, who are carrying along with them that great mass of arts, sciences, vigour, and industry which began long since in the east; they will finish the great circle. The Americans were once scattered all over Europe; here they are incorporated into one of the finest systems of population

*\*Ubi panis ibi patria,* Latin for "Where the bread is is where my country is."

which has ever appeared, and which will hereafter become distinct
by the power of the different climates they inhabit. The American
ought therefore to love this country much better than that wherein
either he or his forefathers were born. Here the rewards of his industry follow with equal steps the progress of his labor; his labor is
founded on the basis of nature, self-interest; can it want a stronger allurement? Wives and children, who before in vain demanded of him
a morsel of bread, now, fat and frolicsome, gladly help their father to
clear those fields whence exuberant crops are to arise to feed and to
clothe them all; without any part being claimed, either by a despotic
prince, a rich abbot, or a mighty lord. Here religion demands but
little of him; a small voluntary salary to the minister, and gratitude
to God; can he refuse these? The American is a new man, who acts
upon new principles; he must therefore entertain new ideas, and
form new opinions. From involuntary idleness, servile dependence,
penury, and useless labor, he has passed to toils of a very different
nature, rewarded by ample subsistence.—This is an American.

[. . .]

As I have endeavoured to shew you how Europeans become
Americans; it may not be disagreeable to shew you likewise how
the various Christian sects introduced, wear out, and how religious
indifference becomes prevalent. When any considerable number of
a particular sect happen to dwell contiguous to each other, they immediately erect a temple, and there worship the Divinity agreeably
to their own peculiar ideas. Nobody disturbs them. If any new sect
springs up in Europe, it may happen that many of its professors will
come and settle in America. As they bring their zeal with them, they
are at liberty to make proselytes if they can, and to build a meeting and to follow the dictates of their consciences; for neither the
government nor any other power interferes. If they are peaceable
subjects, and are industrious, what is it to their neighbors how and in
what manner they think fit to address their prayers to the Supreme
Being? But if the sectaries are not settled close together, if they are
mixed with other denominations, their zeal will cool for want of
fuel, and will be extinguished in a little time. Then the Americans
become as to religion, what they are as to country, allied to all. In
them the name of Englishman, Frenchman, and European is lost, and
in like manner, the strict modes of Christianity as practised in Europe
are lost also. This effect will extend itself still farther hereafter, and
though this may appear to you as a strange idea, yet it is a very true

one. I shall be able perhaps hereafter to explain myself better, in the meanwhile, let the following example serve as my first justification.

Let us suppose you and I to be traveling; we observe that in this house, to the right, lives a Catholic, who prays to God as he has been taught, and believes in transubstantion; he works and raises wheat, he has a large family of children, all hale and robust; his belief, his prayers offend nobody. About one mile farther on the same road, his next neighbor may be a good honest plodding German Lutheran, who addresses himself to the same God, the God of all, agreeably to the modes he has been educated in, and believes in consubstantia- tion; by so doing he scandalizes nobody; he also works in his fields, embellishes the earth, clears swamps, &c. What has the world to do with his Lutheran principles? He persecutes nobody, and nobody persecutes him, he visits his neighbors, and his neighbors visit him. Next to him lives a seceder, the most enthusiastic of all sectaries; his zeal is hot and fiery, but separated as he is from others of the same complexion, he has no congregation of his own to resort to, where he might cabal and mingle religious pride with worldly obstinacy. He likewise raises good crops, his house is handsomely painted, his orchard is one of the fairest in the neighborhood.

How does it concern the welfare of the country, or of the province at large, what this man's religious sentiments are, or really whether he has any at all? He is a good farmer, he is a sober, peaceable, good citizen: William Penn himself would not wish for more. This is the visible character, the invisible one is only guessed at, and is nobody's business. Next again lives a Low Dutchman, who implicitly believes the rules laid down by the synod of Dort. He conceives no other idea of a clergyman than that of an hired man; if he does his work well he will pay him the stipulated sum; if not he will dismiss him, and do without his sermons, and let his church be shut up for years. But not- withstanding this coarse idea, you will find his house and farm to be the neatest in all the country; and you will judge by his wagon and fat horses, that he thinks more of the affairs of this world than of those of the next. He is sober and laborious, therefore he is all he ought to be as to the affairs of this life; as for those of the next, he must trust to the great Creator. Each of these people instruct their children as well as they can, but these instructions are feeble compared to those which are given to the youth of the poorest class in Europe. Their children will therefore grow up less zealous and more indifferent in matters of religion than their parents. The foolish vanity, or rather the fury of making Proselytes, is unknown here; they have no time. The seasons call for all their attention, and thus in a few years, this mixed neighborhood will exhibit a strange religious medley, that will be neither pure Catholicism nor pure Calvinism. A very perceptible indifference even in the first generation, will become apparent; and it may happen that the daughter of the Catholic will marry the son of the seceder, and settle by themselves at a distance from their parents. What religious education will they give their children? A very imperfect one. If there happens to be in the neighborhood any place of worship, we will suppose a Quaker's meeting; rather than not shew their fine clothes, they will go to it, and some of them may perhaps attach themselves to that society. Others will remain in a perfect state of indifference; the children of these zealous parents will not be able to tell what their religious principles are, and their grandchildren still less. The neighborhood of a place of worship generally leads them to it, and the action of going thither, is the strongest evidence they can give of their attachment to any sect.

The Quakers are the only people who retain a fondness for their own mode of worship; for be they ever so far separated from each other, they hold a sort of communion with the society, and seldom depart from its rules, at least in this country. Thus all sects are mixed as well as all nations; thus religious indifference is imperceptibly disseminated from one end of the continent to the other; which is at present one of the strongest characteristics of the Americans. Where this will reach no one can tell, perhaps it may leave a vacuum fit to receive other systems. Persecution, religious pride, the love of contradiction, are the food of what the world commonly calls religion. These motives have ceased here: zeal in Europe is confined; here it evaporates in the great distance it has to travel; there it is a grain of powder inclosed, here it burns away in the open air, and consumes without effect.

[...]

It is no wonder that this country has so many charms, and presents to Europeans so many temptations to remain in it. A traveler in Europe becomes a stranger as soon as he quits his own kingdom; but it is otherwise here. We know, properly speaking, no strangers; this is every person's country; the variety of our soils, situations, climates, governments, and produce, hath something which must please every body. No sooner does an European arrive, no matter of what condition, than his eyes are opened upon the fair prospect;

he hears his language spoke, he retraces many of his own country manners, he perpetually hears the names of families and towns with which he is acquainted; he sees happiness and prosperity in all places disseminated; he meets with hospitality, kindness, and plenty everywhere; he beholds hardly any poor, he seldom hears of punishments and executions; and he wonders at the elegance of our towns, those miracles of industry and freedom. He cannot admire enough our rural districts, our convenient roads, good taverns, and our many accommodations; he involuntarily loves a country where everything is so lovely. When in England, he was a mere Englishman; here he stands on a larger portion of the globe, not less than its fourth part, and may see the productions of the north, in iron and naval stores; the provisions of Ireland, the grain of Egypt, the indigo, the rice of China. He does not find, as in Europe, a crowded society, where every place is over-stocked; he does not feel that perpetual collision of parties, that difficulty of beginning, that contention which oversets so many. There is room for every body in America; has he any particular talent, or industry? he exerts it in order to procure a livelihood, and it succeeds. Is he a merchant? The avenues of trade are infinite; is he eminent in any respect? He will be employed and respected. Does he love a country life? pleasant farms present themselves; he may purchase what he wants, and thereby become an American farmer. Is he a laborer, sober and industrious? He need not go many miles, nor receive many informations before he will be hired, well fed at the table of his employer, and paid four or five times more than he can get in Europe. Does he want uncultivated lands? Thousands of acres present themselves, which he may purchase cheap. Whatever be his talents or inclinations, if they are moderate, he may satisfy them.

I do not mean that everyone who comes will grow rich in a little time; no, but he may procure an easy, decent maintenance, by his industry. Instead of starving he will be fed, instead of being idle he will have employment; and these are riches enough for such men as come over here. The rich stay in Europe, it is only the middling and the poor that emigrate. Would you wish to travel in independent idleness, from north to south, you will find easy access, and the most chearful reception at every house; society without ostentation, good cheer without pride, and every decent diversion which the country affords, with little expense. It is no wonder that the European who has lived here a few years, is desirous to remain; Europe with all its pomp, is not to be compared to this continent, for men of middle stations, or laborers.

An European, when he first arrives, seems limited in his intentions, as well as in his views; but he very suddenly alters his scale; two hundred miles formerly appeared a very great distance, it is now but a trifle; he no sooner breathes our air than he forms schemes, and embarks in designs he never would have thought of in his own country. There the plenitude of society confines many useful ideas, and often extinguishes the most laudable schemes which here ripen into maturity. Thus Europeans become Americans.

But how is this accomplished in that crowd of low, indigent people, who flock here every year from all parts of Europe? I will tell you; they no sooner arrive than they immediately feel the good effects of that plenty of provisions we possess: they fare on our best food, and they are kindly entertained; their talents, character, and peculiar industry are immediately inquired into; they find countrymen everywhere disseminated, let them come from whatever part of Europe. Let me select one as an epitome of the rest; he is hired, he goes to work, and works moderately; instead of being employed by a haughty person, he finds himself with his equal, placed at the substantial table of the farmer, or else at an inferior one as good; his wages are high, his bed is not like that bed of sorrow on which he used to lie: if he behaves with propriety, and is faithful, he is caressed, and becomes as it were a member of the family. He begins to feel the effects of a sort of resurrection; hitherto he had not lived, but simply vegetated; he now feels himself a man, because he is treated as such; the laws of his own country had overlooked him in his insignificancy; the laws of this cover him with their mantle.

Judge what an alteration there must arise in the mind and thoughts of this man; he begins to forget his former servitude and dependence, his heart involuntarily swells and glows; this first swell inspires him with those new thoughts which constitute an American. What love can he entertain for a country where his existence was a burthen to him; if he is a generous good man, the love of this new adoptive parent will sink deep into his heart. He looks around, and sees many a prosperous person, who but a few years before was as poor as himself. This encourages him much, he begins to form some little scheme, the first, alas, he ever formed in his life. If he is wise he thus spends two or three years, in which time he acquires knowledge, the use of tools, the modes of working the lands, felling trees, &c. This prepares the foundation of a good name, the most useful acquisition he can make. He is encouraged, he has gained friends; he is advised and directed, he feels bold, he purchases some land; he gives all the money he has brought over, as well as what he has earned, and trusts to the God of harvests for the discharge of the rest. His good name procures him credit. He is now possessed of the deed, conveying to him and his posterity the fee simple and absolute property of two hundred acres of land, situated on such a river.

What an epocha in this man's life! He is become a freeholder, from perhaps a German boor—he is now an American, a Pennsylvanian, an English subject. He is naturalized, his name is enrolled with those of the other citizens of the province. Instead of being a vagrant, he has a place of residence; he is called the inhabitant of such a county, or of such a district, and for the first time in his life counts for something; for hitherto he has been a cypher. I only repeat what I have heard man say, and no wonder their hearts should glow, and be agitated with a multitude of feelings, not easy to describe. From nothing to start into being; from a servant to the rank of a master; from being the slave of some despotic prince, to become a free man, invested with lands, to which every municipal blessing is annexed! What a change indeed! It is in consequence of that change that he becomes an American. This great metamorphosis has a double effect, it extinguishes all his European prejudices, he forgets that mechanism of subordination, that servility of disposition which poverty had taught him; and sometimes he is apt to forget too much, often passing from one extreme to the other. If he is a good man, he forms schemes of future prosperity, he proposes to educate his children better than he has been educated himself; he thinks of future modes of conduct, feels an ardor to labor he never felt before. Pride steps in and leads him to everything that the laws do not forbid: he respects them; with a heartfelt gratitude he looks toward the east, toward that insular government from whose wisdom all his new felicity is derived, and under whose wings and protection he now lives. These reflections constitute him the good man and the good subject. . . .

SOURCE: J. Hector St. John Crevecoeur. *Letters from an American Farmer.* New York: Fox, Duffield. 1904.

# FRANK LECOUVREUR

## From East Prussia to the Golden Gate
(Prussia; 1852)

*This excerpt is from Letter VII, describing the first two weeks after Lecou-*
*vreur's arrival in San Francisco, when he was twenty. He knew he was too*
*late for the 1849 gold rush, but he planned to try out the life of a miner. His*
*widow had his letters and diary translated and published after his death. His*
*impressions of San Francisco as well as his youthful excitement about his*
*new world are captivating.*

*San Francisco, Jan. 29th, 1852.*

At last I am at my destination and, if I may be permitted to judge
from the impression which the short stay has given me, I shall have
reason to congratulate myself upon the choice of my second fatherland. . . .

[On January 14ᵗʰ . . .] By half-past five we sailed around "Punta de
los Lobos Marinos" (Seal Rocks), passing the Fort right after sunset.
At five minutes past six we anchored close to the American Revenue
Cutter and just outside of North Beach, in the outer harbor of San
Francisco.

Thursday, the fifteenth of January, 1852, at high noon: We weighed
anchor once more, about nine this morning, and sailed slowly under
light westwind into the inner-harbor of the Western Metropolis. The
weather is beautiful. We reached the California wharf at twelve and anchored opposite. Thus ended my trip in two hundred sixty-five days,
five hours and fifty-five minutes since my departure from Konigsberg,
on board of the steamer *Konigsberg* . . . two hundred twenty-three
days, eighteen hours and ten minutes since my departure from Hamburg in the bark *Victoria*, fifty-nine days, one hour and twenty-five
minutes since my departure from Valparaiso in the brig *Aurora* . . .

ON AMERICAN SOIL!

No sooner had we anchored than I at once went ashore to visit
Boettcher, who received me very kindly. It was from his place that

I dispatched my letter No. 11 (including strictly personal notes), which informed you in few words of my safe arrival and well-being. You will now doubtless be exceedingly curious as to the impression which San Francisco has made upon me; and therefore a description of the city and its people will be in order.

San Francisco is, to begin with, an American city. "Every third grade pupil can tell us that," will be your impatient suggestion, "but what is in reality an American city?" . . .

This is a new country and San Francisco is of the latest birth, in what is commonly known as the "Wild Western" region. Everything consequently is yet done for a commercial purpose, and beauty, so far, counts for little. And still one has to admit San Francisco has its attractions. Though the appearance of the city, were I to describe a bird's-eye view from one of the hilltops, is not a very symmetrical one, nor does it present to us the beautiful architecture of ancient Greece, but one finds therein a rare liveliness and an ever changing aspect. San Francisco compares with Berlin as a bright, rosy-cheeked maiden might be compared with a marble Juno. No two houses have a similar front; not ten are alike in general architecture. Each house has its peculiarity, indicating the taste and nationality of its owner and is built in accordance with the requirements of the respective material used. One naturally finds the strangest contrasts of architectural products, mostly imitations of foreign ideas, brought hither from every civilized and uncivilized nation of the world. Buildings, representing the styles of Holland, Australia, East India, Germany, China, Belgium, North America, England, France, Chile, Switzerland and many other countries stand peacefully alongside of each other.

The materials used differ as much as do the countries which their styles represent. Most buildings are of wooden material, many others of brick, iron, zinc and copper. Brick houses with metal roofs, iron doors and window casings are very much the style here and those who are able to afford the great outlay generally favor the latter, because they offer better resistance in case of fire than any of wholly metal structure, which have proven impracticable during great conflagrations. . . .

The streets which run through this gay appearing map of edifices are still very hilly, but time will change that easily and soon enough. As soon as the American finds out that hills do not suit his purpose, he will find means of moving them without much ado. He will not try to bring that about, like Mohammed, by faith, but by machines of the most varied and unheard-of construction, which, however, have or seem to have all one common feature, that of being very much "for the purpose." One of said machines is at present, working at leveling a sand hill, about one hundred feet high, near Rincon point, the Southern end of the harbor. . . .

[. . .]

Let us now describe the people. It was in Valparaiso where a young Frenchman—one of the satirical kind, who ridicule everybody and everything that does not strike their particular fancy at any particular hour—for the French, as a nation as well as individuals, are very much subject to the impulse of the moment—expressed himself about San Francisco and its inhabitants as follows: *"Vous n'y trouverez pas des hommes, seulement des sacs a l'argent, ou remplis ou vides."* ("You will not find any human beings there, only money bags, either filled or empty.") I have not been here sufficiently long to know exactly how far this man's sarcastic saying may be justified but, judging from the kind welcome I have received everywhere so far, I am rather inclined to take his words at a discount as an intended bon-mot rather than as absolute truth.

Variegated as is this metropolis of the West itself, are the many people who crowd the streets, be they afoot, in carriages or on horseback. I do not think that there is a nation, representatives of which are not to be found in every sphere of local society: Yankees, Mexicanos, Peruvians, Chileans, Firelanders, Italians, Malays, Siamese, Creoles, Mulattoes, Negroes, Chinese, Indians—in short, Jews and Gentiles of all nations.people the ever-crowded streets in their respective national costumes.

No matter where the stranger may hail from, he is sure to find sooner or later some congenial countryman with whom he can chat in his mother tongue. Of course, English being the language of this country is the most spoken, but German, French and Spanish are heard almost as often, so that one ought to be able to converse fluently in four languages in order to move with ease among all classes of local society, and there is no doubt in my mind that every retail merchant of this city is daily or even hourly called upon to answer in at least three of the above named languages. No wonder therefore that almost everyone of them—though he may be often unable to go beyond "yes" or "no" and to count (on his fingers)—has a very conspicuous sign in his show window announcing his linguistic ability in words like: "Aqui se habla espanol"; "Ici on parle francais"; and

"Hier spricht man Deutsch." In this respect most seaports are alike. Considering the great mixture of elements, each one representing different modes of living, thinking, acting, each individual educated and raised in different zones from those of his neighbors, impressed from childhood with different principles, different ideas of right and wrong; they are united only in one purpose, namely, a desire to become rich as quickly as possible. Does it or should it astonish you that one's personal safety and that of his property are not as yet as firmly assured as in other civilized states? ...

[...]

As already mentioned, safety to life on our streets is at present as effectually assured as it is anywhere in large cities; and although the majority of citizens continue to go about armed, it is more from the force of habit acquired than by reason of fear. It is true, however, that one has to be on one's guard and avoid quarrel, as the least word-duel is apt to end in a pistolade, as there seems yet to be much inclination to meet an insult with a bullet. But all peaceably minded persons who go quietly about their daily occupation, avoiding everything that is not part of their legitimate line of work, but who seek only to earn daily bread will seldom be annoyed by ruffians.

It cannot naturally be expected of me to have gained a reliable insight into the business affairs of this great Western city during my short stay of a fortnight. Merchants, however, are heard to complain at present of considerable pressure brought about by overproduction and scarcity in the money market. It thus happened that my many efforts, aided by most excellent recommendations and personal endeavors of newly found friends, failed to secure for me a position as clerk. But there are thousands of ways and means of support in America, which, if they do not serve for anything better, will at least surely keep the wolf from the door.

Mercantile establishments are mostly in the hands of either North Americans, Englishmen or Germans, while there are likewise some very rich and respected Chilean firms, but very few French and Mexican business houses. The Chinese, too, go into business ventures once in a while, but rarely on a large scale, though many of them are very rich and could easily have the largest establishments in the city, if money were the sole factor. Each nationality tries to preserve its own peculiar character and, as will be readily understood, the general hunt for money and riches does not always bring out the better qualities of men to advantage, but rather tends to bring the weak ones into daily display. While it cannot be denied that some acquire riches in comparatively few years, most foreigners remain but a short time, only to return home with disappointed hopes and shattered expectations; they, however, make room for newcomers; new elements take the vacant places, and the merry war for earthly possessions continues.

The sooner the European realizes that the only safe way toward accumulating money is to work for it, the better for him. There is not one out of a hundred who grows rich rapidly, and here as elsewhere the old adage: "Honesty is the best paying policy," is in reality the only "golden rule" one should follow in business as well as in private life. Though we generally believe that time is all-powerful in smoothing conditions and harmonizing difficulties and national peculiarities, there seems to be astonishingly little assimilation between the different nations; they seem to remain intentionally and distinctly foreign to each other. . . .

As to myself, I cannot tell you just yet what I may choose to do in case my endeavors to obtain a paying position in this city should not be crowned with success within the next few days, though I shall very likely take the next best chance to try my luck in the mines. To do this will be, if nothing else, an educating experiment, and without overworking one's self, one can easily make the necessary expenses of daily life and in the meantime gain an opportunity of making a wholesome study of the natural conditions of the country. There is, of course, no more hope for immense riches for miners, as in days gone by, when a globe trotter would accidentally stumble over a lump of pure gold. Still, by industry, persevering and saving, one can yet accumulate a moderate sum in a longer or shorter time, as fortune may permit.

I board at present . . . about a (German) mile from San Francisco, in a charming place, which is well named "Pleasant Valley." There are several young clerks from the city, all Germans, rooming in the same house, so that we number a round dozen at the dinner table. The walk to town is very agreeable and takes but half an hour.

My expenditure amounts to twelve dollars a week for room and board, which will prove to you that living expenses are not nearly as high as in days gone by. I live well at that, and, as far as eating and drinking goes, far better than at home. Life in hotels and saloons, however, is very expensive; so are the three best theaters of this city— the American Theater, the "Jenny Lind" and the Theatre Francais— where tickets for seats in the loges or dress circles are three dollars apiece. Wine seems to be cheaper here than in the large vineyards. For instance, a gallon—about five bottles and a half of good table wine—costs but four bits or one-half dollar, and the best champagne no more than four dollars a gallon, which makes it possible for the poorest day laborer who shoves a hand cart or carries a hod to include half a bottle of wine in his bill of fare. And the California wine is fully as good as the French wines, so-called, which we purchase at home; at any rate you get what you pay for. Business men, as a rule, eat after what is called the American plan, and which is a very sensible one, in my estimation. About eight o'clock in the morning one starts with a good warm breakfast, consisting of beefsteak, chops, roast beef or something of that sort, winding up with a cup of good coffee. About noon one indulges in a so-called lunch, that means a glass or two of wine, bread and cheese or cold viands, and enjoys the principal meal at six o'clock, after the cares and worries of the day are over and the office is closed. This mode of living suits me exceedingly well, yes, even better than our home method with its five meals. By this method the day is not much divided, and one can follow one's pursuits without being interrupted every two or three hours, and the natural consequence is that the American accomplishes more in a day than his European competitor.

Though we are said to live in the midst of the rainy season, I confess that so far I have not seen a drop. The air is warm and most agreeable in daytime, the sky clear and of a tropical blue, and Mother Nature is clad in a pretty green; the nights, however, are decidedly cold and remind me quite often of the dear ones at the fireside at home. . . .

One of the finest spots just outside the city is Monte Dolores, a hill of about twelve to eighteen hundred feet in height; from its summit, which it is not difficult to reach, the visitor has a beautiful panorama before him: San Francisco with its fine harbor and the Golden Gate; the bay with its attractive islands on one side and the Pacific Ocean, in all its majesty, on the other. There is a boulevard, laid out with planks, which leads from the Mission Dolores to the foot of the hill and is frequented on Sundays by pleasure seekers, promenading families, ladies in elegant carriages, people on horseback, all bent upon enjoying the sights which Mother Nature presents. "Were it not for an occasional redman (Indian) or the ever present yellow Mongolian with his long, coal black queue, one would fancy one's self transported to one of the much sought promenades of a German city . . . instead of being on the far away Western coast of North America. . . .

*San Francisco, California, the 31st of January, 1852.*

As there remain but a few more minutes until the closing of the European mail, I shall make use of them by adding a few more words to those, who I know, will enjoy them. It is so difficult to tear one's self from a letter, which is homeward bound, across the many thousands of miles, that I cannot let go until "time sets my nails afire" (German idiom). I am at this hour quite determined to try my luck in the mines and shall leave for the interior next Tuesday, the third of February, via Benicia and Stockton, in order to continue along the Stanislaus, a branch of the San Joaquin River, then passing Sonora City, enter the Sierra Nevada as far as I possibly can.

In all probability I shall not return to civilization very soon and, as you will easily comprehend, postal facilities are absolutely unknown in those regions, many of which have never been visited by a paleface before. Of course, it remains an open question how soon you will receive my next letter, while this one, I trust, will keep you busy reading and re-reading for many a day.

Do not worry about me, dear parents, and do not forget that California has ceased to be a nest of robbers and highwaymen. The severe laws, which the miners have enacted in their own behalf and for the preservation of order in their own camps, and which they execute with unrelenting vigor, frighten away criminals from the most remote camps. Even the petty thief, if caught in the act, is sent into eternity by the "rope-route." As the miners—rough and ready—are in the habit of doing those things quickly, we should not be surprised that their method has a wholesome effect upon the long-fingered gentry, most of whom are cowards by nature, and the miner, though he generally carries a warm, yea, philanthropically-disposed heart under a rough exterior, cordially detests cowardice.

The next Panama steamer is due since yesterday and is expected to arrive at almost any moment. I await her with impatience, hoping sincerely for long-missed news from you, which would expel the feeling of uncertainty as to the personal welfare of every one of my loved ones at home. I have openly to confess my great disappointment at the strange fact of not receiving a single letter from you upon landing here and cannot deny that it has depressed and discouraged me for many an hour, and to a great extent emphasized my disappointment at not obtaining employment. Please make up for it by writing long letters and real often. It will be advisable to direct the outer envelope as follows: Messrs. Gent, Schott, Boettcher & Co., San Francisco, Upper California. And then put the closed letter into it. The mail will thus receive quicker attention at the post-office than if it were directed to me in care of Boettcher. Please give my very best regards and many thousand greetings to all the loved ones.

Do not worry if you do not hear from me within the next few months, but write diligently that I may have plenty to read. I embrace and kiss you all. God be with you!

*Franz Lecouvreur*

SOURCE: *From East Prussia to the Golden Gate: Letters and Diary of the California Pioneer.* Edited by Josephine Rosana Lecouvreur. Translated by Julius C. Behnke. New York: Angelina Book Concern. 1906.

# EMMA LAZARUS

*The New Colossus*
(United States; 1883)

*Born in New York City, the poet Emma Lazarus (1849–1887) wrote this
sonnet, the most famous in American literature, to help raise money for the
pedestal at the base of the Statue of Liberty. The poem appears on a plaque
on an inner wall of that very pedestal.*

Not like the brazen giant of Greek fame,
With conquering limbs astride from land to land;
Here at our sea-washed, sunset gates shall stand
A mighty woman with a torch, whose flame
Is the imprisoned lightning, and her name
Mother of Exiles. From her beacon-hand
Glows world-wide welcome; her mild eyes command
The air-bridged harbor that twin cities frame.
"Keep, ancient lands, your storied pomp!" cries she
With silent lips. "Give me your tired, your poor,
Your huddled masses yearning to breathe free,
The wretched refuse of your teeming shore.
Send these, the homeless, tempest-tost to me,
I lift my lamp beside the golden door!"

SOURCE: Emma Lazarus. *The Poems of Emma Lazarus*, Vol. 1. Boston:
Houghton Mifflin and Company. 1889.

# HANS MATTSON

*Reminiscences: The Story of an Emigrant*
(Sweden; 1891)

*Mattson arrived in the United States in 1851 when he was eighteen. He faced one difficulty after another, and only learned English when working on a merchant ship that sailed between Boston and South Carolina. During the Civil War he became a colonel in the Union Army and later served as a United States consul general in India. He died in 1893.*

When I was sixteen years old, an event took place which had a decisive influence on my whole life.

A captain of the army boarded at my father's home, and was regarded as a member of the family. Among his acquaintances was a young man of my own age, who also had the same christian name as I. One day this young man came to see the captain, and as he approached the house my mother and sister observing him, both exclaimed at the same time, "There is Hans!" He heard this, and was greatly surprised that they knew him, while the fact was that they mistook him for me. At that time I was in the city, but the next day this second Hans visited me, and told me of the incident. If there is such a thing as affinity between men, it certainly existed between him and me; we felt ourselves irresistibly drawn towards each other, and from that day we have been more than brothers, and nothing but death can separate us. We are of the same size, complexion and age. He had already served a short time as cadet in the artillery, but had been compelled to resign on account of poor health. Now he had recovered and entered service again as a volunteer in the infantry.

The events of my life are so closely interwoven with this man and his life, that the reader will often hear of him in these pages. Right here I wish to state, that a more faithful friend and a more noble character cannot be found; he has always been a help and a comfort to me in the many and strange vicissitudes which we have shared

34

together. His name is Hans Eustrom, better known in Minnesota as Captain Eustrom.

The first Danish–German war broke out about this time, and I, with many other youths, felt a hearty sympathy for the Danes. The Swedish government resolved to send troops to help their neighbors, and a few regiments marching through our city fanned our youthful enthusiasm into flame. Finally, a detachment of the artillery, quartered in the city, was ordered to leave for the seat of war, and now I could no longer restrain myself, but besieged my parents to let me join that part of the army which was going to the battlefield, and to clinch the argument I was cruel enough to send word to my distressed mother that if she would not consent I would run away from home and join the army anyway. This last argument made her yield, and in the fall of 1849 I became an artillery cadet, being then in my seventeenth year. But although I won this victory over my mother, whose greatest desire was that I should become a clergyman, she in turn gained a victory over me by persuading the surgeon of the battalion, who was also our family physician, to declare me sick and send me to the hospital, although I had only a slight cold; thus my plan to go with the army to Schleswig-Holstein was frustrated. This did not make much difference, however, as the war was virtually closed before our troops arrived at the place of destination, and my time could now be more profitably employed in learning the duties of a soldier, and in taking a course of mathematics and other practical branches at the regimental school.

I remained in the army a year and a half, during which time I received excellent instruction in gymnastics, fencing and riding, besides the regular military drill. Two winters were thus devoted to conscientious and thorough work at the military school.

Knowing that the chances for advancement in the Swedish army during times of peace were at this time very slim for young men not favored with titles of nobility, and being also tired of the monotonous garrison life, my friend Eustrom and myself soon resolved to leave the service and try our luck in a country where inherited names and titles were not the necessary conditions of success.

At that time America was little known in our part of the country, only a few persons having emigrated from the whole district. But we knew that it was a new country, inhabited by a free and independent people, that it had a liberal government and great natural resources, and these inducements were sufficient for us. My parents readily consented to my emigration, and, having made the necessary preparations, my father took my friend Eustrom and myself down to the coast with his own horses, in the first part of May, 1851. It was a memorable evening, and I shall never forget the last farewell to my home, in driving out from the court into the village street, how I stood up in the wagon, turned towards the dear home and waved my hat with a hopeful hurrah to the "folks I left behind." A couple of days' journey brought us to a little seaport, where we took leave of my father and boarded a small schooner for the city of Gothenburg.

At that time there were no ocean steamers and no emigrant agents; but we soon found a sailing vessel bound for America on which we embarked as passengers, furnishing our own bedding, provisions and other necessaries, which our mothers had supplied in great abundance. About one hundred and fifty emigrants from different parts of Sweden were on board the brig *Ambrosius*. In the middle of May she weighed anchor and glided out of the harbor on her long voyage across the ocean to distant Boston.

We gazed back at the vanishing shores of the dear fatherland with feelings of affection, but did not regret the step we had taken, and our bosoms heaved with boundless hope. At the age of eighteen, the strong, healthy youth takes a bright and hopeful view of life, and so did we. Many and beautiful were the air-castles we built as we stood on deck, with our eyes turned towards the promised land of the Nineteenth century. To some of these castles our lives have given reality, others are still floating before us.

★ ★ ★

The good brig *Ambrosius* landed us in Boston on June 29, 1851, but during the voyage about one-half of the passengers were attacked by small-pox and had to be quarantined outside the harbor. My good friend and I were fortunate enough to escape this plague; but instead of this I was taken sick with the ague on our arrival at Boston.

Now, then, we were in America! The new, unknown country lay before us, and it seemed the more strange as we did not understand a word of the English language. For at that time the schools of Sweden paid no attention to English, so that although I had studied four languages, English, the most important of all tongues, was entirely unknown to me.

The first few weeks of our stay in Boston passed quietly and quickly, but the ague grew worse and my purse was getting empty. My friend, however, had more money than I, and as long as he had a dollar left he divided it equally between us. I cannot resist the temptation to relate a serio-comical escapade of this period, one that to many will recall similar occurrences in their own experience as immigrants ignorant of the language of the country.

In Gothenburg we had become acquainted with a bright young man from Vexio, Janne Tenggren by name, who had also served in the army. When we met him he had already bought a ticket on a sailing vessel bound for New York, so that we could not make the voyage together. But we agreed to hunt each other up after our arrival in America. We left Sweden about the same time with the understanding that if we arrived first we should meet him in New York, and if he arrived first he should go to Boston to meet us there.

About a week after our arrival in Boston, we heard that the vessel on which he had embarked had arrived, and I immediately left for New York to fulfill our promise. But, unfortunately, I found he had already gone west, so I bought a return ticket to Boston the same day. The journey was by steamboat to Fall River, thence by rail to Boston. We left New York in the evening. I remained on the deck, and went to sleep about ten o'clock on some wooden boxes. About eleven o'clock I awoke, saw the steamer laying too, and, supposing we were at Fall River, hurried off and followed the largest crowd, expecting thus to get to the railroad depot. Striking no depot, however, I returned to the harbor, only to find the steamer gone, and everybody but myself had vanished from the pier.

There I stood, in the middle of the night, without money, ignorant of the language, and not even knowing where I was! Tired and discouraged I finally threw myself down on a wooden box on the sidewalk, and went to sleep. About five o'clock in the morning a big policeman aroused me by poking at me with his club. This respectable incarnation of social order evidently took me for a tramp or a madman, and as he could not obtain any intelligible information from me in any language known to him, he took me to a small shoe store kept by a German.

Fortunately, my acquaintance with the German language was sufficient to enable me to explain myself, and I soon found that I had left the steamer several hours too early; that the name of this place was New London, that another steamer would come past at the same time the next night, so that all I had to do was to wait for that steamer and go to Boston on the same ticket.

I spent the day in seeing the city and chatting with my friend, the shoe maker, and in the evening returned to the wharf to watch for the Boston steamer.

This being my ague day, I had violent attacks of ague and fever, so that I was again forced to lie down to rest on the same wooden box, and again went to sleep. After a while I was aroused by the noise of the approaching steamer; rushed on board in company with some other passengers, and considered myself very fortunate when reflecting that I would surely be in Boston the next morning. I had made myself familiar with the surroundings during the day, and when the steamer started, I noticed that it directed its course towards New York, instead of Boston. I had no money to pay my fare to New York, could neither borrow nor beg, and so I crawled down in a little hole in the fore part of the steamer, where the tackles and ropes were kept, thus, fortunately, escaping the notice of the ticket collector.

The next evening I again embarked for Boston and finally arrived safely at my destination.

We stayed in Boston several weeks, and during that time my ague caused a heavy drain on our small treasury. We had no definite plan, did not know what to do, and as we had never been used to any kind of hard work, matters began to assume a serious aspect, especially in regard to myself. But then, as now, the hope of many a young man was the Great West which, at that time, was comparatively little known even in Boston. Toward the close of the month of July we, therefore, went to Buffalo, which was as far as our money would carry us. Here we put up at a cheap boarding house kept by a Norwegian by name of Larson, with whom we stopped while trying to get work. But having learned no trade and being unused to manual labor, we soon found that it was impossible to get a job in the city; so we left our baggage at the boarding house and started on foot for a country place named Hamburg, some ten miles distant, where we learned that two of our late companions across the ocean had found employment. On the road to Hamburg, about dusk, we reached a small house by the wayside, where we asked for food and shelter. I was so exhausted that my friend had to support me in order to reach the house. We found it occupied by a Swedish family, which had just sat down to a bountiful supper. Telling them our condition, we were roughly told to clear out; in Sweden, they said, they had had enough of gentlemen and would have nothing to do with them here.

We retraced our steps with sad hearts until a short distance beyond the house we found an isolated barn partly filled with hay. There was no one to object, so we took possession and made it our temporary home. I am glad to say that during a long life among all classes of people, from the rudest barbarians to the rulers of nations, that family of my own countrymen were the only people who made me nearly lose faith in the nobler attributes of man. I have an excuse, however, for this conduct in the fact that in the mother-country, which they had left a year before, they had probably been abused and exasperated on account of the foolish class distinction then existing there. They evidently belonged to that class of tenants who were treated almost like slaves. The following day we found our late companions a mile from our barn, both working for a farmer at $15.00 per month, which was then considered big wages. They were older men and accustomed to hard labor, so that their situation was comparatively easy. They received us kindly and procured work for Eustrom with the same farmer, while I, still suffering with the ague, could not then attempt to work, and therefore returned to my castle in the meadow (the haybarn). There I remained about a week living on berries which I found in the neighboring woods and a slice of bread and butter, which Eustrom brought me in the evening, when, with blistered hands and sore back, he called to comfort me and help build better air castles for the future.

A council was finally held among us four, and it was decided to send me back to Buffalo with a farmer who was going there the following morning. One of the men, Mr. Abraham Sandberg, on parting gave me a silver dollar, with the injunction to give it to someone who might need it worse than I, whenever I could do so. I have never met Abraham again; but I have regarded it as a sacred duty to comply with his request, and, in case these lines should come before his eyes I wish to let him know that my debt has been honestly paid.

On reaching the old boarding house in Buffalo the landlord promised that he would send me to a hospital where I could receive proper treatment and care. I made up a little bundle of necessary underwear, and in an hour a driver appeared at the door; I was lifted into the cart and off we went through the muddy streets to the outskirts of the city, where I was duly delivered at a large building which I supposed to be the hospital. It was near evening, and I was brought into a large dining-room, with a hundred others or more, served with supper, corn mush and molasses water, after which I was shown to a bed in a large room among many others. I suffered with fever, and for the first time in my life with loneliness. Exhausted nature finally took out its due, and I slept soundly until awakened in the morning by a loud sound of a gong. As soon as dressed I walked out in the yard, or lawn, back of the building. On one side was a high plank fence, behind which I heard some strange sounds. I found a knot-hole, and, peeping through this, I observed another lawn, on which were many people. They were strange looking; I never saw any like them before. Some were swinging, some dancing, others shouting, singing and weeping and behaving in a most out-of-the-way manner. I wondered and wondered, and finally it dawned upon me that it must be a lunatic asylum. It was, in fact, as I since learned, the county poor farm, where one part was used for the lunatics and the other for paupers like myself.

*Has it come to this?* I asked myself; *is this the goal of all my ambition and hopes?* Going back to the room, where I had slept, I stealthily took my little bundle, slipped out through a side door into a back yard, found a gate open and was soon in the street. I started on a run with all the power in me, as if pursued by all the furies of paupers and lunatics, never stopping until I was near the old boarding house, where I was taken in exhausted and in deep despair. I would have killed the landlord for deceiving me if I had been able to do so. One good thing resulted from the sad experience of that day: the mental shock on discovering where I was cured me for the time being of the ague.

The next day my friend returned from Hamburg, where he could no longer get any employment on account of his blistered hands, and poor health in general. We now put our wise heads together and agreed that we had already had enough of the West for the time being. Having plenty of good clothes, bedding, revolvers and other knick-knacks, we sold to our landlord whatever we could spare, in order to raise money enough to pay our way back to Boston.

During our stay in Buffalo, our renowned countrywoman, Jenny Lind, happened to give a concert there. We were standing on the street where we could see the people crowd into the theatre, but that was all we could afford, and we never heard her sing. Our host advised us to go and ask her for help; but our pride forbade it.

At this time the Swedes were so little known, and Jenny Lind, on the other hand, so renowned in America, that the Swedes were frequently called "Jenny Lind men," this designation being often applied to myself.

Having purchased tickets for Albany, we returned East in the month of August. I still remember how we rode all night in a crowded second-class car, listening to the noisy merry-making of our fellow-passengers; but we understood very little of it, for up to this time we had lived exclusively among our own countrymen, and learned only a few English words—a mistake, by the way, which thousands of immigrants have made and are still making.

Arriving at Albany, we sat down by an old stone wall near the railroad depot, to talk over our affairs. Fate had been against us while we remained together, and we probably depended too much upon each other. Accordingly, we decided to part for some time and try our luck separately; and if one of us met with success he would, of course, soon be able to find a position for the other. We decided by drawing lots that Eustrom should go to Boston and I to New York. When we had bought our tickets there remained one dollar, which we divided, and we left for our respective places of destination the same evening.

Our landlord in Buffalo had given us the address of a sailors' boarding-house in New York, which was also kept by a Norwegian by the same name of Larson. So when I left the Hudson River steamer early the next morning, I paid my half-dollar to a drayman, who took me to said boarding house. I found Mr. Larson to be a kind, good-natured man, told him my difficulties right out, and asked him to let me stop at his house until I could find something to do. He agreed to this, and for a week or so I tried my best to get work. But, when asked what kind of work I could do, I was compelled to answer that I had learned no trade, but that I would gladly try to learn anything and do anything whatever, even sweep the streets, if necessary. As a result of my protracted sickness, I was so weak and exhausted that nobody thought I would be able even to earn my bread. As to easy or intellectual work, I had no earthly chance, as long as I did not know the English language. Finally Mr. Larson took me to a ship-owner's office. I still remember that a Norwegian captain was cruel enough to remark in my hearing, that he did not intend to take any half-dead corpses along with him to sea.

After two weeks of fruitless efforts to get work for me, my host finally declared that he could not very well keep me any longer, because his accommodations were crowded with paying customers;

nevertheless, he allowed me to sleep in the attic free of charge, while I had to procure my food as best I could, which I also did for another two weeks. Being a convalescent, I had a ravenous appetite, and, indeed, I found how hard it is to obtain food without having anything to pay for it. Of the few articles of clothing which I brought with me from Buffalo, I had to sacrifice one after another for subsistence. When all other means were exhausted, I was compelled to go to the kitchen-doors and tell my desperate and unfortunate condition by signs, and more than one kind-hearted cook gave me a solid meal.

Tramps! In our day there is a great deal of talk about tramps, and it has become customary, to brand as a tramp, any poor wandering laborer who seeks work. There are undoubtedly many who justly deserve this title; but I think there are tramps who are not to blame for their deplorable condition, and who deserve encouragement and friendly assistance, for I have been one of them myself, without any fault or neglect on my part. It always provokes me to hear a young or inexperienced person use the expression "tramp" so thoughtlessly, and in such a sweeping manner. Long ago I made up my mind that no tramp should ever leave my door without such aid as my resources would allow. It is better to give to a thousand undeserving than to let one unfortunate but deserving suffer.

My good host, like his Buffalo namesake, finally contrived to get rid of me by representing me as a sailor, and hiring me to the captain of the bark *Catherine*, a coasting vessel bound for Charleston, S.C., telling me that I was to serve as cabin boy. My wages were to be five dollars a month, of which he received seven dollars and a-half in advance, so that I could pay my debts and buy a sailor's suit of clothes.

On the second day of our voyage we encountered a storm. I was on deck with the sailors and the captain stood on the quarter-deck. We were coursing against the wind and were just going to turn when the captain called on me to untie some ropes. Understanding very little English, and being no sailor, I naturally knew nothing about the names of the different ropes, and I grabbed one after another, but invariably missed the right one. The captain was swearing with might and main in English. Seeing that I did not understand him he suddenly roared out angrily the name of the rope in good Swedish and added: "Do you understand me now, you confounded block-head!" Turning to him, cap in hand, I answered: "No, captain, I do not know the name of a single rope." "And still," he continued "you have followed the sea three years, what a dunce you are." I answered:

"Indeed, Mr. Captain, I have never been a sailor, and will never be worth anything at sea. But I am willing and anxious to do all you ask if within my power." The captain, whose name was Wilson, was a Swedish American and, although somewhat gruff, he was in fact one of the noblest men who ever commanded a ship. He immediately saw how the matter stood; the boarding house man had cheated both him and me and from that hour Captain Wilson became my friend and benefactor.

Afterwards I found out of the whole crew, which numbered twenty-six men, nine-tenths were Scandinavians, but they always used the English language while on board the ship. Captain Wilson told me to see him in his cabin as soon as the work was performed. Here he asked me about my circumstances, and I told him the short story of my life, which elicited his sympathy to such an extent that he even asked me to pardon his rude behavior toward me. He assigned me to a place to sleep in the cabin; told the officers not to give me any orders as he was going to do that himself, and treated me with the utmost kindness and consideration in every respect.

After this I was excused from all work properly belonging to a sailor, but kept the cabin in order, and helped the steward in waiting at the table, and the officers with their calculations. During my spare hours I read and conversed with the captain and his two mates, one of whom was a Dane and the other an Irishman, both splendid fellows. The first mate was preparing the second mate for a captain's examination, and I, having recently taken a course in mathematics, at a military school, was able to assist them in their studies.

On the table in the cabin was a large English Bible, with which I spent many happy hours, and by which I learned the English language. At first I used to pick out chapters of the New Testament, which I knew almost by heart, so that I could understand them without a dictionary or an interpreter. After my first conversation with the captain I did not speak another word in the Swedish language during the voyage, and when I returned to Boston, three months afterwards, it seemed to me that I could talk and read English about as well as Swedish.

I made two trips with the captain from New York to Charleston and back again. At the wharf of Charleston, I was, for the first time in my life, brought face to face with American Negro slavery in its most odious aspect. Crowds of Negroes were running along the pier pulling long ropes, by means of which the ships were loaded and unloaded. Each gang of Negroes was under the charge of a brutal overseer, riding on a mule, and brandishing a long cowhide whip, which he applied vigorously to the backs of the half-naked Negroes. During the night they were kept penned up in sheds, which had been erected for that purpose near the wharf. They were treated like cattle, in every respect. This sight influenced me in later life to become a Republican in politics.

After our second return to New York, Capt. Wilson assumed the command of one of the first clipper ships which carried passengers to California in those days. This was at the most stirring time of the gold fever, and the captain kindly offered to take me along and let me stay out there, an offer which thousands would have accepted. But I was never smitten with the gold fever, and, having a distaste for the sea, I said good-bye to the kind captain, never to see him again. My wages were to have been only five dollars a month, but he generously paid me eight dollars, so that I had earned enough money to pay my way to Boston, whence my friend Eustrom had written me and urged me to come.

I arrived in Boston about the middle of December, and, when I returned to the old boarding house, I spoke English so well that my acquaintances hardly believed it possible that I could be the same person. Mr. Eustrom was now working as wood polisher. He had made many friends and lived happily and contented on $4 a week. By strict economy these wages sufficed for board, lodging, and clothes. It happened to be an unfavorable time of the year when I arrived, however, and many men who had been employed during the summer were now discharged at the approach of winter. Mr. Eustrom's employer had a good friend in New Hampshire, an old Swedish sailor, Anderson by name, who was farming up there. He promised to let me come and live with him and do whatever chores I could until something might turn up the next spring.

A few days afterwards I went by rail to Contocook, where I was met by Mr. Anderson, who took me out to his hospitable home a couple of miles from the town. This Anderson was a remarkable man. Having no education to speak of, he was a better judge of human nature and practical affairs of life than any other man I ever met. He was pleased with me, and said he wished I would sit down in the evening and tell him about Sweden, and explain to him what I had learned at school. Poor Anderson! He had one fault, rum got the better of him, and it was cheap in New England at that time, only sixteen cents a gallon. He bought a barrel of it at a time, and did not taste water as long as the rum lasted.

The day after my arrival he asked me if I would like to go with him into the woods to help cut some logs. Of course I would, and we took our axes and started off. It was a very cold December day, and I had thin clothes and no mittens. Mr. Anderson went to cut down a tree, and I commenced to work at one which was already felled. This was the first time I swung an axe in earnest, and after a short while I felt that my hands were getting cold. But I made up my mind not to stop until the log was finished. By holding the axe handle very tight it stopped the circulation of the blood through my fingers, and when I finally stopped and dropped the axe I could not move my fingers, for eight of them were frozen stiff. Mr. Anderson now took off his cap, filled it with snow, put my hands into the snow, and thus we ran to the house as fast as our legs would carry us. The doctor tried his very best; but, nevertheless, in a few days the flesh and the nails began to peel off, and two doctors decided to amputate all the fingers on my right hand. Fortunately I did not give my consent, but told them that I would rather die of gangrene than live without hands, for my future depended exclusively on them.

My friend Eustrom, having heard of my misfortune, soon came to visit me, and brought with him an old Irish woman who was something of a doctor, and cured my hands by means of a very simple plaster which she prepared herself. But I was forced into complete inactivity for more than three months, during which time I was entirely helpless, and had to be washed, dressed, and fed like an infant. But, as to me, the old proverb has always proved true: "When things are at the worst they'll mend." There were men and women in my accidental home who willingly tended to me in my trouble. May God bless them for it! In the latter part of March, Mr. Anderson, who had always treated me with the greatest kindness, quite unexpectedly told me that I was now able to work again and could try to get a place with some other family in the neighborhood, because he could not keep me any longer.

Our nearest neighbor was a genuine Yankee, Daniel Dustin by name. He was very rich, well read, liberal minded, respectable and honest, but so close that he would scarcely let his own family have enough food to eat, and his wife was even more stingy. Mr. Dustin agreed to let me work for my board until spring, and then he would give me five dollars a month, which offer I cheerfully accepted. He immediately took me out into the woods to chop wood for the summer, and he was to haul it home. The new, tender muscles and nails on my fingers made wood chopping very painful to me, and I could feel every blow of the axe through my entire body. Never has any man worked so hard for me, when I afterwards hired help for good wages, as I worked for my board here; and, by the way, this board consisted chiefly of potatoes and corn meal cake. When the spring work commenced I got five dollars a month, and had to get up at five o'clock in the morning to do the chores, and then work in the field from seven in the morning until dark.

In the beginning of June I got a letter from my parents, stating that my father and brother were going to leave for New York immediately, and they asked me to meet them there and go West with them. I had never complained in my letters to my parents, but, on the other hand, I had not advised them to come to America, either. They had been advised to do so by some of my fellow-passengers on the *Ambrosius*, who went to Illinois, and were highly pleased with their prospects. So I went to Boston again. My father's voyage had been delayed, and I had to wait for him over a month, during which time I got sick, and would have been in a sorry plight, indeed, if it had not been for my friend Eustrom, who now felt like a rich man, with his six dollars a week. A couple of years later he became the partner of his employer.

SOURCE: Hans Mattson. *Reminiscences: The Story of an Emigrant*. St. Paul: D. D. Merrill Co. 1891.

# SADIE BROWNE

*The Life Story of a Polish Sweatshop Girl*
(Poland; 1906)

*An American magazine called* The Independent, *apparently based in New York, ran a series of seventy-five articles and later published some of them in an intriguingly titled volume,* The Life Stories of Undistinguished Americans As Told by Themselves. *A writer, Sydney Reid, took dictation and laid out the stories, many of them extraordinary, all of them well told. Sadie Browne was a sixteen-year-old Jewish immigrant from Poland. She attended night school in Manhattan while working during the day in New York City sweatshops.*

My mother was a tall, handsome, dark complexioned woman with red cheeks, large brown eyes and a great quantity of jet black, wavy hair. She was well educated, being able to talk in Russian, German, Polish and French, and even to read English print, though of course she did not know what it meant. She kept a little grocer's shop in the little village where we lived at first. That was in Poland, somewhere on the frontier, and mother had charge of a gate between the countries, so that everybody who came through the gate had to show her a pass. She was much looked up to by the people, who used to come and ask her for advice. Her word was like law among them.

She had a wagon in which she used to drive about the country, selling her groceries, and sometimes she worked in the fields with my father.

The grocer's shop was only one story high, and had one window, with very small panes of glass. We had two rooms behind it, and were happy while my father lived, although we had to work very hard. By the time I was six years of age I was able to wash dishes and scrub floors, and by the time I was eight I attended to the shop while my mother was away driving her wagon or working in the fields with my father. She was strong and could work like a man.

When I was a little more than ten years of age my father died. He was a good man and a steady worker, and we never knew what it was to be hungry while he lived. After he died troubles began, for the rent of our shop was about $6 a month and then there were food and clothes to provide. We needed little, it is true, but even soup, black bread and onions we could not always get.

We struggled along till I was nearly thirteen years of age and quite handy at housework and shop-keeping, so far as I could learn them there. But we fell behind in the rent and mother kept thinking more and more that we should have to leave Poland and go across the sea to America where we heard it was much easier to make money. Mother wrote to Aunt Fanny, who lived in New York, and told her how hard it was to live in Poland, and Aunt Fanny advised her to come and bring me. I was out at service at this time and mother thought she would leave me—as I had a good place—and come to this country alone, sending for me afterward. But Aunt Fanny would not hear of this. She said we should both come at once, and she went around among our relatives in New York and took up a subscription for our passage.

We came by steerage on a steamship in a very dark place that smelt dreadfully. There were hundreds of other people packed in with us, men, women and children, and almost all of them were sick. It took us twelve days to cross the sea, and we thought we should die, but at last the voyage was over, and we came up and saw the beautiful bay and the big woman with the spikes on her head and the lamp that is lighted at night in her hand (Goddess of Liberty).

Aunt Fanny and her husband met us at the gate of this country and were very good to us, and soon I had a place to live out (domestic servant), while my mother got work in a factory making white goods.

I was only a little over thirteen years of age and a greenhorn, so I received $9 a month and board and lodging, which I thought was doing well. Mother, who, as I have said, was very clever, made $9 a week on white goods, which means all sorts of underclothing, and is high class work.

But mother had a very gay disposition. She liked to go around and see everything, and friends took her about New York at night and she caught a bad cold and coughed and coughed. She really had hasty consumption, but she didn't know it, and I didn't know it, and she tried to keep on working, but it was no use. She had not the strength. Two doctors attended her, but they could do nothing, and at last she died and I was left alone. I had saved money while out at service, but mother's sickness and funeral swept it all away and now I had to begin all over again.

Aunt Fanny had always been anxious for me to get an education, as I did not know how to read or write, and she thought that was wrong. Schools are different in Poland from what they are in this country, and I was always too busy to learn to read and write. So when mother died I thought I would try to learn a trade and then I could go to school at night and learn to speak the English language well.

So I went to work in Allen Street (Manhattan) in what they call a sweatshop, making skirts by machine. I was new at the work and the foreman scolded me a great deal.

"Now, then," he would say, "this place is not for you to be looking around in. Attend to your work. That is what you have to do."

I did not know at first that you must not look around and talk, and I made many mistakes with the sewing, so that I was often called a "stupid animal." But I made $4 a week by working six days in the week. For there are two Sabbaths here—our own Sabbath, that comes on a Saturday, and the Christian Sabbath that comes on Sunday. It is against our law to work on our own Sabbath, so we work on their Sabbath.

In Poland I and my father and mother used to go to the synagogue on the Sabbath, but here the women don't go to the synagogue much, though the men do. They are shut up working hard all the week long and when the Sabbath comes they like to sleep long in bed and afterward they must go out where they can breathe the air. The rabbis are strict here, but not so strict as in the old country.

I lived at this time with a girl named Ella, who worked in the same factory and made $5 a week. We had the room all to ourselves, paying $1.50 a week for it, and doing light housekeeping. It was in Allen Street, and the window looked out of the back, which was good, because there was an elevated railroad in front, and in summer time a great deal of dust and dirt came in at the front windows. We were on the fourth story and could see all that was going on in the back rooms of the houses behind us, and early in the morning the sun used to come in our window.

We did our cooking on an oil stove, and lived well, as this list of our expenses for one week will show:

*Ella and Sadie for Food (One Week):* Tea $0.06; Cocoa .10; Bread and rolls .40; Canned vegetables .20; Potatoes .10; Milk .21; Fruit .20; Butter .15; Meat .60; Fish .15; Laundry .25; Total: $2.42; Add rent 1.50; Grand total: $8.92.

Of course, we could have lived cheaper, but we are both fond of good things and felt that we could afford them.

We paid 18 cents for a half pound of tea so as to get it good, and it lasted us three weeks, because we had cocoa for breakfast. We paid 5 cents for six rolls and 5 cents a loaf for bread, which was the best quality. Oatmeal cost us 10 cents for three and one-half pounds, and we often had it in the morning, or Indian meal porridge in the place of it, costing about the same. Half a dozen eggs cost about 13 cents on an average, and we could get all the meat we wanted for a good hearty meal for 20 cents—two pounds of chops, or a steak, or a bit of veal, or a neck of lamb—something like that. Fish included butter fish, porgies, codfish and smelts, averaging about 8 cents a pound.

Some people who buy at the last of the market, when the men with the carts want to go home, can get things very cheap, but they are likely to be stale, and we did not often do that with fish, fresh vegetables, fruit, milk or meat. Things that kept well we did buy that way and got good bargains. I got thirty potatoes for 10 cents one time, though generally I could not get more than fifteen of them for that amount. Tomatoes, onions and cabbages, too, we bought that way and did well, and we found a factory where we could buy the finest broken crackers for 3 cents a pound, and another place where we got broken candy for 10 cents a pound. Our cooking was done on an oil stove, and the oil for the stove and the lamp cost us 10 cents a week.

It cost me $2 a week to live, and I had a dollar a week to spend on clothing and pleasure, and saved the other dollar. I went to night school, but it was hard work learning at first as I did not know much English.

Two years ago I came to Brownsville, where so many of my people are, and where I have friends. I got work in a factory making underskirts—all sorts of cheap underskirts, like cotton and calico for the summer and woolen for the winter, but never the silk, satin or velvet underskirts. I earned $4.50 a week and lived on $2 a week, the same as before.

I got a room in the house of some friends who lived near the factory. I pay $1 a week for the room and am allowed to do light housekeeping—that is, cook my meals in it. I get my own breakfast in the morning, just a cup of coffee and a roll, and at noon time I come home to dinner and take a plate of soup and a slice of bread with the lady of the house. My food for a week costs a dollar, just as it did in Allen Street, and I have the rest of my money to do as I like with. I am earning $5.50 a week now, and will probably get another increase soon.

It isn't piecework in our factory, but one is paid by the amount of work done just the same. So it is like piecework. All the hands get different amounts, some as low as $3.50 and some of the men as high as $16 a week. The factory is in the third story of a brick building. It is in a room twenty feet long and fourteen broad. There are fourteen machines in it. I and the daughter of the people with whom I live work two of these machines. The other operators are all men, some young and some old.

At first a few of the young men were rude. When they passed me they would touch my hair and talk about my eyes and my red cheeks, and make jokes. I cried and said that if they did not stop I would leave the place. The boss said that that should not be, that no one must annoy me. Some of the other men stood up for me, too, especially Henry, who said two or three times that he wanted to fight. Now the men all treat me very nicely. It was just that some of them did not know better, not being educated.

Henry is tall and dark, and he has a small mustache. His eyes are brown and large. He is pale and much educated, having been to school. He knows a great many things and has some money saved. I think nearly $400. He is not going to be in a sweatshop all the time, but will soon be in the real estate business, for a lawyer that knows him well has promised to open an office and pay him to manage it.

Henry has seen me home every night for a long time and makes love to me. He wants me to marry him, but I am not seventeen yet, and I think that is too young. He is only nineteen, so we can wait.

I have been to the fortune teller's three or four times, and she always tells me that though I have had such a lot of trouble I am to be very rich and happy. I believe her because she has told me so many things that have come true. So I will keep on working in the factory for a time. Of course it is hard, but I would have to work hard even if I was married.

I get up at half-past five o'clock every morning and make myself a cup of coffee on the oil stove. I eat a bit of bread and perhaps some fruit and then go to work. Often I get there soon after six o'clock so as to be in good time, though the factory does not open till seven. I have heard that there is a sort of clock that calls you at the very time you want to get up, but I can't believe that because I don't see how the clock would know.

At seven o'clock we all sit down to our machines and the boss brings to each one the pile of work that he or she is to finish during the day, what they call in English their "stint." This pile is put down beside the machine and as soon as a skirt is done it is laid on the other side of the machine. Sometimes the work is not all finished by six o'clock and then the one who is behind must work overtime. Sometimes one is finished ahead of time and gets away at four or five o'clock, but generally we are not done till six o'clock.

The machines go like mad all day, because the faster you work the more money you get. Sometimes in my haste I get my finger caught and the needle goes right through it. It goes so quick, though, that it does not hurt much. I bind the finger up with a piece of cotton and go on working. We all have accidents like that. Where the needle goes through the nail it makes a sore finger, or where it splinters a bone it does much harm. Sometimes a finger has to come off. Generally, though, one can be cured by a salve.

All the time we are working the boss walks about examining the finished garments and making us do them over again if they are not just right. So we have to be careful as well as swift. But I am getting so good at the work that within a year I will be making $7 a week, and then I can save at least $3.50 a week. I have over $200 saved now.

The machines are all run by foot-power, and at the end of the day one feels so weak that there is a great temptation to lie right down and sleep. But you must go out and get air, and have some pleasure. So instead of lying down I go out, generally with Henry. Sometimes we go to Coney Island, where there are good dancing places, and sometimes we go to Ulmer Park to picnics. I am very fond of dancing, and, in fact, all sorts of pleasure. I go to the theater quite often, and like those plays that make you cry a great deal. *The Two Orphans* is good. Last time I saw it I cried all night because of the hard times that the children had in the play. I am going to see it again when it comes here.

For the last two winters I have been going to night school. I have learned reading, writing and arithmetic. I can read quite well in English now and I look at the newspapers every day. I read English books, too, some times. The last one that I read was *A Mad Marriage*, by Charlotte Braeme. She's a grand writer and makes things just like real to you. You feel as if you were the poor girl yourself going to get married to a rich duke.

I am going back to night school again this winter. Plenty of my friends go there. Some of the women in my class are more than forty years of age. Like me, they did not have a chance to learn anything in the old country. It is good to have an education; it makes you feel higher. Ignorant people are all low. People say now that I am clever and fine in conversation.

We recently finished a strike in our business. It spread all over and the United Brotherhood of Garment Workers was in it. That takes in the cloakmakers, coatmakers, and all the others. We struck for shorter hours, and after being out four weeks won the fight. We only have to work nine and a half hours a day and we get the same pay as before. So the union does good after all in spite of what some people say against it—that it just takes our money and does nothing.

I pay 25 cents a month to the union, but I do not begrudge that because it is for our benefit. The next strike is going to be for a raise of wages, which we all ought to have. But though I belong to the Union I am not a Socialist or an Anarchist. I don't know exactly what those things mean. There is a little expense for charity, too. If any worker is injured or sick we all give money to help.

Some of the women blame me very much because I spend so much money on clothes. They say that instead of a dollar a week I ought not to spend more than twenty-five cents a week on clothes, and that I should save the rest. But a girl must have clothes if she is to go into good society at Ulmer Park or Coney Island or the theater. Those who blame me are the old country people who have old-fashioned notions, but the people who have been here a long time know better. A girl who does not dress well is stuck in a corner, even if she is pretty, and Aunt Fanny says that I do just right to put on plenty of style.

I have many friends and we often have jolly parties. Many of the young men like to talk to me, but I don't go out with any except Henry.

Lately he has been urging me more and more to get married—but I think I'll wait.

SOURCE: *The Life Stories of Undistinguished Americans As Told by Themselves.* Edited by Hamilton Holt. New York: James Pott and Company. 1906.

# LEE CHEW

### *The Life Story of a Chinese Businessman*
(China; 1906)

*Chew arrived in America shortly before the Chinese Exclusion Act of 1882, when he was sixteen. He tells the story of his jobs in San Francisco, the Midwest, Detroit, Buffalo, and finally New York City. In conclusion, angry at the prejudices that he and other Chinese immigrants have faced, he expresses his national and cultural pride as well as, unfortunately, his own prejudices against other immigrants.*

The village where I was born is situated in the province of Canton, on one of the banks of the Si-Kiang River. It is called a village, although it is really as big as a city, for there are about 5,000 men in it over eighteen years of age—women and children and even youths are not counted in our villages.

All in the village belonged to the tribe of Lee. They did not intermarry with one another, but the men went to other villages for their wives and brought them home to their fathers' houses, and men from other villages—Wus and Wings and Sings and Pongs, etc.—chose wives from among our girls.

When I was a baby I was kept in our house all the time with my mother, but when I was a boy of seven I had to sleep at nights with other boys of the village—about thirty of them in one house. The girls are separated the same way—thirty or forty of them sleeping together in one house away from their parents—and the widows have houses where they work and sleep, though they go to their fathers' houses to eat.

My father's house is built of fine blue brick, better than the brick in the houses here in the United States. It is only one story high, roofed with red tiles and surrounded by a stone wall which also encloses the yard. There are four rooms in the house, one large living room which serves for a parlor and three private rooms, one occupied by my grandfather, who is very old and very honorable; another by my father and mother, and the third by my oldest brother and his wife and two little children. There are no windows, but the door is left open all day.

All the men of the village have farms, but they don't live on them as the farmers do here; they live in the village, but go out during the day time and work their farms, coming home before dark. My father has a farm of about ten acres, on which he grows a great abundance of things—sweet potatoes, rice, beans, peas, yams, sugar cane, pineapples, bananas, lychee nuts and palms. The palm leaves are useful and can be sold. Men make fans of the lower part of each leaf near the stem, and waterproof coats and hats, and awnings for boats, of the parts that are left when the fans are cut out.

So many different things can be grown on one small farm, because we bring plenty of water in a canal from the mountains thirty miles away, and every farmer takes as much as he wants for his fields by means of drains.

He can give each crop the right amount of water.

Our people all working together make these things, the mandarin has nothing to do with it, and we pay no taxes, except a small one on the land. We have our own Government, consisting of the elders of our tribe—the honorable men. When a man gets to be sixty years of age he begins to have honor and to become a leader, and then the older he grows the more he is honored. We had some men who were nearly one hundred years, but very few of them.

In spite of the fact that any man may correct them for a fault, Chinese boys have good times and plenty of play. We played games like tag, and other games like shinny and a sort of football called yin.

We had dogs to play with—plenty of dogs and good dogs—that understand Chinese as well as American dogs understand American language. We hunted with them, and we also went fishing and had as good a time as American boys, perhaps better, as we were almost always together in our house, which was a sort of boys' club house, so we had many playmates. Whatever we did we did all together, and our rivals were the boys of other club houses, with whom we sometimes competed in the games. But all our play outdoors was in the daylight, because there were many graveyards about and after dark, so it was said, black ghosts with flaming mouths and eyes and long claws and teeth would come from these and tear to pieces and devour anyone whom they might meet.

It was not all play for us boys, however. We had to go to school, where we learned to read and write and to recite the precepts of

Kong-foo-tsze and the other Sages, and stories about the great Emperors of China, who ruled with the wisdom of gods and gave to the whole world the light of high civilization and the culture of our literature, which is the admiration of all nations.

I went to my parents' house for meals, approaching my grandfather with awe, my father and mother with veneration and my elder brother with respect. I never spoke unless spoken to, but I listened and heard much concerning the red-haired, green-eyed foreign devils with the hairy faces, who had lately come out of the sea and clustered on our shores. They were wild and fierce and wicked, and paid no regard to the moral precepts of Kong-foo-tsze and the Sages; neither did they worship their ancestors, but pretended to be wiser than their fathers and grandfathers. They loved to beat people and to rob and murder. In the streets of Hong Kong many of them could be seen reeling drunk. Their speech was a savage roar, like the voice of the tiger or the buffalo, and they wanted to take the land away from the Chinese. Their men and women lived together like animals, without any marriage or faithfulness, and even were shameless enough to walk the streets arm in arm in daylight. So the old man said.

All this was very shocking and disgusting, as our women seldom were on the street, except in the evenings, when they went with the water jars to three wells that supplied all the people. Then if they met a man they stood still, with their faces turned to the wall, while he looked the other way when he passed them. A man who spoke to a woman on the street in a Chinese village would be beaten, perhaps killed.

My grandfather told how the English foreign devils had made wicked war on the Emperor, and by means of their enchantments and spells had defeated his armies and forced him to admit their opium, so that the Chinese might smoke and become weakened and the foreign devils might rob them of their land.

My grandfather said that it was well known that the Chinese were always the greatest and wisest among men. They had invented and discovered everything that was good. Therefore the things which the foreign devils had and the Chinese had not must be evil. Some of these things were very wonderful, enabling the red-haired savages to talk with one another, though they might be thousands of miles apart. They had suns that made darkness like day, their ships carried earthquakes and volcanoes to fight for them, and thousands of demons that lived in iron and steel houses spun their cotton and silk, pushed their boats, pulled their cars, printed their newspapers and did other work for them. They were constantly showing disrespect for their ancestors by getting new things to take the place of the old.

I heard about the American foreign devils, that they were false, having made a treaty by which it was agreed that they could freely come to China, and the Chinese as freely go to their country. After this treaty was made China opened its doors to them and then they broke the treaty that they had asked for by shutting the Chinese out of their country.

When I was ten years of age I worked on my father's farm, digging, hoeing, manuring, gathering and carrying the crop. We had no horses, as nobody under the rank of an official is allowed to have a horse in China, and horses do not work on farms there, which is the reason why the roads there are so bad. The people cannot use roads as they are used here, and so they do not make them.

I worked on my father's farm till I was about sixteen years of age, when a man of our tribe came back from America and took ground as large as four city blocks and made a paradise of it. He put a large stone wall around and led some streams through and built a palace and summer house and about twenty other structures, with beautiful bridges over the streams and walks and roads. Trees and flowers, singing birds, water fowl and curious animals were within the walls.

The man had gone away from our village a poor boy. Now he returned with unlimited wealth, which he had obtained in the country of the American wizards. After many amazing adventures he had become a merchant in a city called Mott Street, so it was said.

When his palace and grounds were completed he gave a dinner to all the people who assembled to be his guests. One hundred pigs roasted whole were served on the tables, with chickens, ducks, geese and such an abundance of dainties that our villagers even now lick their fingers when they think of it. He had the best actors from Hong Kong performing, and every musician for miles around was playing and singing. At night the blaze of the lanterns could be seen for many miles.

Having made his wealth among the barbarians this man had faithfully returned to pour it out among his tribesmen, and he is living in our village now very happy, and a pillar of strength to the poor.

The wealth of this man filled my mind with the idea that I, too, would like to go to the country of the wizards and gain some of their wealth, and after a long time my father consented, and gave me his blessing, and my mother took leave of me with tears, while my grandfather laid his hand upon my head and told me to remember and live up to the admonitions of the Sages, to avoid gambling, bad women and men of evil minds, and so to govern my conduct that when I died my ancestors might rejoice to welcome me as a guest on high.

My father gave me $100, and I went to Hong Kong with five other boys from our place and we got steerage passage on a steamer, paying $50 each. Everything was new to me. All my life I had been used to sleeping on a board bed with a wooden pillow, and I found the steamer's bunk very uncomfortable, because it was so soft. The food was different from that which I had been used to, and I did not like it at all. I was afraid of the stews, for the thought of what they might be made of by the wicked wizards of the ship made me ill. Of the great power of these people I saw many signs. The engines that moved the ship were wonderful monsters, strong enough to lift mountains. When I got to San Francisco, which was before the passage of the Exclusion act, I was half starved, because I was afraid to eat the provisions of the barbarians, but a few days' living in the Chinese quarter made me happy again. A man got me work as a house servant in an American family, and my start was the same as that of almost all the Chinese in this country.

The Chinese laundryman does not learn his trade in China; there are no laundries in China. The women there do the washing in tubs and have no washboards or flat irons. All the Chinese laundrymen here were taught in the first place by American women just as I was taught.

When I went to work for that American family I could not speak a word of English, and I did not know anything about housework. The family consisted of husband, wife and two children. They were very good to me and paid me $3.50 a week, of which I could save $3.

I did not know how to do anything, and I did not understand what the lady said to me, but she showed me how to cook, wash, iron, sweep, dust, make beds, wash dishes, clean windows, paint and brass, polish the knives and forks, etc., by doing the things herself and then overseeing my efforts to imitate her. She would take my hands and show them how to do things. She and her husband and children laughed at me a great deal, but it was all good natured. I was not confined to the house in the way servants are confined here, but when my work was done in the morning I was allowed to go out till lunch time. People in California are more generous than they are here.

In six months I had learned how to do the work of our house quite well, and I was getting $5 a week and board, and putting away about $4.25 a week. I had also learned some English, and by going to a Sunday school I learned more English and something about Jesus, who was a great Sage, and whose precepts are like those of Kong-foo-tsze.

It was twenty years ago when I came to this country, and I worked for two years as a servant, getting at the last $35 a month. I sent money home to comfort my parents, but though I dressed well and lived well and had pleasure, going quite often to the Chinese theater and to dinner parties in Chinatown, I saved $50 in the first six months, $90 in the second, $120 in the third and $150 in the fourth. So I had $410 at the end of two years, and I was now ready to start in business.

When I first opened a laundry it was in company with a partner, who had been in the business for some years. We went to a town about 500 miles inland, where a railroad was building. We got a board shanty and worked for the men employed by the railroads. Our rent cost us $10 a month and food nearly $5 a week each, for all food was dear and we wanted the best of everything—we lived principally on rice, chickens, ducks and pork, and did our own cooking. The Chinese take naturally to cooking. It cost us about $50 for our furniture and apparatus, and we made close upon $60 a week, which we divided between us. We had to put up with many insults and some frauds, as men would come in and claim parcels that did not belong to them, saying they had lost their tickets, and would fight if they did not get what they asked for. Sometimes we were taken before Magistrates and fined for losing shirts that we had never seen. On the other hand, we were making money, and even after sending home $3 a week I was able to save about $15. When the railroad construction gang moved on we went with them. The men were rough and prejudiced against us, but not more so than in the big Eastern cities. It is only lately in New York that the Chinese have been able to discontinue putting wire screens in front of their windows, and at the present time the street boys are still breaking the windows of Chinese laundries all over the city, while the police seem to think it a joke.

We were three years with the railroad, and then went to the mines, where we made plenty of money in gold dust, but had a hard time, for many of the miners were wild men who carried revolvers and after drinking would come into our place to shoot and steal shirts, for which we had to pay. One of these men hit his head hard against a flat iron and all the miners came and broke up our laundry, chasing us out of town. They were going to hang us. We lost all our property and $365 in money, which members of the mob must have found.

Luckily most of our money was in the hands of Chinese bankers in San Francisco. I drew $500 and went East to Chicago, where I had a laundry for three years, during which I increased my capital to $2,500. After that I was four years in Detroit. I went home to China in 1897, but returned in 1898, and began a laundry business in Buffalo. But Chinese laundry business now is not as good as it was ten years ago. American cheap labor in the steam laundries has hurt it. So I determined to become a general merchant, and with this idea I came to New York and opened a shop in the Chinese quarter, keeping silks, teas, porcelain, clothes, shoes, hats and Chinese provisions, which include shark's fins and nuts, lily bulbs and lily flowers, lychee nuts and other Chinese dainties, but do not include rats, because it would be too expensive to import them. The rat which is eaten by the Chinese is a field animal which lives on rice, grain and sugar cane. Its flesh is delicious. Many Americans who have tasted shark's fin and bird's nest soup and tiger lily flowers and bulbs are firm friends of Chinese cookery. If they could enjoy one of our fine rats they would go to China to live, so as to get some more.

American people eat ground hogs, which are very like these Chinese rats and they also eat many sorts of food that our people would not touch. Those that have dined with us know that we understand how to live well.

The ordinary laundry shop is generally divided into three rooms. In front is the room where the customers are received, behind that a bedroom and in the back the work shop, which is also the dining room and kitchen. The stove and cooking utensils are the same as those of the Americans.

Work in a laundry begins early on Monday morning—about seven o'clock. There are generally two men, one of whom washes while the other does the ironing. The man who irons does not start in till Tuesday, as the clothes are not ready for him to begin till that time. So he has Sundays and Mondays as holidays. The man who does the washing finishes up on Friday night, and so he has Saturday and Sunday. Each works only five days a week, but those are long days—from seven o'clock in the morning till midnight.

During his holidays the Chinaman gets a good deal of fun out of life. There's a good deal of gambling and some opium smoking, but not so much as Americans imagine. Only a few of New York's Chinamen smoke opium. The habit is very general among rich men and officials in China, but not so much among poor men. I don't think it does as much harm as the liquor that the Americans drink. There's nothing so bad as a drunken man. Opium doesn't make people crazy.

Gambling is mostly fan-tan, but there is a good deal of poker, which the Chinese have learned from Americans and can play very well. They also gamble with dominoes and dice.

The fights among the Chinese and the operations of the hatchet men are all due to gambling. Newspapers often say that they are feuds between the six companies, but that is a mistake. The six companies are purely benevolent societies, which look after the Chinaman when he first lands here. They represent the six southern provinces of China, where most of our people are from, and they are like the German, Swedish, English, Irish and Italian societies which assist emigrants. When the Chinese keep clear of gambling and opium they are not blackmailed, and they have no trouble with hatchet men or any others.

About 500 of New York's Chinese are Christians, the others are Buddhists, Taoists, etc., all mixed up. These haven't any Sunday of their own, but keep New Year's Day and the first and fifteenth days of each month, when they go to the temple in Mott Street.

In all New York there are less than forty Chinese women, and it is impossible to get a Chinese woman out here unless one goes to China and marries her there, and then he must collect affidavits to prove that she really is his wife. That is in case of a merchant. A laundryman can't bring his wife here under any circumstances, and even the women of the Chinese Ambassador's family had trouble getting in lately.

Is it any wonder, therefore, or any proof of the demoralization of our people if some of the white women in Chinatown are not of good character? What other set of men so isolated and so surrounded by alien and prejudiced people are more moral? Men, wherever they may be, need the society of women, and among the white women of Chinatown are many excellent and faithful wives and mothers.

Some fault is found with us for sticking to our old customs here, especially in the matter of clothes, but the reason is that we find American clothes much inferior, so far as comfort and warmth go.

The Chinaman's coat for the winter is very durable, very light and very warm. It is easy and not in the way. If he wants to work he slips out of it in a moment and can put it on again as quickly. Our shoes and hats also are better, we think, for our purposes, than the American clothes. Most of us have tried the American clothes, and they make us feel as if we were in the stocks.

I have found out, during my residence in this country, that much of the Chinese prejudice against Americans is unfounded, and I no longer put faith in the wild tales that were told about them in our village, though some of the Chinese, who have been here twenty years and who are learned men, still believe that there is no marriage in this country, that the land is infested with demons and that all the people are given over to general wickedness.

I know better. Americans are not all bad, nor are they wicked wizards. Still, they have their faults and their treatment of us is outrageous.

The reason why so many Chinese go into the laundry business in this country is because it requires little capital and is one of the few opportunities that are open. Men of other nationalities who are jealous of the Chinese, because he is a more faithful worker than one of their people, have raised such a great outcry about Chinese cheap labor that they have shut him out of working on farms or in factories or building railroads or making streets or digging sewers. He cannot practice any trade, and his opportunities to do business are limited to his own countrymen. So he opens a laundry when he quits domestic service.

The treatment of the Chinese in this country is all wrong and mean. It is persisted in merely because China is not a fighting nation. The Americans would not dare to treat Germans, English, Italians or even Japanese as they treat the Chinese, because if they did there would be a war.

There is no reason for the prejudice against the Chinese. The cheap labor cry was always a falsehood. Their labor was never cheap, and is not cheap now. It has always commanded the highest market price. But the trouble is that the Chinese are such excellent and faithful workers that bosses will have no others when they can get them. If you look at men working on the street you will find an overseer for every four or five of them. That watching is not necessary for Chinese. They work as well when left to themselves as they do when someone is looking at them.

It was the jealousy of laboring men of other nationalities—especially the Irish—that raised all the outcry against the Chinese. No one would hire an Irishman, German, Englishman or Italian when he could get a Chinese, because our countrymen are so much more honest, industrious, steady, sober and painstaking. Chinese were persecuted, not for their vices, but for their virtues. There never was any honesty in the pretended fear of leprosy or in the cheap labor scare, and the persecution continues still, because Americans make a mere practice of loving justice. They are all for money making, and they want to be on the strongest side always. They treat you as a friend while you are prosperous, but if you have a misfortune they don't know you. There is nothing substantial in their friendship.

Irish fill the almshouses and prisons and orphan asylums, Italians are among the most dangerous of men, Jews are unclean and ignorant. Yet they are all let in, while Chinese, who are sober, or duly law-abiding, clean, educated and industrious, are shut out. There are few Chinamen in jails and none in the poor houses. There are no Chinese tramps or drunkards. Many Chinese here have become sincere Christians, in spite of the persecution which they have to endure from their heathen countrymen. More than half the Chinese in this country would become citizens if allowed to do so, and would be patriotic Americans. But how can they make this country their home as matters are now? They are not allowed to bring wives here from China, and if they marry American women there is a great outcry.

All Congressmen acknowledge the injustice of the treatment of my people, yet they continue it. They have no backbone.

Under the circumstances, how can I call this my home, and how can anyone blame me if I take my money and go back to my village in China?

SOURCE: *The Life Stories of Undistinguished Americans As Told by Themselves.* Edited by Hamilton Holt. New York: James Pott and Company. 1906.

# ROCCO CORRESCA

## The Life Story of an Italian Bootblack
(Italy; 1906)

*Corresca is nineteen years old when he tells his already amazing life story. As an orphaned boy in Italy, he was taken in by a crook in Naples who sent him and others boys out to beg and steal. At age fifteen or sixteen, Corresca sailed to New York, where he was claimed as kin by an Italian immigrant but then made to pick through garbage for rags and bones. Never daunted for long, he set out on his own with a friend and opened a shoeshine stand.*

When I was a very small boy I lived in Italy in a large house with many other small boys, who were all dressed alike and were taken care of by some nuns. It was a good place, situated on the side of the mountain, where grapes were growing and melons and oranges and plums.

They taught us our letters and how to pray and say the catechism, and we worked in the fields during the middle of the day. We always had enough to eat and good beds to sleep in at night, and sometimes there were feast days, when we marched about wearing flowers.

Those were good times and they lasted till I was nearly eight years of age. Then an old man came and said he was my grandfather. He showed some papers and cried over me and said that the money had come at last and now he could take me to his beautiful home. He seemed very glad to see me and after they looked at his papers he took me away and we went to the big city—Naples. He kept talking about his beautiful house, but when we got there it was a dark cellar that he lived in and I did not like it at all. Very rich people were on the first floor. They had carriages and servants and music and plenty of good things to eat, but we were down below in the cellar and had nothing. There were four other boys in the cellar and the old man said they were all my brothers. All were larger than I and they beat

64

me at first till one day Francisco said that they should not beat me any more, and then Paolo, who was the largest of all, fought him till Francisco drew a knife and gave him a cut. Then Paolo, too, got a knife and said that he would kill Francisco, but the old man knocked them both down with a stick and took their knives away and gave them beatings.

Each morning we boys all went out to beg and we begged all day near the churches and at night near the theaters, running to the carriages and opening the doors and then getting in the way of the people so that they had to give us money or walk over us. The old man often watched us and at night he took all the money, except when we could hide something.

We played tricks on the people, for when we saw some coming that we thought were rich I began to cry and covered my face and stood on one foot, and the others gathered around me and said:

"Don't cry! Don't cry!"

Then the ladies would stop and ask: "What is he crying about? What is the matter, little boy?"

Francisco or Paolo would answer: "He is very sad because his mother is dead and they have laid her in the grave."

Then the ladies would give me money and the others would take most of it from me.

The old man told us to follow the Americans and the English people, as they were all rich, and if we annoyed them enough they would give us plenty of money. He taught us that if a young man was walking with a young woman he would always give us silver because he would be ashamed to let the young woman see him give us less. There was also a great church where sick people were cured by the saints, and when they came out they were so glad that they gave us money.

Begging was not bad in the summer time because we went all over the streets and there was plenty to see, and if we got much money we could spend some buying things to eat. The old man knew we did that. He used to feel us and smell us to see if we had eaten anything, and he often beat us for eating when we had not eaten.

Early in the morning we had breakfast of black bread rubbed over with garlic or with a herring to give it a flavor. The old man would eat the garlic or the herring himself, but he would rub our bread with it, which he said was as good. He told us that boys should not be greedy and that it was good to fast and that all the saints had fasted. He had a figure of a saint in one corner of the cellar and prayed night and morning that the saint would help him to get money. He made us pray, too, for he said that it was good luck to be religious.

We used to sleep on the floor, but often we could not sleep much because men came in very late at night and played cards with the old man. He sold them wine from a barrel that stood on one end of the table that was there, and if they drank much he won their money. One night he won so much that he was glad and promised the saint some candles for his altar in the church. But that was to get more money. Two nights after that the same men who had lost the money came back and said that they wanted to play again. They were very friendly and laughing, but they won all the money and the old man said they were cheating. So they beat him and went away. When he got up again he took a stick and knocked down the saint's figure and said that he would give no more candles.

I was with the old man for three years. I don't believe that he was my grandfather, though he must have known something about me because he had those papers.

It was very hard in the winter time for we had no shoes and we shivered a great deal. The old man said that we were no good, that we were ruining him, that we did not bring in enough money. He told me that I was fat and that people would not give money to fat beggars. He beat me, too, because I didn't like to steal, as I had heard it was wrong.

"Ah!" said he, "that is what they taught you at that place, is it? To disobey your grandfather that fought with Garibaldi! That is a fine religion!"

The others all stole as well as begged, but I didn't like it and Francisco didn't like it either.

Then the old man said to me: "If you don't want to be a thief you can be a cripple. That is an easy life and they make a great deal of money."

I was frightened then, and that night I heard him talking to one of the men that came to see him. He asked how much he would charge to make me a good cripple like those that crawl about the church. They had a dispute, but at last they agreed and the man said that I should be made so that people would shudder and give me plenty of money.

I was much frightened, but I did not make a sound and in the morning I went out to beg with Francisco. I said to him: "I am going to run away. I don't believe Tony is my grandfather. I don't believe that he fought for Garibaldi, and I don't want to be a cripple, no matter how much money the people may give."

"Where will you go? "Francisco asked me. "I don't know," I said; "somewhere." He thought awhile and then he said: "I will go, too."

So we ran away out of the city and begged from the country people as we went along. We came to a village down by the sea and a long way from Naples and there we found some fishermen and they took us aboard their boat. We were with them five years, and though it was a very hard life we liked it well because there was always plenty to eat. Fish do not keep long and those that we did not sell we ate.

The chief fisherman, whose name was Ciguciano, had a daughter, Teresa, who was very beautiful, and though she was two years younger than I, she could cook and keep house quite well. She was a kind, good girl and he was a good man. When we told him about the old man who told us he was our grandfather, the fisherman said he was an old rascal who should be in prison for life. Teresa cried much when she heard that he was going to make me a cripple. Ciguciano said that all the old man had taught us was wrong—that it was bad to beg, to steal and to tell lies. He called in the priest and the priest said the same thing and was very angry at the old man in Naples, and he taught us to read and write in the evenings. He also taught us our duties to the church and said that the saints were good and would only help men to do good things, and that it was a wonder that lightning from heaven had not struck the old man dead when he knocked down the saint's figure.

We grew large and strong with the fisherman and he told us that we were getting too big for him, that he could not afford to pay us the money that we were worth. He was a fine, honest man—one in a thousand.

Now and then I had heard things about America—that it was a far-off country where everybody was rich and that Italians went there and made plenty of money, so that they could return to Italy and live in pleasure ever after. One day I met a young man who pulled out a handful of gold and told me he had made that in America in a few days.

I said I should like to go there, and he told me that if I went he would take care of me. and see that I was safe. I told Francisco and he wanted to go, too. So we said good-bye to our good friends. Teresa cried and kissed us both and the priest came and shook our hands and told us to be good men, and that no matter where we went God and his saints were always near us and that if we lived well we should all meet again in heaven. We cried, too, for it was our home, that place. Ciguciano gave us money and slapped us on the back and said that we should be great. But he felt bad, too, at seeing us go away after all that time.

The young man took us to a big ship and got us work away down where the fires are. We had to carry coal to the place where it could be thrown on the fires. Francisco and I were very sick from the great heat at first and lay on the coal for a long time, but they threw water on us and made us get up. We could not stand on our feet well, for everything was going around and we had no strength. We said that we wished we had stayed in Italy no matter how much gold there was in America. We could not eat for three days and could not do much work. Then we got better and sometimes we went up above and looked about. There was no land anywhere and we were much surprised. How could the people tell where to go when there was no land to steer by?

We were so long on the water that we began to think we should never get to America or that, perhaps, there was not any such place, but at last we saw land and came up to New York.

We were glad to get over without giving money, but I have heard since that we should have been paid for our work among the coal and that the young man who had sent us got money for it. We were all landed on an island and the bosses there said that Francisco and I must go back because we had not enough money, but a man named Bartolo came up and told them that we were brothers and he was our uncle and would take care of us. He brought two other men who swore that they knew us in Italy and that Bartolo was our uncle. I had never seen any of them before, but even then Bartolo might be my uncle, so I did not say anything. The bosses of the island let us go out with Bartolo after he had made the oath.

We came to Brooklyn, New York, to a wooden house in Adams Street that was full of Italians from Naples. Bartolo had a room on the third floor and there were fifteen men in the room, all boarding with Bartolo. He did the cooking on a stove in the middle of the room and there were beds all around the sides, one bed above another. It was very hot in the room, but we were soon asleep, for we were very tired.

The next morning, early, Bartolo told us to go out and pick rags and get bottles. He gave us bags and hooks and showed us the ash barrels. On the streets where the fine houses are the people are very careless and put out good things, like mattresses and umbrellas, clothes, hats and boots. We brought all these to Bartolo and he made them new again and sold them on the sidewalk; but mostly we brought rags and bones. The rags we had to wash in the back yard and then we hung them to dry on lines under the ceiling in our room. The bones we kept under the beds till Bartolo could find a man to buy them.

Most of the men in our room worked at digging the sewer. Bartolo got them the work and they paid him about one-quarter of their wages. Then he charged them for board and he bought the clothes for them, too. So they got little money after all.

Bartolo was always saying that the rent of the room was so high that he could not make anything, but he was really making plenty. He was what they call a padrone and is now a very rich man. The men that were living with him had just come to the country and could not speak English. They had all been sent by the young man we met in Italy. Bartolo told us all that we must work for him and that if we did not the police would come and put us in prison.

He gave us very little money, and our clothes were some of those that were found on the street. Still we had enough to eat and we had meat quite often, which we never had in Italy. Bartolo got it from the butcher—the meat that he could not sell to the other people—but it was quite good meat. Bartolo cooked it in the pan while we all sat on our beds in the evening. Then he cut it into small bits and passed the pan around, saying:

"See what I do for you and yet you are not glad. I am too kind a man, that is why I am so poor."

We were with Bartolo nearly a year, but some of our countrymen who had been in the place a long time said that Bartolo had no right to us and we could get work for a dollar and a half a day, which, when you make it lire is very much. So we went away one day to Newark and got work on the street. Bartolo came after us and make a great noise, but the boss said that if he did not go away soon the police would have him. Then he went, saying that there was no justice in this country.

We paid a man five dollars each for getting us the work and we were with that boss for six months. He was Irish, but a good man and he gave us our money every Saturday night. We lived much better than with Bartolo, and when the work was done we each had nearly $200 saved. Plenty of the men spoke English and they taught us, and we taught them to read and write. That was at night, for we had a lamp in our room, and there were only five other men who lived in that room with us.

We got up at half-past five o'clock every morning and made coffee on the stove and had a breakfast of bread and cheese, onions, garlic and red herrings. We went to work at seven o'clock and in the middle of the day we had soup and bread in a place where we got it for two cents a plate. In the evenings we had a good dinner with meat of some kind and potatoes. We got from the butcher the meat that other people would not buy because they said it was old, but they don't know what is good. We paid four or five cents a pound for it and it was the best, though I have heard of people paying sixteen cents a pound.

When the Newark boss told us that there was no more work Francisco and I talked about what we would do and we went back to Brooklyn to a saloon near Hamilton Ferry where we got a job cleaning it out and slept in a little room upstairs. There was a bootblack named Michael on the corner and when I had time I helped him and learned the business. Francisco cooked the lunch in the saloon and he, too, worked for the bootblack and we were soon able to make the best polish.

Then we thought we would go into business and we got a basement on Hamilton Avenue, near the Ferry, and put four chairs in it. We paid $75 for the chairs and all the other things. We had tables and looking glasses there and curtains. We took the papers that have the pictures in and made the place high toned. Outside we had a big sign that said:

## THE BEST SHINE FOR TEN CENTS

Men that did not want to pay ten cents could get a good shine for five cents, but it was not an oil shine. We had two boys helping us and paid each of them fifty cents a day. The rent of the place was $20 a month, so the expenses were very great, but we made money from the beginning. We slept in the basement, but got our meals in the saloon till we could put a stove in our place, and then Francisco cooked for us all. That would not do, though, because some of our customers said that they did not like to smell garlic and onions and red herrings. I thought that was strange, but we had to do what the customers said. So we got the woman who lived upstairs to give us our meals and paid her $1.50 a week each. She gave the boys soup in the middle of the day—five cents for two plates.

We remembered the priest, the friend of Ciguciano, and what he had said to us about religion, and as soon as we came to the country we began to go to the Italian church. The priest we found here was a good man, but he asked the people for money for the church. The Italians did not like to give because they said it looked like buying religion. The priest says it is different here from Italy because all the churches there are what they call endowed, while here all they have is what the people give. Of course I and Francisco understand that, but the Italians who cannot read and write shake their heads and say that it is wrong for a priest to want money.

We had said that when we saved $1,000 each we would go back to Italy and buy a farm, but now that the time is coming we are so busy and making so much money that we think we will stay. We have opened another parlor near South Ferry, in New York. We have to pay $30 a month rent, but the business is very good. The boys in this place charge sixty cents a day because there is so much work.

At first we did not know much of this country, but by and by we learned. There are here plenty of Protestants who are heretics, but they have a religion, too. Many of the finest churches are Protestant, but they have no saints and no altars, which seems strange.

These people are without a king such as ours in Italy. It is what they call a Republic, as Garibaldi wanted, and every year in the fall the people vote. They wanted us to vote last fall, but we did not. A man came and said that he would get us made Americans for fifty cents and then we could get two dollars for our votes. I talked to some of our people and they told me that we should have to put a paper in a box telling who we wanted to govern us.

I went with five men to the court and when they asked me how long I had been in the country I told them two years. Afterward my countrymen said I was a fool and would never learn politics.

"You should have said you were five years here and then we would swear to it," was what they told me.

I and Francisco are to be Americans in three years. The court gave us papers and said we must wait and we must be able to read some things and tell who the ruler of the country is.

There are plenty of rich Italians here, men who a few years ago had nothing and now have so much money that they could not count all their dollars in a week. The richest ones go away from the other Italians and live with the Americans.

We have joined a club and have much pleasure in the evenings. The club has rooms down in Sackett Street and we meet many people and are learning new things all the time. We were very ignorant when we came here, but now we have learned much.

On Sundays we get a horse and carriage from the grocer and go down to Coney Island. We go to the theaters often, and other evenings we go to the houses of our friends and play cards.

I am now nineteen years of age and have $700 saved. Francisco is twenty-one and has about $900. We shall open some more parlors soon. I know an Italian who was a bootblack ten years ago and now bosses bootblacks all over the city, who has so much money that if it was turned into gold it would weigh more than himself.

Francisco and I have a room to ourselves and some people call us "swells." Ciguciano said that we should be great men. Francisco bought a gold watch with a gold chain as thick as his thumb. He is a very handsome fellow and I think he likes a young lady that he met at a picnic out at Ridgewood.

I often think of Ciguciano and Teresa. He is a good man, one in a thousand, and she was very beautiful. Maybe I shall write to them about coming to this country.

SOURCE: *The Life Stories of Undistinguished Americans As Told by Themselves.* Edited by Hamilton Holt. New York: James Pott and Company. 1906.

# JACOB RIIS

*The Making of an American*
(Denmark; 1908)

*Jacob Riis (1849–1914) was one of the great newspaper crusaders; his book*
How the Other Half Lives *(1890) called attention to the plight of the*
*underclass and immigrants in New York City. In these excerpts from his*
*memoir, he recounts his own experiences as a recent down-and-out immigrant.*

The steamer *Iowa,* from Glasgow, made port after a long and stormy
voyage, on Whitsunday, 1870. She had come up during the night,
and cast anchor off Castle Garden. It was a beautiful spring morning,
and as I looked over the rail at the miles of straight streets, the green
heights of Brooklyn, and the stir of ferryboats and pleasure craft on
the river, my hopes rose high that somewhere in this teeming hive
there would be a place for me. What kind of a place I had myself no
clear notion of. I would let that work out as it could. Of course I had
my trade to fall back on, but I am afraid that is all the use I thought
of putting it to. The love of change belongs to youth, and I meant to
take a hand in things as they came along. I had a pair of strong hands,
and stubbornness enough to do for two; also a strong belief that in
a free country, free from the dominion of custom, of caste, as well as
of men, things would somehow come right in the end, and a man
get shaken into the corner where he belonged if he took a hand in
the game. I think I was right in that. If it took a lot of shaking to get
me where I belonged, that was just what I needed. Even my mother
admits that now . . .

I made it my first business to buy a navy revolver of the largest size,
investing in the purchase exactly one-half of my capital. I strapped
the weapon on the outside of my coat and strode up Broadway,
conscious that I was following the fashion of the country. I knew it
upon the authority of a man who had been there before me and had
returned, a gold digger in the early days of California; but America
was America to us. We knew no distinction of West and East. By

rights there ought to have been buffaloes and red Indians charging up and down Broadway. I am sorry to say that it is easier even today to make lots of people over there believe that than that New York is paved, and lighted with electric lights, and quite as civilized as Copenhagen. They will have it that it is in the wilds. I saw none of the signs of this, but I encountered a friendly policeman, who, sizing me and my pistol up, tapped it gently with his club and advised me to leave it home, or I might get robbed of it. This, at first blush, seemed to confirm my apprehensions; but he was a very nice policeman, and took time to explain, seeing that I was very green. And I took his advice and put the revolver away, secretly relieved to get rid of it. It was quite heavy to carry around.

I had letters to the Danish Consul and to the president of the American Banknote Company, Mr. Goodall. I think perhaps he was not then the president, but became so afterward. Mr. Goodall had once been wrecked on the Danish coast and rescued by the captain of the lifesaving crew, a friend of my family. But they were both in Europe, and in just four days I realized that there was no special public clamor for my services in New York, and decided to go West.

A missionary in Castle Garden was getting up a gang of men for the Brady's Bend Iron Works on the Allegheny River, and I went along. We started a full score, with tickets paid, but only two of us reached the Bend. The rest calmly deserted in Pittsburgh and went their way. . . .

The [iron works] company mined its own coal. Such as it was, it cropped out of the hills right and left in narrow veins, sometimes too shallow to work, seldom affording more space to the digger than barely enough to permit him to stand upright. You did not go down through a shaft, but straight in through the side of a hill to the bowels of the mountain, following a track on which a little donkey drew the coal to the mouth of the mine and sent it down the incline to run up and down a hill a mile or more by its own gravity before it reached the place of unloading. Through one of these we marched in, Adler and I, one summer morning, with new pickaxes on our shoulders and nasty little oil lamps fixed in our hats to light us through the darkness, where every second we stumbled over chunks of slate rock, or into pools of water that oozed through from above. An old miner whose way lay past the fork in the tunnel where our lead began showed us how to use our picks and the timbers to brace the slate that roofed over the vein, and left us to ourselves in a chamber perhaps ten feet wide and the height of a man.

We were to be paid by the ton—I forget how much, but it was very little—and we lost no time getting to work. We had to dig away the coal at the floor without picks, lying on our knees to do it, and afterward drive wedges under the roof to loosen the mass. It was hard work, and, entirely inexperienced as we were, we made but little headway. As the day wore on, the darkness and silence grew very oppressive, and made us start nervously at the least thing. The sudden arrival of our donkey with its cart gave me a dreadful fright. The friendly beast greeted us with a joyous bray and rubbed its shaggy sides against us in the most companionable way. In the flickering light of my lamp I caught sight of its long ears waving over me—I don't believe I had seen three donkeys before in my life; there were none where I came from—and heard that demoniac shriek, and I verily believe I thought the evil one had come for me in person. I know that I nearly fainted.

That donkey was a discerning animal. I think it knew when it first set eyes on us that we were not going to overwork it; and we didn't. When, toward evening, we quit work, after narrowly escaping being killed by a large stone that fell from the roof in consequence of our neglect to brace it up properly, our united efforts had resulted in barely filling two of the little carts, and we had earned, if I recollect aright, something like sixty cents each. The fall of the roof robbed us of all desire to try mining again. It knocked the lamps from our hats, and, in darkness that could almost be felt, we groped our way back to the light along the track, getting more badly frightened as we went. The last stretch of way we ran, holding each other's hands as though we were not men and miners, but two frightened children in the dark ...

*[A short time later he learned of the outbreak of the Franco-Prussian War, and at once determined to enlist.]*

I reached New York with just one cent in my pocket, and put up at a boarding-house where the charge was one dollar a day. In this no moral obliquity was involved. I had simply reached the goal for which I had sacrificed all, and felt sure that the French people or the Danish Consul would do the rest quickly. But there was evidently something wrong somewhere. The Danish Consul could only register my demand to be returned to Denmark in the event of war. They have my letter at the office yet, he tells me, and they will call me out with the reserves. The French were fitting out no volunteer army that I could get on the track of, and nobody was paying the passage of fighting men. The end of it was that, after pawning my revolver and my top-boots, the only valuable possessions I had left, to pay for my lodging, I was thrown on the street, and told to come back when I had more money. That night I wandered about New York with a gripsack that had only a linen duster and a pair of socks in it, turning over in my mind what to do next. Toward midnight I passed a house in Clinton Place that was lighted up festively. Laughter and the hum of many voices came from within. I listened. They spoke French. A society of Frenchmen having their annual dinner, the watchman in the block told me. There at last was my chance. I went up the steps and rang the bell. A flunkey in a dress-suit opened, but when he saw that I was not a guest, but to all appearances a tramp, he tried to put me out. I, on my part, tried to explain. There was an altercation and two gentlemen of the society appeared. They listened impatiently to what I had to say, then, without a word, thrust me into the street, and slammed the door in my face.

It was too much. Inwardly raging, I shook the dust of the city from my feet and took the most direct route out of it, straight up Third Avenue. I walked till the stars in the east began to pale, and then climbed into a wagon that stood at the curb, to sleep. I did not notice that it was a milk-wagon. The sun had not risen yet when the driver came, unceremoniously dragged me out by the feet, and dumped me into the gutter. On I went with my gripsack, straight ahead, until toward noon I reached Fordham College, famished and footsore. I had eaten nothing since the previous day, and had vainly tried to make a bath in the Bronx River do for breakfast. Not yet could I cheat my stomach that way.

The college gates were open, and I strolled wearily in, without aim or purpose. On a lawn some young men were engaged in athletic exercises, and I stopped to look and admire the beautiful shade-trees and the imposing building. So at least it seems to me at this distance. An old monk in a cowl, whose noble face I sometimes recall in my dreams, came over and asked kindly if I was not hungry. I was in all conscience fearfully hungry, and I said so, though I did not mean to. I had never seen a real live monk before, and my Lutheran training had not exactly inclined me in their favor. I ate of the food set before me, not without qualms of conscience, and with a secret suspicion that I would next be asked to abjure my faith, or at least do homage to the Virgin Mary, which I was firmly resolved not to do. But when, the meal finished, I was sent on my way with enough to do me for supper, without the least allusion having been made to my soul, I felt heartily ashamed of myself. I am just as good a Protestant as I ever was. Among my own I am a kind of heretic even, because I cannot put up with the apostolic succession; but I have no quarrel with the excellent charities of the Roman Church, or with the noble spirit that animated them. I learned that lesson at Fordham thirty years ago.

Up the railroad track I went, and at night hired out to a truck-farmer, with the freedom of his hay-mow for my sleeping quarters. But when I had hoed cucumbers three days in a scorching sun, till my back ached as if it were going to break, and the farmer guessed that he would call it square for three shillings, I went farther. A man is not necessarily a philanthropist, it seems, because he tills the soil. I did not hire out again. I did odd jobs to earn my meals, and slept in the fields at night, still turning over in my mind how to get across the sea. An incident of those wanderings comes to mind while I am writing. They were carting in hay, and when night came on, some-where about Mount Vernon, I gathered an armful of wisps that had fallen from the loads, and made a bed for myself in a wagon-shed by the roadside. In the middle of the night I was awakened by a loud outcry. A fierce light shone in my face. It was the lamp of a carriage that had been driven into the shed. I was lying between the horse's feet unhurt. A gentleman sprang from the carriage, more frightened than I, and bent over me. When he found that I had suffered no injury, he put his hand in his pocket and held out a silver quarter. "Go," he said, "and drink it up."

"Drink it up yourself!" I shouted angrily. "What do you take me for?"

They were rather high heroics, seeing where I was, but he saw nothing to laugh at. He looked earnestly at me for a moment, then held out his hand and shook mine heartily. "I believe you," he said; "yet you need it, or you would not sleep here. Now will you take it from me?" And I took the money.

The next day it rained, and the next day after that, and I footed it back to the city, still on my vain quest. A quarter is not a great capital to subsist on in New York when one is not a beggar and has no friends. Two days of it drove me out again to find at least the food to keep me alive; but in those two days I met the man who, long years after, was to be my honored chief, Charles A. Dana, the editor of the *Sun*. There had been an item in the *Sun* about a volunteer regiment being fitted out for France. I went up to the office, and was admitted to Mr. Dana's presence. I fancy I must have appealed to his sense of the ludicrous, dressed in top-boots and a linen duster much the worse for wear, and demanding to be sent out to fight. He knew nothing about recruiting. Was I French? No, Danish; it had been in his paper about the regiment. He smiled a little at my faith, and said editors sometimes did not know about everything that was in their papers. I turned to go, grievously disappointed, but he called me back.

"Have you," he said, looking searchingly at me; "have you had your breakfast?"

No, God knows that I did not; neither that day nor for many days before. That was one of the things I had at last learned to consider among the superfluities of an effete civilization. I suppose I had no need of telling it to him, for it was plain to read in my face. He put his hand in his pocket and pulled out a dollar.

"There," he said, "go and get your breakfast; and better give up the war."

Give up the war! and for a breakfast. I spurned the dollar hotly.

"I came here to enlist, not to beg money for breakfast," I said, and strode out of the office, my head in the air, but my stomach crying out miserably in rebellion against my pride. I revenged myself upon it by leaving my topboots with the "uncle," who was my only friend and relative here, and filling my stomach upon the proceeds. I had one good dinner, anyhow, for when I got through there was only twenty-five cents left of the dollar I borrowed upon my last article of "dress." That I paid for a ticket to Perth Amboy, near which place I found work in Pfeiffer's clay-bank.

Pfeiffer was a German, but his wife was Irish and so were his hands, all except a giant Norwegian and myself. The third day was Sunday, and was devoted to drinking much beer, which Pfeiffer, with an eye to business, furnished on the premises. When they were drunk, the tribe turned upon the Norwegian, and threw him out. It seems that this was a regular weekly occurrence. Me they fired out at the same time, but afterward paid no attention to me. The whole crew of them perched on the Norwegian and belabored him with broomsticks and bales ticks until they roused the sleeping Berserk in him. As I was coming to his relief, I saw the human heap heave and rock. From under it arose the enraged giant, tossed his tormentors aside as if they were so much chaff, battered down the door of the house in which they took refuge, and threw them all, Mrs. Pfeiffer included, through the window. They were not hurt, and within two hours they were drinking more beer together and swearing at one another endearingly. I concluded that I had better go on, though Mr. Pfeiffer regretted that he never paid his hands in the middle of the month. It appeared afterward that he objected likewise to paying them at the end of the month, or at the beginning of the next. He owes me two days' wages yet.

At sunset on the second day after my desertion of Pfeiffer I walked across a footbridge into a city with many spires, in one of which a chime of bells rang out a familiar tune. The city was New Brunswick. I turned down a side street where two stone churches stood side by side. A gate in the picket fence had been left open, and I went in looking for a place to sleep. Back in the churchyard I found what I sought in the brownstone slab covering the tomb of, I know now, an old pastor of the Dutch Reformed Church, who died full of wisdom and grace. I am afraid that I was not overburdened with either, or I might have gone to bed with a full stomach, too, instead of chewing the last of the windfall apples that had been my diet on my two days' trip; but if he slept as peacefully under the slab as I slept on it, he was doing well. I had for once a dry bed, and brownstone keeps warm long after the sun has set. The night dews and the snakes, and the dogs that kept sniffing and growling half the night in the near distance, had made me tired of sleeping in the fields. The dead were much better company. They minded their own business, and let a fellow alone . . .

*[He found no employment in New Brunswick and after six weeks in a neighboring brickyard he returned to New York, to be again disappointed in an effort to enlist.]*

The city was full of idle men. My last hope, a promise of employment in a human-hair factory, failed, and, homeless and penniless, I joined the great army of tramps, wandering about the streets in the daytime with the one aim of somehow stilling the hunger that gnawed at my vitals, and fighting at night with vagrant curs or outcasts as miserable as myself for the protection of some sheltering ash-bin or doorway. I was too proud in all my misery to beg. I do not believe I ever did. But I remember well a basement window at the downtown Delmonico's, the silent appearance of my ravenous face at which, at a certain hour in the evening, always evoked a generous supply of meat-bones and rolls from a white-capped cook who spoke French. That was the saving clause. I accepted his rolls as installment of the debt his country owed me, or ought to owe me, for my unavailing efforts in its behalf.

It was under such auspices that I made the acquaintance of Mulberry Bend, the Five Points, and the rest of the slums, with which there was in the years to come to be a reckoning. . . .

There was until last winter a doorway in Chatham Square, that of the old Barnum clothing store, which I could never pass without recalling those nights of hopeless misery with the policeman's periodic "Get up there! Move on!" reinforced by a prod of his club or the toe of his boot. I slept there, or tried to, when crowded out of the tenements in the Bend by their utter nastiness. Cold and wet weather had set in, and a linen duster was all that covered my back. There was a woollen blanket in my trunk which I had from home—the one, my mother had told me, in which I was wrapped when I was born; but the trunk was in the "hotel" as security for money I owed for board, and I asked for it in vain. I was now too shabby to get work, even if there had been any to get. I had letters still to friends of my family in New York who might have helped me, but hunger and want had not conquered my pride. I would come to them, if at all, as their equal, and, lest I fall into temptation, I destroyed the letters. So, having burned my bridges behind me, I was finally and utterly alone in the city, with the winter approaching and every shivering night in the streets reminding me that a time was rapidly coming when such a life as I led could no longer be endured.

Not in a thousand years would I be likely to forget the night when it came. It had rained all day, a cold October storm, and night found me, with the chill downpour unabated, down by the North River, soaked through and through, with no chance for a supper, forlorn and discouraged. I sat on the bulwark, listening to the falling rain and the swish of the dark tide, and thinking of home. How far it seemed, and how impassable the gulf now between the "castle" with its refined ways, between her in her dainty girlhood and me sitting there, numbed with the cold that was slowly stealing away my senses with my courage. There was warmth and cheer where she was. Here an overpowering sense of desolation came upon me. I hitched a little nearer the edge. What if? Would they miss me or long at home if no word came from me? Perhaps they might never hear. What was the use of keeping it up any longer with, God help us, everything against and nothing to back a lonely lad?

And even then the help came. A wet and shivering body was pressed against mine, and I felt rather than heard a piteous whine in my ear. It was my companion in misery, a little outcast black-and-tan, afflicted with fits, that had shared the shelter of a friendly doorway with me one cold night and had clung to me ever since with a loyal affection that was the one bright spot in my hard life. As my hand stole mechanically down to caress it, it crept upon my knees and licked my face, as if it meant to tell me that there was one who understood; that I was not alone. And the love of the faithful little beast thawed the icicles in my heart. I picked it up in my arms and fled from the tempter; fled to where there were lights and men moving, if they cared less for me than I for them—anywhere so that I saw and heard the river no more . . .

*[After a while he fell in with some Danish friends and there was a period of more prosperous times, including some experiences on the lecture platform. Then came further adventures and finally . . .]*

I made up my mind to go into the newspaper business. It seemed to me that a reporter's was the highest and noblest of all callings; no one could sift wrong from right as he, and punish the wrong. In that I was right. I have not changed my opinion on that point one whit, and I am sure I never shall. The power of fact is the mightiest lever of this or of any day. The reporter has his hand upon it, and it is his grievous fault if he does not use it well. I thought I would make a good reporter. My father had edited our local newspaper, and such little help as I had been of to him had given me a taste for the business. Being of that mind, I went to the *Courier* office one morning and asked for the editor. He was not in. Apparently nobody was. I wandered through room after room, all empty, till at last I came to one in which sat a man with a paste-pot and a pair of long shears. This must be the editor; he had the implements of his trade. I told him my errand while he clipped away.

"What is it you want?" he asked, when I had ceased speaking and waited for an answer.

"Work," I said.

"Work!" said he, waving me haughtily away with the shears; "we don't work here. This is a newspaper office."

I went, abashed. I tried the *Express* next. This time I had the editor pointed out to me. He was just coming through the business office. At the door I stopped him and preferred my request. He looked me over, a lad fresh from the shipyard, with horny hands and a rough coat, and asked:

"What are you?"

"A carpenter," I said.

The man turned upon his heel with a loud, rasping laugh and shut the door in my face. For a moment I stood there stunned. His ascending steps on the stairs brought back my senses. I ran to the door, and flung it open. "You laugh!" I shouted, shaking my fist at him, standing halfway up the stairs; "you laugh now, but wait!" And then I got the grip of my temper and slammed the door in my turn. All the same, in that hour it was settled that I was to be a reporter. I knew it as I went out into the street. . . .

With a dim idea of being sent into the farthest wilds as an operator, I went to a business college on Fourth Avenue and paid $20 to learn telegraphing. It was the last money I had. I attended the school in the afternoon. In the morning I peddled flat-irons, earning money for my board, and so made out . . .

*[But there came again a season of hard times for him and the Newfoundland dog someone had given him, and he had some unhappy experiences as a book agent.]*

It was not only breakfast we lacked. The day before we had had only a crust together. Two days without food is not good preparation for a day's canvassing. We did the best we could. Bob stood by and wagged his tail persuasively while I did the talking; but luck was dead against us, and "Hard Times" stuck to us for all we tried. Evening came and found us down by the Cooper Institute, with never a cent. Faint with hunger, I sat down on the steps under the illuminated clock, while Bob stretched himself at my feet. He had beguiled the cook in one of the last houses we called at, and his stomach was filled. From the corner I had looked on enviously. For me there was no supper, as there had been no dinner and no breakfast. Tomorrow there was another day of starvation. How long was this to last? Was it any use to keep up a struggle so hopeless? From this very spot I had gone, hungry and wrathful, three years before when the dining Frenchmen for whom I wanted to fight thrust me forth from their company. Three wasted years! Then I had one cent in my pocket, I remembered. Today I had not even so much. I was bankrupt in hope and purpose. Nothing had gone right; nothing would ever go right; and worse, I did not care. I drummed moodily upon my book. Wasted! Yes, that was right. My life was wasted, utterly wasted.

A voice hailed me by name, and Bob sat up, looking attentively at me for his cue as to the treatment of the owner of it. I recognized in him the principal of the telegraph school where I had gone until my money gave out. He seemed suddenly struck by something.

"Why, what are you doing here?" he asked. I told him Bob and I were just resting after a day of canvassing.

"Books!" he snorted. "I guess they won't make you rich. Now, how would you like to be a reporter, if you have got nothing better to do? The manager of a news agency downtown asked me today to find him a bright young fellow whom he could break in. It isn't much—$10 a week to start with. But it is better than peddling books, I know."

He poked over the book in my hand and read the title. "*Hard Times*," he said, with a little laugh. "I guess so. What do you say? I think you will do. Better come along and let me give you a note to him now."

As in a dream, I walked across the street with him to his office and got the letter which was to make me, half-starved and homeless, rich as Croesus, it seemed to me. . . .

When the sun rose, I washed my face and hands in a dog's drinking trough, pulled my clothes into such shape as I could, and went with Bob to his new home. That parting over, I walked down to 23 Park Row and delivered my letter to the desk editor in the New York News Association, up on the top floor.

He looked me over a little doubtfully, but evidently impressed with the early hours I kept, told me that I might try. He waved me to a desk, bidding me wait until he had made out his morning book of assignments; and with such scant ceremony was I finally introduced to Newspaper Row, that had been to me like an enchanted land. After twenty-seven years of hard work in it, during which I have been behind the scenes of most of the plays that go to make up the sum of the life of the metropolis, it exercises the old spell over me yet. If my sympathies need quickening, my point of view adjusting, I have only to go down to Park Row at eventide, when the crowds are hurrying homeward and the City Hall clock is lighted, particularly when the snow lies on the grass in the park, and stand watching them a while, to find all things coming right. It is Bob who stands by and watches with me then, as on that night.

The assignment that fell to my lot when the book was made out, the first against which my name was written in a New York editor's book, was a lunch of some sort at the Astor House. I have forgotten what was the special occasion. I remember the bearskin hats of the Old Guard in it, but little else. In a kind of haze I beheld half the savory viands of earth spread under the eyes and nostrils of a man who had not tasted food for the third day. I did not ask for any. I had reached that stage of starvation that is like the still center of a cyclone, when no hunger is left. But it may be that a touch of it all crept into my report; for when the editor had read it, he said briefly:

"You will do. Take that desk, and report at ten every morning, sharp."

That night, when I was dismissed from the office, I went up the Bowery to No. 185, where a Danish family kept a boarding-house up under the roof. I had work and wages now, and could pay. On the stairs I fell in a swoon and lay there till someone stumbled over me in the dark and carried me in. My strength had at last given out.

So began my life as a newspaper man.

SOURCE: *Stories of Achievement*. Edited by Asa Don Dickinson. Volume 4. New York: Doubleday, Page and Company. 1916. [Excerpted from *The Making of an American* by Jacob A. Riis. New York: Macmillan. 1908.]

# ABRAHAM RIHBANY

## Lights and Shadows
(Syria; 1914)

*Abraham Rihbany (1869–1944) was a Christian Arab born in a part of Syria that is now Lebanon. After arriving in the United States in 1891, he began publishing the first Arabic-language newspaper in America. He later became a Unitarian minister and a popular author on religion. This essay is an excerpt from his memoir.*

My struggles with the English language (which have not yet ceased) were at times very hard. It is not at all difficult for me to realize the agonizing inward struggles of a person who has lost the power of speech. When I was first compelled to set aside my mother-tongue and use English exclusively as my medium of expression, the sphere of my life seemed to shrink to a very small disk. My pretentious purpose of suddenly becoming a lecturer on Oriental customs, in a language in which practically I had never conversed, might have seemed to anyone who knew me like an act of faith in the miraculous gift of tongues. My youthful desire was not only to inform but to move my hearers. Consequently, my groping before an audience for suitable diction within the narrow limits of my uncertain vocabulary was often pitiable.

The exceptions in English grammar seemed to be more than the rules. The difference between the conventional and the actual sounds of such words as "victuals" and "colonel" seemed to me to be perfectly scandalous. The letter c is certainly a superfluity in the English language; it is never anything else but either k or s. In my native language, the Arabic, the accent is always put as near the end of the word as possible; in the English, as near the beginning as possible. Therefore, in using my adopted tongue, I was tossed between the two extremes and very often "split the difference" by taking a middle course. The sounds of the letters, *v, p,* and the hard *g,* are not represented in the Arabic. They are symbolized in transliteration by

85

the equivalents of *f, b,* and *k.* On numerous occasions, therefore, and especially when I waxed eloquent, my tongue would mix these sounds hopelessly, to the amused surprise of my hearers. I would say "coal" when I meant "goal," "pig man" for "big man," "buy" for "pie," "ferry" for "very," and vice versa.

For some time I had, of course, to think in Arabic and try to translate my thoughts literally into English, which practice caused me many troubles, especially in the use of the connectives. On one occasion, when an American gentleman told me that he was a Presbyterian, and I, rejoicing to claim fellowship with him, sought to say what should have been, "We are brethren in Christ," I said. "We are brothers, by Jesus." My Presbyterian friend put his finger on his lip in pious fashion, and, with elevated brows and a most sympathetic smile, said, "That is swearing!"

But in my early struggles with English, I derived much negative consolation from the mistakes Americans made in pronouncing my name. None of them could pronounce it correctly—Rih-ba'-ny—without my assistance. I have been called Rib'-beny, Richbany, Ribary, Laborny, Rabonie, and many other names. An enterprising Sunday School superintendent in the Presbyterian Church at Mansfield, Ohio, introduced me to his school by saying, "Now we have the pleasure of listening to Mr. Rehoboam!" The prefixing of "Mr." to the name of the scion of King Solomon seemed to me to annihilate time and space, and showed me plainly how the past might be brought forward and made to serve the present.

But my struggles with the technicalities of language were not the only pains of my second birth into the new environment. The social readjustments were even more difficult to effect. Coming into the house in Syria, a guest removes his shoes from his feet at the door, but keeps his fez or turban on. It was no easy matter, therefore, for me, on going into an American home, to realize instantly which extremity to uncover.

The poetic Oriental mind extends hospitality in a very warm and dramatic manner. The would-be guest, although able and willing to accept an invitation to dinner, expects to be urged repeatedly by the would-be host, to have all his feigned objections overruled, to be even pulled bodily into the house before he gives his consent. By following such tactics in this country, I lost many a precious privilege. The brevity of the American invitation distressed me greatly. Whenever I was told, "We should be much pleased to have you come in and have dinner with us, if you can," I would answer, "No, thank you; I cannot possibly come," when I had it in mind all the time that I would gladly accept if they would only urge me. But they would let me go! They would take me at my word (as they should not do, I thought, in such matters), to my great disappointment. It was not very long, however, before I became on this point thoroughly Americanized. However, eating butter on bread, dessert with every meal, and sitting in rocking-chairs seemed to me to be riotous luxuries. It took me about three years to become accustomed to these seeming superfluities. It would require six now to make me give them up.

The prominence of woman in domestic and social affairs seemed to me, when I first came in close touch with American society, a strange and unnatural phenomenon. While in Syria, contrary to the view which generally prevails in this country, the woman is not considered a slave by the man, yet in all important domestic and social matters she is looked upon as only his silent partner. The American woman is by no means silent; she finds it neither convenient nor necessary to assume such an attitude.

The first opportunity I had of making close observation of the social position of the American woman was at the home of a Methodist minister where I proved sensible and fortunate enough to accept "without controversy" an invitation to dinner. His wife presided at the table with so much grace and dignity that my astonishment at the supreme authority she exercised on the occasion was deeply tinged with respect. How harmonious the husband and wife seemed! What mutual regard! What delicacy of behavior toward each other! But I could not avoid asking, subjectively, "Is all this really genuine? Does this man treat his wife in this manner always, or only when they have company? Why, my host seems to be in the hands of his wife like the clay in the hands of the potter! Why should a woman be given so much latitude?" and so forth.

When, later in the evening, upon retiring, the lady said to her husband, "Good-night, dear," and kissed him in my presence, the act seemed to me distressingly unseemly. It is no longer distressing to me.

It should not be counted against an Oriental that he is unable in a very short period of time to invest such phases of conduct with high idealism. If his instincts are normal, intimate associations with the better class of Americans cannot fail to change his sentiments and clarify his vision. Not many years will be required to reveal to him the elevating beauty of a woman's being the queen of her home, with her husband as a knight-errant by her side; to teach him that America, as the heir to the noblest traditions of northwestern Europe, has discovered that which neither the Oriental peoples, ancient Egypt, Greece, nor Rome succeeded in discovering, namely, that true civilization can arise only from a mutual regard of the equal rights, and, within the family circle, the mutual love of man, woman, and child.

All such discipline, however, was not to be compared with the economic difficulties which beset my way, put my optimism to the severest test, and seriously threatened my stoutest resolutions. In my travels westward, the expressions, "These are very hard times," "The summer is a dull season for the churches," "Not many people care for lectures this time of year," tortured my hearing everywhere. It was so difficult for me to secure money enough to keep soul and body together.

In Oil City, Pennsylvania, I longed for the first time for the "flesh-pots of Egypt" and wished that I had never left Syria. In my search for a cheap lodging-place, I was directed by a police officer to an old house which seemed to me the symbol of desolation. An elderly lady, who appeared very economical in smiling, "showed me into my room" and disappeared. As my weary arm dropped the valise inside the door, every sustaining power in me seemed to give way. Sobs and tears poured forth simultaneously with, "Why did I ever leave Syria?" "Why did I not stay in New York?" "Is this what America has for me?" and other questions with which I besieged the deaf ears of a lonely world. The fact that my hostess served no meals afforded me an excellent excuse to ask her to direct me to a "real" boarding-house. She did so, and I transferred my headquarters to a more cheery dwelling, where the landlady smiled graciously and generously, and the presence of fellow guests helped to lighten my burdens.

The veiling of the future from mortal eyes is, I believe, a divine provision whose purpose seems to be to tap the springs of heroism in human nature and to equip the soul with the wings of hope. Nevertheless, this blessed mystery has its drawbacks. Prolonged uncertainty of the future in those days of loneliness and poverty threatened to sink the goal of life below the horizon and make of me a wanderer in a strange land. The alternation of life between the two extremes, feast and famine, is never conducive to connected planning and constancy of endeavor.

At Columbus, Ohio, I spent a whole week in strenuous but utterly fruitless endeavor to secure opportunities to earn some money.

Having had to pay in advance for my week's keep at a very frugal boarding-house, I had only ten cents left, which I put in the "collection plate," at a Salvation Army meeting. To be penniless was not entirely new to me, but as the week drew to a close, the question where I was going to secure money enough with which to leave Columbus became terribly oppressive. There was one more venture for me to make. I had the name of a Methodist minister, the Rev. John C. Jackson, pastor of the Third Avenue Methodist Episcopal Church, whom I had not yet seen during my sojourn in the capital of Ohio. My courageous plan was to call on this clergyman and request him either to give me the chance to lecture in his church for a small financial compensation or to lend me money enough to enable me to leave Columbus. The distance from my boarding-house to his residence measured, if I may trust my memory, twenty-four blocks, which I walked in what seemed to me the hottest day in the calendar of the years.

My general appearance when I arrived at the parsonage was not exactly what I should call a clear title to confidence and the securing of credit. Nevertheless, I made my application with a creditable show of firmness, placing in the hands of the clergyman, who was just recovering from a long illness, my letters of recommendation. He disposed of my request to lecture in his church by saying, "There is no possible chance for the present." When I applied for a loan of five dollars, his pale face lighted up with a short-lived smile as he asked, "Do you expect you will get it?" "Y-e-s," I answered, "and to return it, also." "When would you return it?" he asked again. Falling back upon the Biblical language of my kinsmen, I said, "If God prolong my life and prosper me, I will pay you." Assuming the attitude of perplexed charity, Mr. Jackson said, "I do not know whether you are the man to whom these letters pertain, nor, if you are the man, how you secured them in the first place; but I am going to try you. Here is five dollars." "Certainly God has not left this world," I said inwardly, as I received the money from the good man's hand. It was only a week thence when God did prosper me just enough so that I was able to return to Mr. Jackson his money and I received a letter from him (which I still treasure) thanking me for my "promptness" and wishing me all kinds of success.

The next point I touched at after leaving Columbus was Mount Vernon, Ohio, where I was much cheered, chiefly by the kindness of the Presbyterian minister and his gracious wife. And it was at

Mount Vernon that I learned my first memory lesson in patriotism. Soon after my arrival in that town I strayed into the public square where stands a fine soldiers' monument. It seems to me that my attention had never been strongly challenged by a similar object in this country before I reached that small Ohio city. Certainly I must have seen soldiers' monuments in other towns, but was not ready to respond to their appeal. Here, as soon as my eyes beheld the significant memorial, I forgot for the moment my weariness and poverty and yielded myself to the mighty challenge of the thought that I was in a country where men died willingly and intelligently for their flag and all it symbolized, and that what the flag did symbolize were ideals worth dying for. I was chained to the spot until I had committed to memory the inscription chiseled on one side of the granite base, and which read—

### OUR COUNTRY

By that dread name we wave the sword on high,
And swear for her to live—for her to die.

These vital words have clung to my memory, in the exact form quoted above, for over twenty years. When I thought of including them in this story, fearing that my recollection of them might be incorrect, I wrote to the commander of the Grand Army post of Mount Vernon, requesting him to send me an exact copy of the inscription, and upon comparing it with my memory picture I found that I was only slightly incorrect in that I had in the first line the word "In" in place of "By," and the word "lift" in place of "wave."

Perhaps the choicest of the events of my Wilderness-of-Sinai discipline since I had left New York, occurred at Elyria, Ohio. I reached that town late in the evening with a very small sum of money in my purse—something less than two dollars. The severe economic struggles of the immediate past had taught me to be abnormally cautious in spending money. Failing to secure accommodation at either of two cheap boarding-houses in the town, I ventured into a hotel with very noticeable timidity. As soon, however, as the clerk told me that my lodging there would cost me seventy-five cents, I departed. I had the name of a prominent minister in the town on whom I thought I would call first, and, if he promised me the opportunity to lecture in his church, I might feel free to indulge in the luxury of lodging at a hotel.

My experience with that divine was not pleasant enough to permit of the mention of his name and denomination. When I stated my case to him, he assumed a decidedly combative attitude. I was so weary that I should have been most grateful for a few minutes' rest in one of the many upholstered chairs which graced the living-room, but the elderly gentleman stood in the door and kept me standing in the hall, while he quizzed me as follows:—"Did you say that your purpose in lecturing in the churches is to secure funds to go to college?" "Yes."

"Well, I doubt it. I have seen many fellows such as you. What college do you expect to enter?"

"I do not yet know, but it will be some good college."

"You don't even know what college you expect to enter? I can say one thing for all of you 'traveling students.' You are very cunning."

"But I can show good letters of recommendation from—"

"It would do no good. Keep your letters to yourself. I have seen many such documents."

"Now, Dr. W., all I ask for is that you give me the chance to prove to you that I am an honest man, for I feel badly hurt by your words."

"Do not trouble yourself about that. At any rate, I am sorry I can do nothing for you. Good-night, sir!"

The unexpected assault upon my integrity and veracity intensified the darkness of the night into which I plunged again, wounded to the heart. It was distressing enough to be homeless, weary, and in want; but to be accused of being a swindler seemed to overshadow all other trials. But hope triumphed over despair and pointed me to the best which was yet to be. I returned to the railway station with the intention of spending the night there. But the ticket agent thought differently. His "orders" required him to lock the doors of the station at a certain hour in the night, leaving no transient lodgers inside. I moved from the station to the park and stretched my weary mortal coil on one of the benches. The air was balmy, and I had as good a pillow (the iron arm of the bench) as my countryman of old, Jacob, had at Peniel. There I would spend the night under the beneficent heavens, meditating while awake upon the time when I should close the doors of some great university behind me, departing not thence until I had become a full-fledged scholar.

At about midnight, the sequel of the balmy air which enabled me to sleep in the park comfortably without extra covering arrived. The heavens wept over me large generous tears which drove me to a pretentious hotel near by, where the "night clerk" met me in a stern, businesslike manner and most cruelly charged me fifty cents for half a night's lodging in the cheapest room he had.

In my Arabic diary of that period, under date of December 29, 1893, I find the following entry which shows what impressions that eventful year left on me, and indicates also my turn of mind and hope for the future:—

"I shall always remember the events of 1893 as distressing and full of bitter pain. At times I really longed for death and loved it. Many were my difficulties and trials, and I had no home where to rest and no real friends to whom to unburden my heart. But God has mysterious purposes beyond our power to know. He has sustained me and led me safely through all my difficulties. It is good that I have been taught by my distresses to better appreciate the comforts of life. Now there is light on my pathway, and I see myself moving steadily toward better things. My hope that the Most High is leading me to that which He knows is best for me and pleasing to Him grows stronger from day to day, and I shall yet reach my goal, by his help, and preach to the world his pure and undefiled religion."

Yes, life's smiles are, on the whole, much more numerous than its frowns, and, notwithstanding all its afflictions, this world is keyed to goodness. My first appearance before an American audience occurred at New Brighton, Pennsylvania, where, if I remember correctly, a minister of the United Presbyterian Church permitted me to speak on the Holy Land at his prayer-meeting. As the meeting (which was not of the ordinary drowsy type) progressed, my whole soul said, "Lord, it is good to be here." The minister, who was past middle age and wore a most benignant countenance, conducted the service with such simple dignity and sweetness of spirit that the whole scene was transformed into a benediction. His lesson was from Acts XII, the story of Peter's miraculous release from prison. I shall never forget the sweet, informing, and persuasive modulations of that preacher's voice as he sought to show that although the band of Christians who were gathered together at the house of Mary, the mother of John, were praying for the release of the imprisoned apostle, yet when they were told by the damsel, Rhoda, that Peter stood at the door, they were afraid to open and receive the answer to their prayer. "They prayed God to bring Peter to them," said the preacher. "God did bring the apostle to the door, but those praying Christians were afraid to open and say, 'Come in!'"

I have never been able to ascertain the initial cause of my decision to enter the ministry, nor to point to the exact time when I was "called" to it. What I am certain of, however, is that the influences of such occasions as the one mentioned above did more than any others I know to lead me to the pulpit. It was the virile and irresistible leaven of the characters of those Christians of the various denominations, who did not so much profess correct creeds as reflect the life of the Master in their own lives, which led me in a mysterious way to add to my decision to enter college the decision to make my life-work the holy ministry of religion.

When I stood up to address the meeting, the cordial, sympathetic attitude of the audience soon calmed the violent beating of my heart and stopped the knocking of my knees together, but it had no appreciable effect on my grammar and diction. The nouns and the verbs often stood at cross-purposes in my remarks, and the adjectives and adverbs interchanged positions, regardless of consequences. My impromptu literal translation of Arabic into English greatly puzzled the minds of my hearers, and, at times, it was difficult even for me to know fully what I was saying or wanted to say. Notwithstanding all that, however, I managed in closing to shift from Syria to America and eulogize George Washington. The minister asked for a contribution for me to help me go to college. As my engagement to speak had not been made known to my hearers before they came to the meeting, many of them were unprepared to give; the contribution was therefore small, but the meeting was rich in good things, and I went away in a happy and optimistic frame of mind.

If anyone had told me on that evening in New Brighton that less than three years later I was to become the regular minister of an American congregation and a "stump speaker" in favor of the "gold standard," I should have considered him a very flighty day-dreamer. But America, the mother of modern wonders, began to reveal itself to me and in me. I soon became possessed by the consciousness that the whole country was a vast university which offered a thousand incentives to progress; that I had the privilege of being born again in a land which more than any other on our planet establishes the truth of the New Testament promise, "Ask, and it shall be given you; seek, and ye shall find; knock, and it shall be opened unto you."

SOURCE: Abraham Mitrie Rihbany. *A Far Journey.* Boston: Houghton Mifflin. 1914.

# EDWARD STEINER

*From Alien to Citizen*
(Slovakia; 1914)

*Edward Steiner was born in 1866 in Slovakia before going to school in Vienna, Bohemia, and Germany. A Jewish convert to Christianity, he moved to the United States when he was in his early twenties. This essay is from the chapters "The Gate into Chicago" and "Among the Bohemians."*

An entanglement of railroad tracks, miles of hot sand dunes, a stretch of inland sea; the sky line assaulted by gigantic elevators and smokestacks, a block or two crowded by houses dropped into an empty prairie—that is the beginning of Chicago. Certainly it began too soon for a certain footsore traveler, who thought he had arrived—then found that the guide-post promised fifteen miles more of labyrinthine tracks, of sand dunes fashioned into scrubby streets, of multiplied elevators and smokestacks and more miles of sporadically settled prairie. Chicago held out no illusions; she promised nothing but toil, grime, sore feet and a ceaseless struggle for just shelter and a mouthful of food. To me, accustomed to the beauties of large cities in the Old World, she seemed forbiddingly, hopelessly ugly and pitiless. Even now, after having discovered the soul and the heart of her—I have a distinct feeling of fear when I arrive there, although I step from a Pullman car and feel safe, at least from want.

The process of selection takes place in hobo land as it does everywhere else, and out of the army of tramps which I met, a rather decent Bohemian attached himself to me. He had been in Chicago before, and failing to gain a foothold at that time was returning to try again. He had some very attractive schemes for beginning to make a fortune for both of us, and the one which seemed to him most alluring was to go into the saloon business under the patronage of some beer-brewer. Neither capital nor character being needed, and having had the necessary experience with liquor on both sides of the bar, his future seemed rosy indeed, and generous fellow that he was, he was ready to share its glow with me.

Being blessed by a temperate ancestry, liquor was repugnant to me, whether to buy or sell; so I did not embark in the saloon business, although for a man situated as I was, entrance into Chicago almost invariably lay through that avenue.

I often wish back the opportunity of receiving the first impression of places and cities I have seen, but never of Chicago.

What the Loop, that congested, noise-girdled shopping district, is to those privileged to spend money, Canal Street and West Madison Street are to those compelled to earn it in the hardest way. How can one describe them?

Solid phalanxes of saloons, reeking from stale beer odors, mechanical music, blatant and harsh; long lines of men leaning over brass trimmed bars, poor, wasted remnants of womanhood, brazen creatures, pitilessly repellent, offering up all that is left them on the altar of man's lust; whirling wheels of chance and poor, duped humanity crowding about, eager to stake the last cent remaining from a hard-earned wage. Anxious groups surrounding bulletin boards which announced hard work for little pay, criers for boarding houses pulling and cajoling their victims, and the watchful Jewish trader eager for bargaining—that was the Chicago to which my hobo comrade introduced me.

He knew where to get the largest schooner of beer and the best free lunch. He opened to me the door into Chicago through that degrading, demoralizing institution, the saloon; and the more I saw of it, the more I became convinced that the selling of liquor was the most harmless of all its functions. Beneath it, above it and in the rear, it dealt out damnation indescribable and unmentionable.

Leaving my comrade absorbed in a free lunch and beer, the drink paid for out of my meagre purse, I started down Canal Street, studying the posters of various labor agencies which at that time were invariably connected with saloons.

A man who evidently had watched me, stopped with me in front of one of those places and cordially invited me to enter and consider an attractive situation. I was eager for work and went in with him. I was asked to step in front of the bar—then I felt something give way and I was hurled into darkness. I knew nothing until late at night I felt myself being dragged out into an alley and abandoned.

No one came in answer to my feeble cries, so I summoned enough strength to crawl back to the street. As I came staggering out of the darkness a policeman caught me by the back of the neck, dragged me to a street lamp and in a few minutes I could hear the tramping of horses. At the time I did not know that it was a patrol wagon into which I was roughly pushed, and after a short ride, during which no explanation was vouchsafed me, I was deposited at the Harrison Street Police Station.

There is a tradition that one ought not to speak ill of the dead; I suppose not even of dead police stations. Fortunately, this horrible man trap is no more—but without slandering the "dear departed," I can say that it was worse than the saloon in which I was knocked down and robbed of the little I had—and that is saying a great deal.

That night I spent in a huge basement cell, a sort of general depository of the day's unsorted human refuse. Men were fighting for room to stretch out and rest their miserable bodies, and they fought like savages. Some were drunk and delirious, some sick and sore, others were hungry and dirty; all were crying, laughing or singing until an insane asylum would have seemed like a child's nursery in comparison with that bedlam. There was just one time when the room was comparatively quiet, when men were sleeping. Then it was more gruesome than the noise, for they talked in their sleep.

I heard snatches of tender words, angry curses, the ravings of men under the spell of hideous dreams; then someone chuckled as if enjoying a brief breath of happiness, and one man woke and began to curse his dreaming neighbor, who too awoke. Blow followed blow and men lived in hell again until daybreak.

I have said that I should not care to have my first impressions of Chicago repeated, yet I have shared with thousands of men and women their experience, more or less like my own.

Until very lately the immigrant in Chicago, unless he had waiting friends, found no gateway open to him except the saloon, the brothel, the cheap lodging house and finally the "lock up."

The agencies which began the assimilative process were all anti-social, greedy for their prey and, worst of all, the police was in league with them and protected them. There was nothing left to do but walk up and down in impotent rage and inveigh against a city which permitted its newest and most potential human material to be polluted, if not corrupted, at the very entrance into its life.

I have repeatedly snatched men from the doors of gambling-rooms, from fake labor agencies and from greedy hotel runners, only to find myself unpleasantly involved with the police; while I usually got a cursing, if not worse, for my pains.

An Immigrant Protective League and the Y.M.C.A. are now doing fine work in directing and sheltering the new-comers. Nevertheless, it is a reflection upon the spirit which governs the city that private individuals had to organize a sort of vigilance committee to do this most elementary work of justice for helpless strangers.

There are now two forces which do the fundamental work for the assimilation of our immigrant. One of them is the anti-social group of agencies which I have mentioned, and until very lately it did its work unchallenged. The other is the privately organized associations which under the recent growth of the social conscience have multiplied and, in a measure at least, checked the enemy.

The American people as a whole clamor with a kind of savage hunger for the assimilation of the immigrant; but the question into what he is to be assimilated has not agitated them to any marked degree. Whether or not we threw the immigrant to the dogs did not matter, so long as he was eaten up and his bones gnawed free of anything foreign which adhered to his nature.

However, when that which is eaten by the dogs becomes dog, sometimes very savage dog, we develop a national hydrophobia which manifests itself in great aversion to the immigrant in general. We load him with all the curses of our civilization and blame him for all its ills, from race suicide to the I.W.W.

When I finally escaped this primary influence which had so rudely touched me, I had as yet no special grievance against society, but I had a clear understanding of the suffering of the new-comer to an American city. I also had a profound sympathy with those who were at war against a government which seemed not only stupid, but venal, and which on the face of it was no better than the most brutal autocracy, although it called itself a "government of the people, by the people, and for the people."

This sympathy I was eager to express, but the immediate physical necessities silenced for a while my burning idealism.

In my aimless wandering I drifted beyond the territory marked by the red line of crime and misery. I walked endless stretches of maddening streets as hopeless as they were straight, hot and ugly. North as far as the picturesque water tower on Lake Michigan, south as far as the city had gone on its conquering way. The few remaining landmarks, whenever I see them, remind me of hunger, weariness and despair.

Chicago is full of friends now. I need never go to a hotel for shelter. I need not even travel on a street car; I have spoken in its fashionable churches and been banqueted in the gilded caverns of its sumptuous hostelries; but best of all, I have been drawn into the blessed circle of those who are giving wealth and time and life for the bettering of the very conditions from which I once suffered.

Yet I have never been able to love Chicago. Perhaps I ought to love it, if only because it reminds me of "how deep the hole out of which I was drawn, and how horrible the pit out of which I was digged."

\* \* \*

After a fruitless search for work which would give me a chance to rehabilitate myself, I returned to the West Side; but fortunately wandered beyond the limits of that awful portal and found myself, to my great delight, in Chicago's "Bohemia."

I shall never forget the joy I felt in reading Czechish names and signs, and hearing again the language which was as familiar to me as my mother tongue.

I always felt a close kinship with the Bohemian people, whose unhappy history I knew and whose genius I understood and valued. I suppose while "blood is thicker than water," language is thicker than blood, and the larger relationship rests more upon ability to understand another people's ideals and share them, than upon general hereditary factors.

Perhaps more than any other people, the Bohemians have been able to transplant their national ideals and characteristics to the new soil, developing them to a marked degree. This may be due to the great difficulties under which they have lived in the Old World, so that when, in this country, they can speak and print their beloved language, they do it with a fierce passion as if to make up for lost time.

The contradictory characteristics of these, the most talented of the Slavic peoples, give them uncommon interest. Their light-heartedness and sadness, hospitality and hostility, industry and idleness, their passionate loves and hates, their devotion to art, their piety, infidelity and materialism—all seemed to be running at full tide when I happened upon "Bohemia in Chicago," in my quest for work. Had there been the least opposition to their expression, these people might have built a mediaeval castle wall around themselves and annexed their territory to the Kingdom of Bohemia.

I was walking through one of those West Side streets which differ from others in nothing but the name, when I saw men digging for the foundation of a house. Upon asking in Bohemian for a job, I got my opportunity, not only to work, but also to enter into the life of the most radical section of the Bohemian community.

The man who employed me was a tailor who, with the thrift of his race, had saved enough money to build a house. It was most fortunate for me that when the evening of the first day's labor came, he had discovered that I was homeless and offered me lodging under his roof, which, of course, I most gratefully accepted.

Not only was the place scrupulously clean, but there were music and good literature. The latter was decidedly radical, ranging from Spencer to Ingersoll. The home also brought me in contact with people of some education.

At that time the social life of the men still centered almost entirely around the saloon, an institution which unfortunately and invariably takes on Anglo-Saxon qualities, no matter with what national elements it is started, or by what name it is called. It might be a matter of some interest to discover why this is so; but whatever the reason, it is certain that the saloon plays an important part in the Americanization of the immigrant. It frequently aims to preserve his social tendencies and usually harbors the national societies which spring up in every immigrant group.

The saloon patronized by my host and employer was located on Halstead Street and bore all the outer marks of its American prototype, although within were the Bohemian elements which gave it something of a home or club atmosphere.

What attracted me was the newspapers which were kept on file and the meetings of a Freethinkers' Club, which had its headquarters there.

I was in the mood to yield myself completely to its influence and rejoiced in its intellectual atmosphere, which meant more to me than bread and meat after my recent stultifying experiences.

This radical movement which seemed so natural to the Bohemian communities at that time was an inevitable reaction from their intolerant past in which Church and State, bishop and king had each been bad, and together did their worst.

Out of an environment of superstition and oppression these people had come into the buoyant atmosphere of religious freedom, and they were breathing like men escaped from a tomb. Much of their speech was like the raving of madmen, but, after all, it was a fine idealism to which they tried to give expression, and this movement, harmful as it must have been in some directions, saved them from a gross materialism to which they were naturally inclined.

This group, which I joined, was then reading the essays of Thomas Paine, and no matter what one may think of his philosophy or his attitude toward traditional religion—it seemed to me wonderful, to see ditch diggers, tailors and cobblers at the end of the day's work discussing such serious literature so earnestly. This movement among the Bohemians has been severely attacked as atheistic. It never deserved that opprobrium, for at its heart it was religious, only it was seeking a high, free level. It never was dangerous, because, in spite of the attempt to inoculate the younger generation, the virus never took.

For some reason, anti-religious movements cannot be propagated in this country. No matter how virile the movement in its beginning, it dwindles and dies, and the second generation of even the most radical propagandists, becomes either respectably religious or blends with that great mass of people who are neither hot nor cold in their attitude toward the things of the spirit.

During this period I came in touch with a number of anarchists and heard their vehement onslaught against organized government. While I never was carried away by their extreme individualism, and never was in danger of becoming an assassin, I felt keenly the injustice they deplored, and sympathized deeply with them in their protest against the brutal hanging of some of their number, which not long before had startled the United States.

In the exercise of justice, governments are apt to be both cruel and unjust, and I am not sure but that the verdict against the Chicago anarchists will one day be revised by a generation of men far enough removed from the hate and prejudice gendered at that time to judge the matter impartially.

I heard Mrs. Parsons, the wife of one of the condemned anarchists, and suffered greatly as I listened to her. While I never plotted violent deeds, I appreciated her desire to avenge what she called judicial murder. After all, it is easy for us who are safely removed from the suffering and need of the toilers to condemn the radicals or label men and movements with a name which smacks of the plague or the pestilence. It was a crowd like that which said of Jesus, "He hath a devil," and joined in the ready cry: "Crucify Him!"

The one thing we are all apt to forget is that anarchy and kindred movements grow out of a soil made stony and hard by injustice. They are symptoms of a disease in the body social, and the ill cannot be cured by jailing or hanging or crucifying the men who feel the hurt most and cry out in their agony.

It was in this Chicago Bohemian saloon that I began to speak in public, and I delivered a series of talks on Bakunin and Tolstoy.

The latter's religious idealism gave no little offence to my auditors, but to me it was the saving element in the situation and kept my soul alive during that most critical period. These talks were exceedingly informal, broken into by questions, jests and ridicule. Although I always began with a definite theme, all the affairs of the universe which needed righting were usually touched upon before I finished.

The startling thing to me was then, and now is, the latent idealism in these immigrant groups which can make of even a saloon something resembling a people's university. Unfortunately, this idealism does not survive long, for in that very saloon where at that time men sat and leisurely drank their beer, while they discussed the philosophy of Bakunin and Tolstoy, they now stand before the bar and make a business of drinking. They may discuss a prize fight or the latest news from the baseball field, but nothing more elevating.

The social settlement which might have given me a grappling place for the higher things, if it existed at all, was in its swaddling clothes, and the so-called respectable people never wandered into my social sphere.

When the house of my Bohemian host was finished I found a job in a machine shop and gradually lifted myself to a position of leadership among my shopmates. During the noon hour they would ask me questions and once I attempted to deliver an address, but the foreman interfered, a quarrel ensued and I was summarily discharged.

I had little money saved, but I had some good clothing and an accumulation of paper-bound books.

Then began a weary journey from shop to mill in a vain search for work; until my last penny was eaten up, all my surplus clothing had become security for my lodging and the books were sold for a pittance.

It was a year of great industrial depression; on one side, over-production, and on the other, under-consumption. Strikes and riots combined to make the situation abnormal, and after even the casual jobs failed I again turned westward, this time to the great harvest fields of Minnesota.

SOURCE: Edward Alfred Steiner. *From Alien to Citizen: The Story of My Life in America.* New York: Fleming H. Revell Company. 1914.

# ANNA HILDA LOUISE WALTHER

*A Pilgrimage with a Milliner's Needle*
(Denmark; 1917)

*This essay includes excerpts from two chapters in her memoir, "The Vantage Ground of America" and "Model Hats." Walther was born in 1878; I have not been able to discover what became of her after the book's publication.*

Our hearts were overwhelmed with grief as I embarked for the United States.

Buoyed up by the spirit of victory, I was confident that I would find in America the conditions that would completely satisfy me. The future held glorious prospects. Hope beckoned. A new era was beyond.

More swiftly the ship moved. I cast aside the unbearable garment of bitterness and donned a fresh one, woven in all the merriment of the ship's company, and yet! and yet! the future life was a series of confused conjectures. One passenger attracted my attention, because he reminded me of Edward* as he looked when I knew him first. His spirit lived again, he seemed to speak when the young man conversed with me. For that reason, perhaps, I could not resist asking him to call on me, when he said that he intended to remain in New York. In my bewildered brain ran the question again. Will the new world cause me to forget Edward?

We entered New York harbor. The city lay almost concealed under a thick mist of heat with countless towers and houses looking as if they were elevated into the sky. The Statue of Liberty rising out of the ocean so free and majestic, thrilled me! An entrance never to be forgotten!

One passenger ("Mephistopheles" I had named him, because his figure, expression and beard resembled pictures of that gentleman),

*Walther's former suitor.

wrapped in his scarlet steamer rug, paced up and down the deck in the evenings speaking to no one. Now he stood beside me wringing his hands, exclaiming "Famous! Famous!" and his face brightened with hope as he gazed toward the statue. The inspiring figure was full of promise. Even for one who brought a wounded heart from the Old World, there were possibilities in this land of freedom. I did not fail to snapshot the big woman and her torch, as an important picture for my collection.

Immediately after landing, I visited some old friends of my parents, an elderly couple who received me most cordially. While talking, Mr. Nielsen suddenly raised his finger at me. "By the by," he said, "running away from home?" Then he referred to an incident when as a little child I had run away, and was later found alone on the street by a patrol who carried me to the police station. I had forgotten the occurrence, but was not surprised at the tale. I have run away on so many adventures since.

It was agreed that I should make my home with them. To find an unexpected home the moment I landed, emboldened me. Thanking them, I added that this had been my mother's wish. While Mrs. Nielsen arranged my room, her husband attended to my luggage. I was sincerely affected. Such prompt hospitality was so easy and natural that I wondered if it were the "American way."

★ ★ ★

During the days that followed I tried to familiarize myself with the city. Almost overpowered by its magnificence, I walked up Fifth Avenue, and feasted my eyes on its display of riches and prosperity. Here were gold and luxury, and just now I desired wealth above everything. I smiled; the seeming endlessness of the streets, the crowds, the splendor of its fashionable sections, made me realize my own insignificance.

Sometimes I felt discouraged, for what was I—a stranger—to do in this city, where no one was interested in me and my plans? On the other hand, I had two hands which, though empty, were willing, and the will which directed me to "ride on over all obstacles and win the race." I scanned the "want advertisements" in the daily papers. To obtain a position was not so easy as I had imagined. My experience in foreign countries, and even my letters of recommendation from well known fashionable establishments, did not help me in the least.

The shops preferred a milliner familiar with New York trade, and one who had worked in the city. Wherever I applied, this information was given, so that I became tired and lost courage. And yet these words "Go ahead" spurred me on. I heard them everywhere. Sometimes they came from a driver; sometimes from an elevator boy, and sometimes from a child. I was told it was slang, but the sentence clung to my memory as words that an American would repeat if he wished to reach his goal; and so they urged me, no matter how weary, to go ahead, making another and another attempt—but with the same result—until at last I entered a store where I asked for an opportunity to show my skill. I said I was willing to work for a small salary. Perhaps pity had something to do with the result, for my proposition was accepted. My face wore rather a dejected look, but, at all events, I was given a chance and directed to work one week "on trial."

The next morning I entered the shop with a heavy heart, for I felt that with six dollars a week, the prospect of becoming wealthy was far off indeed. I determined to do my best, even though the salary was the lowest that had ever been offered me.

The woman in charge was pleased with my efforts, and after the trial week my salary was raised to nine dollars. I soon realized that my work was very satisfactory and worth more than I received. I summoned all my pluck and demanded twenty dollars per week. At first the manager refused. Angry and surprised, she told me in plain words that my demand was so unreasonable that she could not for a moment think of granting it. But, as I happened to know that all the hats I trimmed were "good sellers," I insisted on the twenty dollars, and declared that unless I received it, I would seek a position elsewhere. When she realized that I was in earnest, she granted my demand, and I was proud of my victory.

Two months elapsed. From morning until night I sat in a dirty workroom, lighted by gas, filled with dusty, ragged boxes, frames and customers' discarded hats. Any moment one might expect a box with its contents to drop on one's head from a nearby shelf. No space to move about in. Seated as close together as possible at the work table, with nine common girls, I was forced to listen to never ending empty talk, and to remarks about my persistent silence. One day a girl remarked in vulgar tone to her friend across the table, "Sadie, listen! What do you say to our taking her out some night for a good time and waking her up?" But I kept to myself, did my work, and led a secretly unhappy life; spending the evening in solitude, thinking over my misery, and from time to time comparing the big, sunny African farm [Ed.: i.e., her sister's] to the narrow and poorly gas-lit workroom.

I attended evening school. Here I realized the extent of New York's generosity to the immigrants, who, unfamiliar with the language, were taught without expense. I was astonished to find that the city maintained not only the schools and granted free instruction, but also supplied students with necessary books and material; that the immigrant may not only learn English, but he may even take up various trades. No questions asked about his family or circumstances, as in the Old Country. The schools furnish free education to all who desire to learn. I enlarged my vocabulary of the English language and studied United States history. At the end of the term, I was awarded a prize, a copy of Longfellow's *Evangeline*, for regular attendance—not for cleverness!

SOURCE: Anna Hilda Louise Walther. *A Pilgrimage with a Milliner's Needle*. New York: Frederick A. Stokes. 1917.

# ROSE COHEN

*Out of the Shadow*
(Russia; 1918)

*In these extraordinarily touching episodes from her memoir, Cohen (1880–1925) narrates not her arrival in America but her family's preparations for leaving Russia and her imaginings of what she has in store. Cohen wrote her memoir when she was thirty-eight, at the encouragement of her night-school teacher.*

Father had been in America but a short time when grandmother realized that his emigration had lessened Aunt Masha's prospects of marriage. When she came to this conclusion her peace was gone. She wept night and day. "Poor Masha," she moaned, "what is to become of her? Her chances had been small enough without a dowry. And now, burdened with an aged father and a blind helpless mother, the best she can expect is a middle-aged widower with half a dozen children!"

Mother tried to comfort her by telling her that she would remain in Russia as long as grandmother lived, so that she would not have to live with Masha. But this only irritated her. "You talk like a child," she wept. "You stay here and wait for my death, while my son, at the other end of the world, will be leading a life of loneliness. And as for me, would I have any peace, knowing that I was the cause?"

Mother, seeing that she could do nothing to comfort her, silently awaited results.

One night I woke hearing a muffled sound of crying. I felt for grandmother, with whom I slept. But she was not beside me. Frightened, I sat up and peered into the darkness. The crying came from the foot of the bed. And soon I discerned grandmother sitting there. With her hands clasped about her knees and her face buried in her lap she sat rocking gently and weeping.

I called to her in a whisper to come and lie down, but she did not answer. For a while I sat trembling with cold and fear. Then I slipped far back under the warm comforter and tried to sleep. But the picture of grandmother sitting alone in the dark and cold haunted me. And so again I arose.

Creeping over to her quickly I curled up close to her and put my arms around her cold, trembling form. At first she did not take any notice of me. But after a few minutes she lifted her head and unclasping her hands, she drew me under her shawl, saying as she laid her wet face against mine, "Oh, you little mouse, how you do creep up to one! But you had better go back to your place or you will catch cold."

When I went back and as grandmother tucked me in, I asked her why she cried so. "Never mind, you little busybody," she said, "go to sleep." But I teased her to tell me. And finally she said with a sigh and speaking more to herself than to me, "It is about Masha. Go to sleep now, you will hear all about it tomorrow."

She sat down on the edge of the bed gently patting my shoulder, as she had often done when I was a little child. Soon I fell asleep.

The next day the rings under her eyes were darker, and her eyelids were more red and swollen than usual. But otherwise she seemed more calm than she had been for a long time.

After dinner she said to mother, hesitating at every word as she spoke, "You know, I decided last night, that when you go to America Masha should go with you." This startled mother so that she almost dropped the baby whom she was swinging on her foot.

"What are you saying? Masha go to America and you left here alone?"

"Yes, alone," she sighed, "as if I never had any children. But so it must be. True, I have not had a happy life. But happy or not I have lived it. And now, it is almost at an end. But Masha has just begun to live, and in America she will have a better chance, for there are fewer women there, they say. As for me, I shall not be without comfort in my last days. When I am lonely, I shall think of her happily married and surrounded by dear little children like yours. And now listen to this plan. Of course I can not be left here alone, though my needs are few. And so before you start for America you will take me to my niece in the city. She is a very pious woman and so I am sure she will give me a little space in some corner of her house. Of course you will pay her for a year of my board. And after that perhaps you will send her money. But I hope it won't be necessary. Indeed, I feel that I won't trouble this world much longer."

Mother tried to dissuade her from this plan but she turned a deaf ear and insisted that we write to father at once. And we did.

About a month passed before we received an answer. The letter was heavier than usual. And when we opened it, two yellow tickets fell out from among the two closely-written sheets.

"What is this?" we all asked at once. "Not money. And this writing must be English."

We handed the tickets to grandmother who held out her hand for them. Suddenly her hand began to tremble and she said, "Perhaps these are steamer tickets. Quickly read the letter."

After the usual greetings father wrote, "Since Masha is to come to America she might as well start as soon as she can get ready. And Rahel had better come with her. I am sure she can earn at least three dollars a week. With her help I'll be able to bring the rest of the family over much sooner, perhaps in a year or so. And besides, now she can still travel on half a ticket, which I am enclosing with the one for Masha."

Quite bewildered, I looked at mother. Her lips were opening and closing without making a sound. Suddenly she caught me into her arms and burst into tears.

* * *

For many days mother could not look at the steamer tickets without tears in her eyes. And even then though she tried to speak cheerfully about my going to America, I noticed that the anxious look which came into her eyes while the letter was being read, never left them. Also I felt her eyes following me about on every step. But once only, she gave way to her feelings openly.

One morning while she was fastening the back of my dress I caught a few disconnected words, which she uttered low as though she were speaking to herself.

"Good Heavens! child twelve years old—care—herself." Then came those inward tearless sobs and I felt her hands tremble on my back.

But grandmother took the news in a manner that astonished us all. When I looked at her over my mother's shoulder, after the letter was read, I saw her sitting at the table in her usual position. Her head was bent low and a little to one side, and her hands were folded in her lap. Very quietly she sat, not a word, not a tear came from her.

Even grandfather, who never took any notice of her except to scold, looked at her in surprise.

"Well, Baila!" he said. "Have you wept yourself dry? Or perhaps you have come to your senses at last and realize how useless tears are. Remember, that you are sending your child away yourself. I can always take care of my needs but will die in the poorhouse."

Grandfather and grandmother were always quarrelling. Grandfather claimed that she wept her eyes out. And grandmother said that all her troubles came because of his impiety. But when I grew older I learned that there was a deeper reason for their quarrels.

As a rule when grandfather scolded, grandmother would retort with great spirit. But this time it was as if she did not hear him.

She called me and dictated a letter to Aunt Masha, to come home at once. Then she went to her trunk and took out the ball of fine linen thread which she had been saving for years. And while starting a pair of stockings for Aunt Masha I heard her figuring quietly, what we would need for the journey, how long it would take us to get ready, and what day we would start.

As for me, I became suddenly a very important person. At home I was looked upon as a guest. Now mother never pressed me to do any work. On the contrary, as soon as I would start to do something, she would say,

"Run out and play, you will work hard enough pretty soon." Neither did I find it necessary to feign illness as I had often done before that I might be fondled and caressed. No, indeed; now mother would often put baby down to take me on her lap.

And the young women of the village, who never took any notice of me before, would stop to speak to me.

One day, at sundown, I sat on our gate munching a bit of carrot, and watching the red sun disappearing gradually behind the treetops, when I became aware of someone standing in back of me. I turned around and saw Miriam. She was a pretty, gypsy-like young woman whose dark eyes always looked moist and a little red as though she had just been crying.

"So you are going to America," she said, looking at me wistfully, "you are very fortunate. Of course you are too young to realize it now but you will, later, when you grow older and think of this." She pointed to Siomka's half-tumbled hut, and the little pig who stood at the door and squealed to be let in.

"No," she continued, almost in a whisper, "your life won't be wasted like————." Here Siomka's little pig squealed louder than ever and Miriam turned suddenly and went away. I sat for a long while wondering what the last word might have been. Then I jumped down from the gate and ran into the house to look at the steamer tickets, perhaps for the tenth time that day.

I do not know whether I considered myself fortunate in going to America or not. But I do remember that when I convinced myself, by looking at the tickets often, that it was not a dream like many others I had had, that I would really start for America in a month or six weeks, I felt a great joy. Of course I was a little ashamed of this joy. I saw that mother was unhappy. And grandmother's sorrow, very awful, in its calmness, was double now. For I felt that I was almost as dear to her as Aunt Masha.

When a week passed we cleaned the house as thoroughly as if it were for Easter, in honor of Aunt Masha's coming.

During the five years that she had been away she visited us twice. The last time had been three years before. And so we were all excited and eager to see her.

As the days passed and the time drew near for her coming, grandmother became so impatient and nervous that she would jump at the least outdoor sound, asking excitedly,

"What is that? I think I hear the rumbling of wheels. Isn't that someone coming?" Then we would all rush to the door and windows and find that it was only a cart passing on the road, or a pig scratching his back against the sharp corner of the house.

One day we really heard a cart drive up to the door. When we ran out we saw a small, plump, pretty young woman in a brown dress jump lightly to the ground.

"Oh, grandmother, quickly come, it is Aunt Masha."

In a moment grandmother tumbled out of bed, but before she could reach the door she was in Aunt Masha's arms. And for a while there was sobbing in every corner of the room.

★ ★ ★

We children scarcely knew Aunt Masha. All I remembered of her two visits, was that both times she had come to stay a month, but went away at the end of a week, and that we felt depressed afterwards, and grandmother cried for days and days.

And so it was only now that we began to know her. When she had been home a short time we found that she was affectionate, but also severe, and hot-tempered. If we did not obey her promptly she scolded severely; or worse still, stopped speaking to us. Aunt Masha was also a painfully clean person and spent a great deal of time in washing us. Brother, whose skin was dark, often appeared, after she was through with him, with his neck red and tears in his eyes.

But the greatest trouble was caused by Aunt Masha's personal belongings. Nothing of hers must be touched. And as we were very curious about things that came from the city there was a world of trouble.

One morning I arose earlier than usual. All were asleep except mother and grandfather, who were out. As I passed Aunt Masha's bed I was attracted by her little shoes which stood close together on the floor beside her bed, looking like two soldiers keeping watch. They were the smallest things with high tops, pointed toes and elastic sides. Often I had longed to try them on. And once I even asked Aunt Masha if I might. But she said, "No, you would burst them." Now as I stood looking at them and at my own clumsy lace shoes, made by our village shoemaker, I thought, "Yes, they would fit. Oh, how I should like to try them on, just for a moment."

I glanced at Aunt Masha's face. The wrinkle between her eyebrows was there even now, and it was saying to me, "No!" But the lips which were partly open showing the white strong teeth, seemed to smile, "Yes."

Very quietly I tiptoed over to the bed, took the shoes and hastened to the bench near the oven. My fingers trembled so, that I could not open my laces. They became knotted and it took me a long time to break them open. But at last my shoes were off.

I remember how rapidly my heart beat when I began to draw one of hers on. I thought, "If it does not go on easily, I won't force it." But it did, and felt comfortable. And the elastic fitted snugly around the ankles. With a feeling of pleasure I stepped down on the floor to see how much taller I looked with high heels. As I stood up I glanced anxiously toward Aunt Masha's bed. What I saw sent the blood rushing to my face.

She was sitting up in bed looking as though she saw a ghost.

"I suppose you have burst them. I told you not to put them on," she said and frowned. This frown brought back my earliest recollections of her. I remembered how I feared it. Now as I stood looking at her it deepened and deepened until it seemed to darken her whole face, and reminded me of an angry cloud.

Quickly I took off her shoes, put them near her bed and ran from her as from an approaching storm.

Outside I met mother, who saw that something had happened, the minute she looked at me. When I told her she scolded.

"You should not have tried on the shoes when you were told not to do it. Now I think you had better go and apologize."

I had never apologized in my life. In the days when I was given the choice between apologising and a spanking, I always chose the spanking. Now when I knew that no spanking was coming I certainly refused to do it. But mother coaxed and begged, and reasoned,

"You are going out into the wide world alone, among strangers. Don't harden your heart against your only friend. Oh, how I wish you had more sense!" She turned away and cried like a little child.

I was miserable. The very thought of apologising made my face burn. But here stood mother crying.

"I won't have many more chances of pleasing her," I thought.

"Mother, I'll apologize, but—not now," I begged. She turned to me. "That is a dear child," she said, looking brighter, "but if you do it at all, do it now."

"What shall I say?" I asked.

"Oh, just say you are sorry you disobeyed."

We went into the house. Aunt Masha was dressed and stood at the window, combing out her beautiful brown hair. It fell all about her, covering almost half of her small body. When she heard the door close she parted her hair in front, as if it were a curtain, and looked. She dropped it quickly when she saw me and went on combing carefully. Slowly I went over to her. "Aunt Masha," I said. My voice sounded strange to me. Again she parted her hair and looked at me. I thought I saw an expression of triumph in her steel grey eyes. This hurt me. And almost before I could think I blurted out, angrily,

"Aunt Masha, I'll never, never, touch anything of yours again, as if it were—swine!"

Aunt Masha fairly gasped. And mother looked horrified. Indeed, I was horrified myself at what I had done. I turned to mother and tried to explain. But I could not make her understand me. I was not good at explanations when I myself was concerned. Quite miserable, I ran out of the house and wandered about in the fields for the rest of the morning.

Aunt Masha did not speak to me for three days. During that time when our eyes happened to meet, I tried to tell her, in a dumb way, that I was sorry. But she always turned her face away quickly. Once when we met near the door, our shoulders almost touching, I saw a smile come quivering to her lips. And so I waited, hoping she would speak to me. But the next moment she frowned it down and passed on as if she did not know me. On the fourth day, at twilight, I came up on her so suddenly, while she was outside, that she gave a little scream of fright. I, too, was frightened, and caught hold of her hand. And she let it stay in mine.

★ ★ ★

All through the Spring, while mother, grandmother and Aunt Masha were sewing and knitting stockings for Aunt Masha and me to take along to America, I wandered about in the fields, restless and unable to play at anything.

Early, while the flowers were still heavy with the morning dew, I would take baby, who was a little over a year old, on my back, tie him on to me with a shawl, so that I could rest my arms when they grew tired, and start out followed by the rest of the children. For hours we would wander about like gypsies.

More often than anywhere we went to the lake, where it was very lively at that time of the year, as the peasant women were bleaching their linens. There, sister and brother would go off digging for flag-root. And I would put the two little ones on the flat rock near the edge and climbing up beside them, we would all sit quietly for the longest while, watching, listening.

It was a pleasant spot. The clear blue water lay quietly rippling and sparkling in the sun. On the edge were the women with red kerchiefs on their heads and beads of many colors around their necks, swinging their wooden mallets in unison. And the neighborhood rang with the echoes which seemed to come from the dense, mysterious looking forest across the lake. While through the air floated the sweet odor of new wet linen.

But the time I loved this spot best was late in the afternoon, when the light grew soft and the women went away to their homes. Then came a peculiar hush, and yet there seemed to be a thousand voices in the air whispering softly. They came from everywhere, from the tall stately forest trees across the lake, the hazelnut bushes, the flags as the wind passed over them. And the lake, a deeper blue now in the soft light, rippled gently as if with laughter. Sometimes these fairy-like voices would be lost for a moment in the louder sound of a dry twig breaking and falling to the ground, the cuckoo of a bird or the splash of a fish.

I do not know what effect this had on the children. It made me unspeakably happy and sad at the same time. I remember that I used to want to laugh and cry and sing and dance, and very often I did. To dance I would clasp hands with the children, and we would spin around, and around, until we fell down breathless and dizzy.

At twilight we would start for home, walking very slowly and feeling very sad at the thought of bed time.

So the Spring passed.

As the second of June, the day for our departure to America, drew near, I stayed more in the house and followed mother about more closely. Gradually I became conscious of two things. One was the fear of going out into the world. Just what I feared I did not know. And the other was regret. I had not realized how dear to me were my people and home until I was about to leave them. But the one whom I regretted to leave most was grandmother.

Grandfather was not fond of me and so he cared little about my going away. And mother and the children I should see again. But that grandmother cared I knew. And I also knew and she knew that her I should never see again.

One day grandmother and I were alone in the house, at least, I think we were alone. For as I look back now I can see no one but the two of us. I am standing at the window, and she is walking across the room, with her slow, hesitating step, and her hands stretched in front of her for protection. Coming upon a bench in the middle of the room she sat down heavily, saying, with a sigh, "It is strange, but the room seems to have grown larger."

"What is that shadow at the window, Rahel? Come, child, let me lean on you. There, your shoulder just fits under my arm. Do you remember when you first began to lead me about? That was when you still called yourself by name."

When we reached the window she raised her hand, shaded her eyes from the strong light and stood quietly for a while, looking out. Then she said, "This must be a beautiful day. For my eyelids are not as heavy when it is clear."

"Oh, grandmother, it is glorious! There is not a cloud in the sky. And, that thing waving in front of the window, can you make out what it is?"

"I see a black, shapeless mass. What is it?"

"It is the wild apple tree, white with blossoms."

"H-m-m—yes," she said, meditatively, "it was a day just like this."

"When, grandmother?"

She did not answer for a long while and when she spoke at last her voice was low and passionate.

"When God took my sight from me. My eyes had never been strong. One day in the Spring, it was beautiful like today, I was digging in the garden, but a little while it seemed to me, when I was startled by a crash of thunder so that the very earth under my feet seemed to tremble. I looked up. The sun was gone and a black angry cloud hung over our house. Quickly I gathered up the tools and hastened toward home. I was but a few steps away when a wind-storm came. It rocked the trees, blew the loosened shingles from the roof, and swept the dry sand in a whirl before me. At the same moment I felt a stinging pain in my eyes so that I could not see the door. In darkness I groped about for long time, till I found it. For twenty-four hours I was beside myself with pain. At the end of that time it went away as suddenly as it came. When your father, who was a little boy then, untied the kerchief from my eyes I asked him if it were night.

"'Why, mother,' I heard his frightened voice, 'it is daylight. Don't you see the sun across your bed?' Then I knew."

She stood silent and motionless for a while. Then she said more calmly, "But I must not sin. For if God has taken my sight, He has given me dear little grandchildren who have been everything I wanted. Ah, if I had only been worthy enough to keep them with me!" Here she turned to me suddenly and taking my face between her cold soft hands she said entreatingly, "Rahel, promise me that you won't cry when you are starting. You hear? It is bad luck to cry when one is starting on a journey. And—I want you to write me whether there are any synagogues in America."

"I promise!"

Still holding my face between her hands she bent over it and looked at it intently. I saw a strained expression come into her face and the eyes move about restlessly under the heavy red lids, as though she were trying to see. Then came a pitiful moan, and tears rolled down her cheeks and fell on mine.

What happened after this I do not remember until the very minute of starting on the second of June. And even then, as I look back I can see nothing at first, but a thick grey mist. But the sounds I recall very distinctly.

There was Aunt Masha's voice crying, a crack of a whip, horses' hoofs striking against stones. Then there was a sudden jolt and I felt myself falling backwards. And now I remember what I saw, too.

When I rose I found myself sitting in a straw-lined wagon, with my back to the horse. Besides me were mother and the baby, who were coming to the city with us, and Aunt Masha who was lying with her face hidden in the straw, crying aloud.

I remembered grandmother's warning, "Nothing but bad luck could come to one who is crying while starting on a journey," and felt sorry for Aunt Masha. But as we were pulling out through the gate and I saw grandmother looking so lonely and forsaken, as she stood leaning against the house, and when I saw grandfather and the children who stood at the gate, looking after us and crying, I could not keep my own tears back, though I opened my eyes wide and blinked hard.

We were still but a short distance from the house when I saw grandmother go in through the open door, and close it behind her with unusual quickness. As she was passing the window I caught a last glimpse of her white kerchief tied about her head.

When we turned the corner I could not see grandfather's and the children's faces any more but I still heard their voices carried over by the wind.

One by one we passed the dear familiar places. Each one brought back sad and happy recollections. As I looked at my favourite bush while we were passing it, I saw my little make-believe companions spring up in it one after another. And among them I saw the swarthy face of my imaginary brother Ephraim. I waved my hand to him, and then hid my face on mother's shoulder.

When I looked up again the road was unknown to me.

SOURCE: Rose Cohen. *Out of the Shadow: A Russian Jewish Girlhood on the Lower East Side.* New York: George H. Doran Company. 1918.

# EDWARD BOK

## Where America Fell Short with Me
(Holland; 1922)

*Edward Bok (1863–1930) reflects on his childhood discovery of cultural differences between Holland and America and how those differences continued to grate on him in his adult professional life.*

When I came to the United States as a lad of six, the most needful lesson for me, as a boy, was the necessity for thrift. I had been taught in my home across the sea that thrift was one of the fundamentals in a successful life. My family had come from a land (the Netherlands) noted for its thrift; but we had been in the United States only a few days before the realization came home strongly to my father and mother that they had brought their children to a land of waste.

Where the Dutchman saved, the American wasted. There was waste, and the most prodigal waste, on every hand. In every streetcar and on every ferryboat the floors and seats were littered with newspapers that had been read and thrown away or left behind. If I went to a grocery store to buy a peck of potatoes, and a potato rolled off the heaping measure, the groceryman, instead of picking it up, kicked it into the gutter for the wheels of his wagon to run over. The butcher's waste filled my mother's soul with dismay. If I bought a scuttle of coal at the corner grocery, the coal that missed the scuttle, instead of being shoveled up and put back into the bin, was swept into the street. My young eyes quickly saw this; in the evening I gathered up the coal thus swept away, and during the course of a week I collected a scuttleful. The first time my mother saw the garbage pail of a family almost as poor as our own, with the wife and husband constantly complaining that they could not get along, she could scarcely believe her eyes. A half pan of hominy of the preceding day's breakfast lay in the pail next to a third of a loaf of bread. In later years, when I saw, daily, a scow loaded with the garbage of Brooklyn householders being towed through New York harbor out to sea, it was an easy

118

calculation that what was thrown away in a week's time from Brooklyn homes would feed the poor of the Netherlands.

At school, I quickly learned that to "save money" was to be "stingy"; as a young man, I soon found that the American disliked the word "economy," and on every hand as plenty grew spending grew. There was literally nothing in American life to teach me thrift or economy; everything to teach me to spend and to waste.

I saw men who had earned good salaries in their prime, reach the years of incapacity as dependents. I saw families on every hand either living quite up to their means or beyond them; rarely within them. The more a man earned, the more he—or his wife—spent. I saw fathers and mothers and their children dressed beyond their incomes. The proportion of families who ran into debt was far greater than those who saved. When a panic came, the families "pulled in"; when the panic was over, they "let out." But the end of one year found them precisely where they were at the close of the previous year, unless they were deeper in debt.

It was in this atmosphere of prodigal expenditure and culpable waste that I was to practice thrift: a fundamental in life! And it is into this atmosphere that the foreign-born comes now, with every inducement to spend and no encouragement to save. For as it was in the days of my boyhood, so it is today—only worse. One need only go over the experiences of the past two years, to compare the receipts of merchants who cater to the working-classes and the statements of savings banks throughout the country, to read the story of how the foreign-born are learning the habit of criminal wastefulness as taught them by the American.

Is it any wonder, then, that in this, one of the essentials in life and in all success, America fell short with me, as it is continuing to fall short with every foreign-born who comes to its shores?

As a Dutch boy, one of the cardinal truths taught me was that whatever was worth doing was worth doing well: that next to honesty came thoroughness as a factor in success. It was not enough that anything should be done: it was not done at all if it was not done well. I came to America to be taught exactly the opposite. The two infernal Americanisms "That's good enough" and "That will do" were early taught me, together with the maxim of quantity rather than quality.

It was not the boy at school who could write the words in his copy-book best who received the praise of the teacher; it was the boy who could write the largest number of words in a given time. The acid test in arithmetic was not the mastery of the method, but the number of minutes required to work out an example. If a boy abbreviated the month January to "Jan." and the word Company to "Co." he received a hundred per cent mark, as did the boy who spelled out the words and who could not make the teacher see that "Co." did not spell "Company."

As I grew into young manhood, and went into business, I found on every hand that quantity counted for more than quality. The emphasis was almost always placed on how much work one could do in a day, rather than upon how well the work was done. Thoroughness was at a discount on every hand; production at a premium. It made no difference in what direction I went, the result was the same: the cry was always for quantity, quantity! And into this atmosphere of almost utter disregard for quality I brought my ideas of Dutch thoroughness and my conviction that doing well whatever I did was to count as a cardinal principle in life.

During my years of editorship, save in one or two conspicuous instances, I was never able to assign to an American writer work which called for painstaking research. In every instance, the work came back to me either incorrect in statement, or otherwise obviously lacking in careful preparation.

One of the most successful departments I ever conducted in *The Ladies' Home Journal* called for infinite reading and patient digging, with the actual results sometimes almost negligible. I made a study of my associates by turning the department over to one after another, and always with the same result: absolute lack of a capacity for patient research. As one of my editors, typically American, said to me: "It isn't worth all the trouble that you put into it." Yet no single department ever repaid the searcher more for his pains. Save for assistance derived from a single person, I had to do the work myself for all the years that the department continued. It was apparently impossible for the American to work with sufficient patience and care to achieve a result.

We all have our pet notions as to the particular evil which is "the curse of America," but I always think that Theodore Roosevelt came closest to the real curse when he classed it as a lack of thoroughness.

Here again, in one of the most important matters in life, did America fall short with me; and, what is more important, she is falling short with every foreigner that comes to her shores.

In the matter of education, America fell far short in what should be the strongest of all her institutions: the public school. A more inadequate, incompetent method of teaching, as I look back over my seven years of attendance at three different public schools, it is difficult to conceive. If there is one thing that I, as a foreign-born child, should have been carefully taught, it is the English language. The individual effort to teach this, if effort there was, and I remember none, was negligible. It was left for my father to teach me, or for me to dig it out for myself. There was absolutely no indication on the part of teacher or principal of responsibility for seeing that a foreign-born boy should acquire the English language correctly. I was taught as if I were American-born, and, of course, I was left dangling in the air, with no conception of what I was trying to do.

My father worked with me evening after evening; I plunged my young mind deep into the bewildering confusions of the language— and no one realizes the confusions of the English language as does the foreign-born—and got what I could through these joint efforts. But I gained nothing from the much-vaunted public-school system which the United States had borrowed from my own country, and then had rendered incompetent—either by a sheer disregard for the thoroughness that makes the Dutch public schools the admiration of the world, or by too close a regard for politics.

Thus, in her most important institution to the foreign-born, America fell short. And while I am ready to believe that the public school may have increased in efficiency since that day, it is, indeed, a question for the American to ponder, just how far the system is efficient for the education of the child who comes to its school without a knowledge of the first word in the English language. Without a detailed knowledge of the subject, I know enough of conditions in the average public school today to warrant at least the suspicion that Americans would not be particularly proud of the system, and of what it gives for which annually they pay millions of dollars in taxes.

I am aware in making this statement that I shall be met with convincing instances of intelligent effort being made with the foreign-born children in special classes. No one has a higher respect for those efforts than I have—few, other than educators, know of them better than I do, since I did not make my five-year study of the American public school system for naught. But I am not referring to the exceptional instance here and there. I merely ask of the American, interested as he is or should be in the Americanization of the strangers within his gates, how far the public school system, as a whole, urban and rural, adapts itself, with any true efficiency, to the foreign-born child. I venture to color his opinion in no wise; I simply ask that he will inquire and ascertain for himself, as he should do if he is interested in the future welfare of his country and his institutions; for what happens in America in the years to come depends, in large measure, on what is happening today in the public schools of this country.

SOURCE: Edward Bok. *The Americanization of Edward Bok: The Autobiography of a Dutch Boy Fifty Years After.* New York: Charles Scribner's Sons. 1922.

# LOUIS ADAMIC

*Amerikansi in Carniola*
(Slovenia; 1932)

*Louis Adamic (1899–1951) became a journalist. In the "Author's Note"*
*to his memoir,* Laughing in the Jungle, *he reminds us: "Immigration was*
*a large factor in the upbuilding of America. The immigrant flood during the*
*last seven or eight decades, and especially from about 1890 to 1914, included*
*large numbers of my countrymen— 'Bohunks,' or 'Hunkies': Slavs from the*
*Balkans and from eastern and central Europe—whose contribution as work-*
*ers to the current material greatness and power of the United States, albeit*
*not generally recognized, is immense." He explains in this excerpt from that*
*memoir how, as a fourteen-year-old, he left Slovenia for America.*

As a boy of nine, and even younger, in my native village of Blato,
in Carniola—then a Slovenian duchy of Austria and later a part of
Yugoslavia—I experienced a thrill every time one of the men of the
little community returned from America.

Five or six years before, as I heard people tell, the man had quietly
left the village for the United States, a poor peasant clad in homespun, with a mustache under his nose and a bundle on his back; now,
a clean-shaven *Amerikanec,* he sported a blue-serge suit, buttoned
shoes very large in the toes and with India-rubber heels, a black
derby, a shiny celluloid collar, and a loud necktie made even louder
by a dazzling horseshoe pin, which, rumor had it, was made of gold,
while his two suitcases of imitation leather, tied with straps, bulged
with gifts from America for his relatives and friends in the village. In
nine cases out of ten, he had left in economic desperation, on money
borrowed from some relative in the United States; now there was talk
in the village that he was worth anywhere from one to three thousand American dollars. And to my eyes he truly bore all the earmarks
of affluence. Indeed, to say that he thrilled my boyish fancy is putting
it mildly. With other boys in the village, I followed him around as he

went visiting his relatives and friends and distributing presents, and hung onto his every word and gesture.

Then, on the first Sunday after his homecoming, if at all possible, I got within earshot of the nabob as he sat in the winehouse or under the linden in front of the winehouse in Blato, surrounded by village folk, ordering wine and *klobase*—Carniolan sausages—for all comers, paying for accordion-players, indulging in tall talk about America, its wealth and vastness, and his own experiences as a worker in the West Virginia or Kansas coal-mines or Pennsylvania rolling-mills, and comparing notes upon conditions in the United States with other local *Amerikansi* who had returned before him.

Under the benign influence of *cvichek*—Lower Carniolan wine— and often even when sober, the men who had been in America spoke expansively, boastfully, romantically of their ability and accomplishments as workers and of the wages they had earned in Wilkes-Barre or Carbondale, Pennsylvania, or Wheeling, West Virginia, or Pueblo, Colorado, or Butte, Montana, and generally of places and people and things and affairs in the New World. The men who returned to the village, either to stay or for a visit, were, for the most part, natural men of labor—men with sinewy arms and powerful backs—"Bohunks," or "Hunkies," so called in the United States— who derived a certain brawny joy and pride from hard toil. Besides, now that they had come home, they were no longer mere articles upon the industrial labor market, "working stiffs" or "wage slaves," as radical agitators in America referred to them, but adventurers, distant kinsmen of Marco Polo safely returned from a far country, heroes in their own eyes and the eyes of the village; and it was natural for them to expand and to exaggerate their own exploits and enlarge upon the opportunities to be found in America. Their boasting, perhaps, was never wholly without basis in fact.

I remember that, listening to them, I played with the idea of going to America when I was but eight or nine.

My notion of the United States then, and for a few years after, was that it was a grand, amazing, somewhat fantastic place—the Golden Country—a sort of Paradise—the Land of Promise in more ways than one—huge beyond conception, thousands of miles across the ocean, untellably exciting, explosive, quite incomparable to the tiny, quiet, lovely Carniola; a place full of movement and turmoil, wherein things that were unimaginable and impossible in Blato happened daily as a matter of course.

In America one could make pots of money in a short time, acquire immense holdings, wear a white collar, and have polish on one's boots like a *gospod*—one of the gentry—and eat white bread, soup, and meat on weekdays as well as on Sundays, even if one were but an ordinary workman to begin with. In Blato no one ate white bread or soup and meat, except on Sundays and holidays, and very few then.

In America one did not have to remain an ordinary workman. There, it seemed, one man was as good as the next. There were dozens, perhaps scores, or even hundreds of immigrants in the United States, one-time peasants and workers from the Balkans—from Carniola, Styria, Carinthia, Croatia, Banat, Dalmatia, Bosnia, Montenegro, and Serbia—and from Poland, Slovakia, Bohemia, and elsewhere, who, in two or three years, had earned and saved enough money working in the Pennsylvania, Ohio, or Illinois coal-mines or steel-mills to go to regions called Minnesota, Wisconsin, and Nebraska, and there buy sections of land each of which was larger than the whole area owned by the peasants in Blato ... Oh, America was immense—*immense*!

I heard a returned *Amerikanec* tell of regions known as Texas and Oklahoma where single farms—*renche* (ranches), he called them—were larger than the entire province of Carniola! It took a man days to ride on horseback from one end of such a ranch to the other. There were people in Blato and in neighboring villages who, Thomas-like, did not believe this, but my boyish imagination was aflame with America, and I believed it. At that time I accepted as truth nearly everything I heard about America. I believed that a single cattleman in Texas owned more cattle than there were in the entire Balkans. And my credulity was not strained when I heard that there were goldmines in California, and trees more than a thousand years old with trunks so enormous that it required a dozen men, clasping each other's hands, to encircle them with their arms.

In America everything was possible. There even the common people were "citizens," not "subjects," as they were in Austria and in most other European countries. A citizen, or even a non-citizen foreigner, could walk up to the President of the United States and pump his hand. Indeed, that seemed to be a custom in America. There was a man in Blato, a former steel-worker in Pittsburgh who claimed that upon an occasion he had shaken hands and exchanged words with Theodore Roosevelt, to whom he familiarly referred as "Tedi"—which struck my mother very funny. To her it seemed as if someone had called the Pope of Rome or the Emperor of Austria by a nickname. But the man assured her, in my hearing, that in America everybody called the President merely "Tedi." Mother laughed about this, off and on, for several days And I laughed with her. She and I often laughed together.

★ ★ ★

One day—I was then a little over ten—I said to Mother: "Some day I am going to America."

Mother looked at me a long moment. She was then a healthy young peasant woman, not yet thirty, rather tall, with a full bust and large hips; long arms and big, capable hands; a broad, sun-browned, wind-creased Slavic face; large, wide-spaced hazel eyes, mild and luminous with simple mirth; and wavy auburn hair which stuck in little gold-bleached wisps from under her colored kerchief, tied below her chin. She had then four children, two boys and two girls; later she bore five more, three boys and two girls. I was the oldest. Years after I came to America my oldest sister wrote me that there was a story in the village that Mother had laughed in her pains at my birth—which probably is not true; mother herself, who is still living, does not remember. But I know that when I was a boy she had—and probably still has—the gift of laughter in a greater measure than most people thereabouts; indeed, than most people anywhere. Hers was the healthy, natural, visceral, body-shaking laughter of Slovenian peasants in Carniola, especially of peasant women—variable laughter; usually mirthful and humorous, clear and outright, but sometimes, too, mirthless and unhumorous, pain-born, and pain-transcending.

"I am going to America," I said again, as Mother continued to look at me in silence.

I imagine she thought that I was a strange boy. Now and then she had remarked in my hearing that I worried her. Often she looked at me with silent concern. In some respects I was a self-willed youngster. I usually had things my way, regardless of opposition.

Finally, Mother smiled at me, although I do not doubt that what I said frightened her. She smiled with her whole face—her mouth, her wrinkles, her eyes, especially her eyes.

I smiled, too. I was a healthy boy, tall and strong for my age. Physically, as Mother often remarked, I resembled Father, who was a peasant in body and soul; but evidently I was not made to be a peasant. If necessary, I could work hard in the fields, but I very much preferred not to. I liked to move about the village, roam in the woods, go to neighboring villages, stand by the side of the highway, and observe things.

With a little catch in her voice, Mother said: "To America? But when are you going?"

"I don't know," I said. "When I grow up, I guess. I am already ten." I had not thought of it in detail, but had merely decided to go some day.

Mother laughed. Her laughter was tremulous with apprehension. She could not make me out.

I realized then that she would not like me to go to America. A cousin of hers had gone there twenty-odd years before, when she was still a little girl. She scarcely remembered him, but had heard other relatives speak of him. The first year he had written a few times. Then Heaven only knew what became of him. And, as it occurred to me later, Mother knew of other men in Blato and the vicinity who had gone to America and had sunk, leaving no trace, in the vastness of America. She knew of men in villages not remote from our own who had returned from the United States without an arm or minus a leg, or in bad health. There was an *Amerikanec* in Gatina, the village nearest Blato, who had come home with a strange, sinful, and un-mentionable disease, which he later communicated to his wife, who, in turn, gave birth to a blind child. There was a widow in Podgora, another village near by, whose husband had been killed in a mine accident in the United States. Mother had only a faint conception of what a mine was; there are no mines in Lower Carniola; but she dreaded the thought that some day one of her children might work underground.

* * *

All of us, parents and children, slept in the *izba*—the large room in a Slovenian peasant house—and that night, soon after we all went to bed, Mother called me by name in a low voice, adding, "Are you asleep?"

I was awake, and almost answered her, but then it occurred to me that she probably meant to discuss me with Father. I kept quiet. The bed which I shared with my brother was in the opposite corner from my parents'.

"He is asleep," mumbled Father. "Why do you call him?"

"I want to tell you what he said to me today," said Mother, in a half-whisper, which I heard clearly. "He said he would go to America when he grew up."

Father grunted vaguely. He was heavy with fatigue. He had worked hard all day. He was one of the better-to-do peasants in Blato, but, with Mother's aid, did nearly all the work on the farm, seldom hiring outside help. He was a large, hard man, in his late thirties; blue-eyed and light-haired; a simple, competent peasant.

He grunted again. "America? He is only a child. How old is he, anyhow?" he asked. He was too busy to keep up with the ages of his children.

"He is ten," said Mother. "But he is like no other boy in the village."

"Only a child," Father grunted again. "Childish talk."

"Sometimes I am afraid to talk with him," said Mother. "I don't know what is going on in his head. He asks me questions and tells me things. Nothing that occurs hereabouts escapes him. And he reads everything he finds in the village."

They were both silent a minute.

"I'll send him to city school, then," said Father, "even if he is our oldest." According to custom in Carniola, as the oldest son, I was supposed to stay home and work on the farm, and after my father's death become its master. "He isn't much good on the farm, anyhow," Father went on. "I'll send him to school in Lublyana"—the provincial capital. "Let him get educated if he has a head for learning."

'That's what Martin says we should do, too," said Mother. Martin was her brother, the priest in charge of the parish of Zhalna, which included the village of Blato.

"They say children are God's blessing," said Father, after a while, "but—"

"Oh, everything will be well in the end," Mother interrupted his misgiving. "There is little to worry about so long as God gives us health." She was a natural, earth-and-sky optimist; a smiling, laughing fatalist. Then, after a few moments, she added: "Maybe—maybe, if we send him to school in Lublyana, he will become a priest, like my brother Martin."

Father said nothing to this. Mother was silent, too.

By and by I heard Father snore lightly, in the first stage of his slumber.

Mother, I believe, did not fall asleep till late that night. She probably smiled to herself in the darkness, yielding her consciousness to delicious thoughts. It was absurd to think that I should go to America! I was only a child, and one should not take seriously a child's chatter.

They would send me to Lublyana; that was settled. Then, after years of schooling, I would become a priest and the bishop might send me to the parish church in Zhalna. "Oh, that would be beautiful!" she exclaimed to herself, half aloud. I heard her clearly, despite Father's snoring, and I imagine that this is what she was thinking to herself. She probably figured that by the time I would be ordained a priest, Uncle Martin would have been promoted to a bigger parish than Zhalna, making a vacancy for me.

*[When he was fourteen, Adamic was expelled from the school in Lublyana for his attendance at a political rally for the Yugoslav Movement in 1913, where his friend was killed. His parents enrolled him in a Jesuit school, from which he fled.]*

No more school for me. I was going to America. I did not know how, but I knew that I would go . . .

In Lublyana, Father searched for me all afternoon.

I walked but a few kilometers on the highway, when a peasant came along in his wagon and gave me a ride all the way to Blato. His destination was some distance beyond our village.

It was already dark when I arrived home. Father had returned by train an hour or two before.

The moment I appeared a storm broke loose. Father burst into a rage and wanted to beat me, but Mother begged him to leave me alone. She told me to go to my room in the attic.

I went. Presently Mother brought me some supper. She was hurt, upset, and sad, but tried to be as sweet to me as ever.

"Eat," she said. Then she left me alone.

As I ate, Father was slamming the doors below, and the younger children, frightened by his anger, were crying. I could also hear Father shout at Mother, who was trying to pacify him.

After a while Mother returned to my room.

"But what do you want to do, son?" she asked me, quietly.

"I want to go to America."

She looked at me startled, frightened.

"Don't worry, Mother," I said. "Nothing will happen to me in America." I thought of Yanko Radin and our talk about the United States. "For some people, I know, America is a bad place, but I can take care of myself there."

"You mustn't go to work in the mines—underground," she said.

"Of course not." I saw that she was already willing to let me go. "But how are you going?"

"Maybe I'll go with Peter Molek," I said. "He is going back, now that his health is so much better. Perhaps Father will loan me the money for the passage. I'll send it back to him from America."

Mother was silent, looking at me. Fatalist that she was, she probably thought to herself that there was no way of stopping me; I seemed to know what I wanted. Now I would never be a priest; and she—no doubt—had told other women in Blato that I might become one. She was disappointed, chagrined. But, peasant-like, she recovered almost at once.

Late that night, as I lay sleepless in the attic, I heard Father and Mother talk below.

In the morning everything was quiet again. The storm was over. Father and Mother bore their parental misfortune with the unconscious dignity of simple people. The effect upon them of my expulsion from school and my subsequent balking at going into the Jesuit School was essentially the same as had been the effect of a severe hailstorm early the previous summer, which, in a few minutes late one afternoon, had ruined most of our growing potatoes and young corn. On that occasion I had seen Mother stare at the swirls of hailstones beating upon the young plants. She had wept and sprinkled holy water from the doorway, while Father, standing by her side, had prayed and cursed in the same breath. But then the storm had passed and in a few minutes the sun had come out, and Mother had ceased weeping and Father had stopped praying and cursing. A half-hour afterward they had walked in the fields, inspecting the ruins. I had walked with them. Suddenly, Mother's sad face had lighted up. "Look," she had said, "here the hail did almost no harm. It passed over. This will grow yet." She had smiled at Father, then at me. "Yes," Father had agreed, "this will grow again."

When I came down that morning, Mother said, simply: "Father says he will give you the money and you may go to America, and God bless you, son."

★ ★ ★

The *Niagara* sailed from Le Havre, France. She was an old ship, rather small, carrying mostly immigrants. Most of the steerage passengers were Poles, Slovaks, Czechs, Croatians, Slovenians, and Bosnians, with a sprinkling of Jews, Greeks, Turks, Germans, and Austrian

Italians; young men and middle-aged men, women and children of all ages, some of them wearing colorful native costumes—all of them headed for the Land of Promise. A few of them were returning to America from visits to their old homelands. Most of these traveled second-class.

Peter Molek and I were the only two Slovenians aboard not traveling steerage. Molek had feared that the bad food and lack of ventilation "down below" might play the devil with his health again, and my father, in his pride, had then insisted on buying me a second-class ticket, too. Molek and I occupied a tiny room together.

The first day on the ocean I had a heavy feeling in my midriff. Through my mind went loose thoughts of home, of Yanko Radin, of Blato and Lublyana, of everything that had lately happened to me.

The best part of the trip, aside from the thrill of being on the ocean for the first time, were the lessons that Peter Molek gave me in the meaning and pronunciation of American words and phrases.

The day before we reached New York Harbor, Molek said to me in English: "You'll be all right in America, even if it is a jungle," which I understood with but slight help from him. He added in Slovenian: "You are going to America for excitement and adventure. Don't fear; you will not be disappointed; you will find plenty of both."

I did not know what to say to that. The heavy feeling in my midriff had left me completely. I ceased thinking of people and things in the Old Country.

SOURCE: Louis Adamic. *Laughing in the Jungle: The Autobiography of an Immigrant in America.* New York: Harper & Row. 1932.

# STOYAN PRIBICHEVICH

*In an American Factory*
(Yugoslavia; 1938)

*Stoyan Pribichevich (1905–1976), who had been a lawyer in Yugoslavia, found his calling in America as a journalist for many prominent publications. In this essay, he accounts for his appreciation of men with mechanical intelligence: "It was this power of quick mechanical diagnosis that my legally, abstractly trained mind could not grasp."*

I came to America in 1934 as a political exile who could hardly speak English. In 1932 I had become involved in Yugoslav university students' riots and in printing pamphlets against King Alexander's dictatorship. I was twenty-seven years of age then, a doctor of political science and a practicing lawyer in Belgrade. Before the political police could seize me I managed to cross the Yugoslav frontier disguised as a peasant. I went to Paris where I spent two years, helping my father—a former member of the Yugoslav cabinet and also an exile—to write a book on democracy. I quarreled with the painters of Montparnasse on art, played the violin, and argued with my exiled countrymen in cafes clouded with tobacco smoke about the perfect democratic society. Then I thought I would visit a relative of mine in New York. I signed under oath a long printed paper in English declaring that I was not a bomb thrower, lunatic, or venereal patient, and landed in Manhattan.

Coming from France, which to me seemed a thoroughly logical country, I was confused by the many incomprehensible contradictions of American life. Yet I found to my astonishment that my American friends thought the French were a crazy people. When they asked me why France has more than twenty political parties, I countered: "Why do you jam Roosevelt, Glass, and Hague all in one party and Hoover, Borah, and La Guardia together in the other?" I could not understand why the country with the largest workers' population in the world should have no labor party; why centralization should be advocated by liberals, and States' Rights defended by big corporations; why Tom Mooney should be in jail for murder and Al Capone for tax evasion; why aliens should be regarded with contempt by the sons of aliens; why religion should be separated from the state, and Darwin's theory of evolution banned by one State in the name of the Bible; why bishops should oppose child-labor regulation; why gangsters and kidnappers should grow up next door to the strange prophets and utopians of the Share-the-Wealth, Epic, Social Justice, and Old-Age-Pension plans; why the dictatorships of Louisiana and Jersey City should flourish under a democratic federal Constitution. Only gradually did I begin to grasp the deep significance of American inconsistencies which so strike the set, static mind of a European: to realize that they were mere symptoms of growth, showing a slow trend of the nation toward ever-increasing democracy.

In this country I experienced for the first time the magnificent feeling of absolute personal freedom. No policeman could stop me in the street or in a restaurant and ask me to show him my papers. I could walk about without carrying an identity card in my pocket, change my address without reporting to the police, and slap a cop on the shoulder just because I was feeling fine. Only a European can appreciate the personal freedom a man enjoys in this country.

I decided to stay here—and went back to France to change my legal clothes. I obtained an immigration visa and, toward the end of 1935, returned to America as an immigrant. I began to look for work. When I had tried to get a job in Europe either I could get no appointment or I was treated rudely. Here I was received very politely by bank directors or the heads of law firms. I was helped out of my overcoat, shown a chair, and offered a cigar. Then I would tell my story to an attentive listener. "Right now there is very little I can do for you," the man behind the desk would say apologetically, "but I shall certainly be glad to get in touch with you if anything should come up." Then he would take my address and telephone number and escort me to the door. It was not until I reached the street that I realized I had not got the job. It is almost a pleasure to be turned down in this country.

Finally I secured work. Despite my four languages and legal training, it was the job of a worker in an Ohio machine shop. It happened this way. Three and a half years ago I met a manufacturer from Cleveland at a party in New York. He teased me, saying that as a newcomer to America I should learn about American life by spending a few months as a worker in his shop. I did not see him again. When, in 1936, I was unable to find a job in New York and found myself penniless, I wrote to him and asked whether he remembered me and his invitation. He replied that he did and renewed his offer. I packed my things and went. Instead of a few months, I spent a whole year in his shop.

When one gray, foggy morning in the beginning of 1937 I got off the train in Cleveland, I became dismayed at the thought of what lay before me. I did not know a soul in this city. I had never done physical work before. I wanted to return to New York where I had friends. But there was no more money for another train fare and no way out. As I stood in the cold, damp mist I felt weak for a moment.

"Which is the way to the X Company?" I asked a passer-by. He pointed to a waiting trolley car.

Rolling along the dingy, interminable avenue, I began to whistle. The morning sun pierced through the torn rags of dirty fog, and slowly a feeling of glory descended upon me. I was following the old trail that for forty years before me had been trodden by those countless thousands of immigrants from Yugoslavia who had helped to build America. With a few borrowed dollars in my pocket I was on my way to work in an American factory. "It's a great thing," I said to myself.

It was bitter cold and a heavy snowfall set in as I walked through the gloomy, smoky industrial district to put on overalls for the first time. The huge plant, covering two blocks, all in steel and concrete, was run by electricity. Passing through enormous rooms, I saw countless machines swinging their metal arms through the air like fantastic octopuses, hissing furiously, and drowning in their roar the voices of men. Over them were bending rough, athletic-looking workers, with rolled-up sleeves and black caps, their faces grim and smeared with oil and grease, their eyes intent.

The so-called "turret lathe" was manufactured in this shop. This is a machine which in its turn makes tools and machine parts. You can fabricate almost anything with it, from automobile parts to bullets.

The factory itself was spotless. I had seen orderly European shops, but they had not gleamed with such beautiful cleanliness. I was assigned to the second shift. Through underground passages I was led to the Assembly, another huge room where the finished parts of turret lathe machines were put together, tested, and taken apart for shipment. The workers cast curious glances at the newcomer. They were amused at my clumsy attempts to punch the clock and showed me a vacant locker along the left wall where I changed clothes. Then, at four o'clock, the note of the factory bell sounded in my ears, and our shift started off like a regiment toward the machines in the center. Holding our tool boxes in our hands, we waited in line for the foreman to assign us our jobs.

I did rough work on that first night. I swept the floor and picked up waste and dirt with my bare hands. I carried heavy machine parts in my arms or on my shoulders. I screwed big pipes together. A compassionate worker showed me how to hold a file, and with it I smoothed off the edges of five push-button plates. Within fifteen minutes my hands were blistered, my arms impregnated with black metal dust and machine oil, and my mouth full of grease. When I was through at midnight the muscles of my feet, legs, fingers, hands, arms, and back ached terribly. I dragged myself home and slept like a dead man.

"How do you feel?" the foreman asked me as we washed up the following night. I shrugged my shoulders. He winked at another worker and laughed: "It'll do him good; in three weeks he'll have muscles like Popeye the Sailor." The factory reminded me of a European dictatorial state, where bureaucrats plan and order and citizens work and obey. The board of the Company was the government, and the workers were the people, ruled through a centralized hierarchy of officials and controlled by a mechanized system of registration, bookkeeping, time cards, and punch clocks. Like citizens of authoritarian states, we did our individual assignments without knowing their purpose or the general plan of work. I met a worker whose specialty was to assemble gear boxes to the turret lathe machines and who had no idea what the machines were for. The foreman was our supreme visible authority. With his superiors we could not communicate. And the president, with his board members and directors, sat high above us like an invisible, unapproachable god. Watchmen were stationed inside and outside the building to let nobody in or out except on a special permit. We even had our numbers. Mine was 1941.

I was struck by the contrast between the American worker's political freedom and the rigid regimentation of his forty-hour week. The French worker cannot conceive a personal freedom which does not include a certain leisureliness at work. So he must work six days a week if the production is not to lag and the production costs to rise. The American worker pays for his two free days by straining his energies under a mechanized discipline during the other five. A German-American worker, who previously had been employed in an automobile plant, said to me: "What are you talking about? This machine shop is a fine place to work. On my last job, after we'd won the sit-down strike, the Company made us punch our cards even when we went to the toilet!" I have often wondered whether the willingness of the American worker to submit to such regimentation might not be due, not only to his sense of efficiency but also to a general American trait. In spite of their fundamental belief in the democratic form of government, Americans show a certain predilection for personal rule and the "one man" system in their group and business activities. In no other free country are the significant terms "chief" and "boss" so frequently heard.

We were only twenty in our group in the Assembly Room, but we were of fourteen different nationalities: Serbs, Slovenes, Croats, Italians, Hungarians, Rumanians, Czechs, Germans, Poles, Swedes, Englishmen, Scotchmen, Irishmen—even Americans. When, later, I was transferred to other departments, I found Slovaks and Lithuanians in addition. Of course only the older men were foreign-born. The young workers were born in this country, mostly of foreign parentage at least on one side. They hardly spoke the native languages of their parents and cared little about their old countries. During an entire year I never witnessed a nationalistic dispute among these people. There was something humorous about our racial differences in this American shop. We cracked jokes at one another and imitated the various foreign accents in our English speech. There was an Italian who never took offense when called "Spaghetti." A pro-Hitler German laughed every time we grotesqued the Nazi salute and yelled "Heil Hitler!" at him. "Hey, you! You took our country!" shouted a Hungarian at me from his machine one day, referring to Yugoslavia's annexation of southern Hungarian provinces after the World War. "Sure!" I retorted, swinging my hammer; "you had us for a thousand years, and it's our turn now!" We both laughed. And yet I knew that in Europe, or even in their native-quarter saloons, these same fellows would fight bitterly on less provocation.

International politics were a daily topic. Most foreign-born workers thought they were safer and better off here than they would be overseas. Some Italians were pro-Mussolini, and of course had to take a lot of chaffing. The anti-Fascist Italians did not speak to them. The Germans were rather silent about their beliefs, and it was difficult to find out whether they were for or against Hitler. The reasonable guess was that those who would not divulge their opinions intimately disapproved of the Nazi regime. All workers regardless of nationality sympathized with China. And, almost without exception, they hated General Franco intensely. Most were anti-Communist, but many expressed interest in Soviet Russia's economic experiment.

At first my fellow-workers showed annoyance at my ignorance of a mechanic's work, but when they realized I had never been in a shop before they were eager to help me. They showed me how to file, hammer, and scrape. They let me use their tools, air hoses, and trucks. They pulled heavy crane chains for me—and fixed up my mistakes. Their sense of comradeship and co-operation was genuine and magnificent. I profited by it greatly—and so did the Company.

A robust Rumanian, after having loaded some eighty pounds on my back one day, said: "So you never work before? I work when I was sixteen!" He obviously considered intellectual occupation as just fooling around. Naturally, they were all curious about my background. No matter how hard I tried to conceal it, I would repeatedly give myself away by some such form of address as "Please," "May I?" or "Thank you." They instinctively regarded such politenesses as the social affectation of an upper class. Correct grammar was also a high-hat pretense to them, and I soon caught myself saying "He don't" or "I says."

Like school children, they loved to throw paper balls and orange peels at one another or to pinch an unsuspecting posterior. After my transfer to the small-tool department I was solemnly escorted to a "weight guesser" who held me on his back, while, surrounded by a roaring crowd of the "brotherhood," I unexpectedly received three burning slaps on my rear. My unpronounceable last name was a cause of great fun. Everybody practiced it with comical variations. My stern-faced foreman was greeted with loud cheers one night when he gave it up and shouted in desperation: "Where's that new fellow, what's his name, Pepperbitch?" Most of my fellow-workers disapproved of drinking but chewed tobacco enthusiastically. Every night in the Assembly I watched, fascinated, a machinist who at regular intervals spat streams of coffee-brown liquid in an arc over his machine and never missed the spittoon.

The stories of some of the immigrant workers were tragic.

There was an emaciated Scotchman with a finely chiseled face and trembling hands, who collapsed nearly every week and had to be sent home, his eyes glassy. Years before he had contracted tropical malaria working for a British company in India. A Swede, with all the symptoms of stomach ulcers, lips tightened, skin earthen, drilled and hammered doggedly. From time to time he crouched down behind his machine to endure silently an intolerable pain. A poor Italian, his wife long dead, had to leave his children without supervision while he worked at night in the shop. Almost every year his eldest daughter brought him an illegitimate child. She had been only sixteen when she had the first one. A Croat with an ambassador's face had been worth fifty thousand dollars before the depression. Left without a cent, he was prevented by his children from committing suicide, and went to work in the shop. Another Croat was picked up in 1903 at the age of nineteen in a desolate mountain region of Croatia by the agents of an American railroad company, who took him away from his sheep and shipped him off to America. On his arrival in Pennsylvania he was lined up with many others in an open field. The foremen stripped off their coats and examined their muscles as if they had been cattle or African slaves. Still another countryman of mine told me that he came here at the age of thirteen to fell trees with the Negroes in the forests of Virginia. He is a fine machinist now and speaks good English. He made a very significant statement to me: "Nobody knows how many dramas are buried in American shops. Most of our people do not prosper in America because they do not take the trouble to learn English. And they never will as long as they live in racial colonies."

Yet most of the immigrants loved America with a peculiar sense of pride. "We are told to go back where we came from," exclaimed a Serbian worker from California. "No, sir! This is our country. And our affection for it is all the more deep for having watered it with the sweat of our labor. We made this country what it is today."

I often hear about the unemployment of men over forty. But in this machine shop wherever skill or experience was needed most men were over forty. And even physically many of them had more resistance than the young fellows. I did not really mind being ignorant of a mechanic's work, I could always ask for help or advice. But unfortunately I belong to that class of persons who become panicky every time they have to hammer a nail or open a stubborn lock. Every worker knew, for instance, how to sharpen a drill on the automatic stone wheel. But in my hands the thing invariably went crooked, and I left part of my skin on the whirling grinder. Stamping numbers on a machine part, I would first hit gently; the number would not come out; then I would gather myself for a terrific whack which, of course, would land right on my knuckles. And the holes I drilled were always cock-eyed. Irritated and impatient, I tried to overcome my subconscious fear of mechanical things by the use of physical force and, naturally, ruined both my work and my hands. It took me a long time to realize that a mechanic's ability resides in a careful deliberation and calculation of movements rather than in brute strength. I began to observe that my fellow-workers used their hands with caution, sized up every load before lifting it, took care to place their fingers in the right places, and then pushed or pulled with just the required physical energy. When their efforts were unsuccessful they repeated them slowly over and over again. It was a superb lesson in self-control and patience. Like a fine racehorse, a machine wants to be treated firmly, but with kindness and intelligence.

"Take your time, my boy," remarked an old Slovene, watching me tighten some screws, "you are going to waste a lot of time hurrying." I was amazed by the tenderness which the workers showed toward the inanimate objects of their labor. "Oh, she'll be all right again," said a youngster of a machine he was repairing, and patted it as though it were a sick person. After "tapping"—cutting screw threads in a big turret—one night, I left it dripping with oil on the bench and turned to my next job. Immediately a bushy-haired fellow ran up to me and shouted angrily: "You can't leave her like that! Are you a machinist?" And he neatly wiped it off with his rag. "See?" he said and looked fondly at the shining metal. I took such rude reprimands without resentment, learning that these men did work of fine quality and that infinite care was the first requirement. Helping to take complicated parts out of the machine "heads" and to replace them, I always had the vivid impression of assisting at an operation on a human body. Even their tools—wrenches, pincers, scrapers, pliers, drills—were similar to a surgeon's or dentist's instruments. A mechanic's work is surgery on metal. In spite of scale and microm- eter, the human eye and hand have the final control. No mechanical device can supplant the craftsman's sensitive fingers in fitting a bar to a hole, in feeling the evenness of a slide, or in the finishing touch of smoothing and polishing.

Whenever I got stuck and called for help, unable to find the cause of trouble, my neighbor would shout over the noise: "Find out! Think!" Then he would come closer, look the machine over, and adjust something at the far opposite end which had made my bar in front fit badly. It was this power of quick mechanical diagnosis that my legally, abstractly trained mind could not grasp. But no worker or instructor ever troubled to give me a theoretical explanation of a job. They would say: "Watch me!" then pull a lever, push a button, turn a wheel, and stand back for me to repeat their movements. They would tell me how, but never why. The invisible control of the worker's activities through bookkeeping and job cards was so ubiquitous and inexorable that the office could at any time find out which worker had put which screw on which part, and on what day.

Once I broke a small handle. "You can't get away with that; they'll find it out," said a man who saw me do the damage. "You'd better go to the foreman and report." Every operation, no matter how small, had to be accomplished within the prescribed standard time, marked on special cards. On my first day in the shop I was warned by fellow-workers not to "ring out" my cards before the allotted time was up, or the office would cut down the standard norm for everybody. This had been tacitly agreed by them all to prevent the management from speeding us up. Whoever "rang" less than one hundred per cent time was a scab. Intelligently, the management took no steps against this. But the collective work of a shift could sometimes be speeded up imperceptibly. One week we were told we were to work six days and be paid time and a half for overtime. When Friday came the foreman said he had changed his mind. Asked why, he answered: "The department has caught up." In other words, under his continual gentle urging during that week we had all worked slightly faster, with the result that the shift accomplished six days' work in five days for five days' pay.

Most men disliked the time-card system. "I like to do a good job but I hate to have a time limit for it," said a German scraper to me. It was easy to keep to time norms either in very simple or in very mechanized jobs; but when the quality of each piece depended on the skill of the worker's hands, the uniform time rules became meaningless bureaucratic measures. Once I took three hours and a half to scrape the slides properly and ream the holes on eight parts. Another time I took nine hours. In spite of the time cards the foremen had to give us individual allowances on all quality jobs.

One night as the "pay man" distributed our checks, a bad-tempered Swede flung his on the floor and spat on it. Shaking his fists he roared: "They deduct money for social security, for the community fund, for hospital insurance, and I have to pay my union dues and the income tax. God damn it, I work for everybody except myself!"

"I am afraid," I tried to pacify him, "you'll have to pick up your check anyway."

The workers work hard all their lives and get enough for a living, sometimes a comfortable living, but never enough to stop working. "Once in a shop, always in a shop," was the gloomy refrain in every department. Sitting on wooden boxes or machine levers at lunch or dinner time, we often exchanged confidences and talked about our intimate ambitions. The old workers would shake their heads telling of twenty, thirty years spent in shops. The young ones would dreamingly speak of their hopes for the future. A fine machine operator said bitterly: "I get sick looking at this machine. Shall I run it when I am fifty? What a life!" Another hoped to get an office job some day. Still another dreamed of becoming a schoolteacher. He had finished high school; then he had got married, had had two children, and had gone into the shop instead of to college. Most wanted to go into "business for themselves" some day. Not one wished to remain a shop worker.

Discussing the reasons for the complete failure of the Marxist class ideology in this country, Mr. George Sokolsky said once that the American worker is merely a capitalist without money. I do not think that this is quite correct. My fellow-workers did not like being laborers but they also had no desire to become employers. They wanted to be on their own, neither hired nor hiring. Their attitude toward life was not proletarian nor was it capitalist; it was typically middle-class.

[. . .]

Years ago I had an ambition to become a concert violinist. I am glad I never became one. But I kept up violin playing with that zeal and determination that distinguishes the stubborn amateur, and after some months in Cleveland I began to be asked to play the violin at musical parties in the evenings. I found that many workers in the shop were musical. Some sang, some played instruments, some were members of choirs and bands. One night in the Assembly I whistled the leading tune from the first movement of the Beethoven violin concerto. A handsome young Pole looked up: "Do you sing?" "No," I replied, "I fiddle." "I sing," he explained, "and I knew you must be a musician the way you whistle." We talked music all night while I washed the machines with rags dipped in kerosene and he screwed bolts on them.

When my people overseas heard that I had been compelled to work in an American factory they were worried not so much about the physical hardships I should have to endure as about the social humiliation I should have to suffer. Professional and class standards are so set in Europe that an intellectual who resorts to physical work for a living is considered declasse. Here I saw the sons of rich lawyers and business men spend their college vacations working in a shop. America—we all know—has long ceased to be a pioneer country; but ideas often survive the facts, and certain social standards of the pioneer era still persist here. One of them is respect for physical work. In no European country could I come home all dirty from shop work, layoff my working clothes, take a bath, put on a dinner coat, and play the Cesar Franck or the Brahms D-Minor violin-piano Sonata before an audience in evening clothes at some private house.

One day I was asked by a prominent local organization to give a series of lectures on Central Europe and the Balkans. I spotted a few of my fellow-workers among the audience. The day after my last lecture I put on my overalls again; but my anonymity in the shop had been completely killed by the newspaper publicity, and I was afraid the workers might resent me. As I took the elevator I was greeted with hearty shouts: "Hey, Doc!" or "Here comes the Doc!" They were interested to know whether there was more money in lecturing than in machine running. I told them that, for the time being, I would rather stick to my machine.

After a full year spent in the factory I returned to New York. Looking back upon my year-long experience in this American shop, I am fully aware that it does not give a general picture of the American industrial life. One can arrive at a just evaluation of it only by comparing it with industrial conditions elsewhere, here and abroad. We were paid at an average rate of 84 cents an hour. We worked 40 hours a week, in clean, healthy surroundings. We were given time and a half for overtime. We had time for rest, amusements, and cultural activities. We had a two weeks' vacation with pay. We were treated fairly as men and as workers. The foremen were willing to make exceptions in emergencies and to help out in trouble. Not seldom they would give us time-saving jobs (the so-called "good jobs") when we were behind on our time cards. But the people whose character left the deepest impression on me were the workers. Humaneness and sympathy were concealed under their brusque ways and manners. On their faces, which sometimes reminded me of those of the peasants in my old country, lines of dishonesty or wickedness were rarely to be found. Many of them came from distant, forlorn corners of the United States, or from far-off, backward countries; they grew into the soil of a new community, excelled at work, and managed to give their children better care than they had enjoyed. When I think how tremendously handicapped they were by lack of means as well as of background and education, I wonder if perhaps they are not more able fellows than I. They were men of simple taste and reasonable, sane attitude toward life. No fanaticism colored their discontent. And their ambitions were undistorted by megalomaniac wishes to make "a career" or do "great things."

Their objectives in life were within the limits of the possible. Again and again I feel compelled to reflect upon the question which that young married worker once put to me: "What are you living for?"

SOURCE: Stoyan Pribichevich, "In an American Factory." *Harper's Magazine.* September 1938.

# ANDRÉS ARAGON

*After the Death of Spain*
(Spain; 1978)

*Aragon (a pseudonym the writer took while working for the American Office of War Information during World War II) became a professor of Spanish literature at a California college. He was from Galicia, Spain, where he fought for the Republicans against Franco in the Spanish Civil War. This oral "essay" was conducted with Aragon by June Namias in March 1976.*

As a student I went to the university at seventeen in Granada, in southern Spain, and I became very active. I moved about and I saw such terrible things in the countryside. I couldn't rationalize these things and I [became] very politically minded.

When the Civil War came about, I was very happy to have a chance to fight. I fought in the fronts of Madrid. At the beginning I was a regular militiaman. Later I got involved with something called *Milicias de la Cultura*; it was to bring political consciousness to the soldiers. I was the editor of a magazine for the front line, also. I was very, very active all through the war, and when the war ended, I felt very bad that I had to cross the border.

I was in Madrid during the first year of the war. And after I was called by the government to go to Valencia, where the government was. From Valencia I went to Barcelona and from Barcelona to France at the end of the war.

I was in charge of the war archives of our commercial relations with Russia, and in the last few months of the war, I was one of the technical secretaries of the undersecretary of war, department of weapons.

In those last months I had to write all the communications to buy weapons and how to pay for the weapons. At the end the head of my office asked me to take the archives out with me to the mountains close to the border in case we lost the war. I went with a group of soldiers to this mountain spot and waited with a radio transmitter to receive orders. Finally one day they told us to burn the whole documentations and to cross the border. The border was closed. This was early February '39. The Pyrenees were completely covered with snow. The people that went with me burned the papers, but the Franco troops were very close and began to fire all over when they saw the fires going on at night.

When we decided to go to the border we were between the French and Franco's forces. People were dying of cold and hunger, thousands of persons. We spent one night in the open there and people would die like flies. The French had the *gendarmerie* at the border. We threatened that if they didn't allow us to enter peacefully we'd enter forcibly. Finally the French allowed us to enter. Several thousand people were there. There was a small village close by. We started going to the next village without knowing what to do or anything. Before reaching the village we were ordered to wait in a tremendous line. Little by little we were registered and looked over, made to undress, lots of things. Finally we were divided, men one side, women another and sent to improvised concentration camps. It was snowing.

In my camp there were already probably two thousand, three thousand people. The first day in that camp they threw pieces of cooked horse meat above the wire for people to pick up and eat if they wanted. That was all. No disposition for a place to sleep or anything else. The following morning they took out of that single camp between two hundred and three hundred bodies that died of cold that night and that repeated several times in the first days. But this is written in the histories. There were 120,000 in the Argles sur Mer camp and for fifteen days an average of five hundred died.

A few of us escaped. We were protected by an old woman who took pity on us. Finally after fifteen days of being in hiding we left the place. I never went back to the concentration camp. I managed to reach Paris. I had a rich uncle in Havana, that's why. He opened me an account in a French bank. Then I decided to rent a castle close to Paris and take with me as many as I could and hide there. I took ten or twelve friends.

It was a ruined castle, a big house, only a few rooms with furniture. The rest was in very bad shape. When I signed the contract I didn't know who the owner was but after the first month the owner appeared and was the head of the police of a nearby town. He told me I had to pay double the amount or he'd send all of us to a concentration camp.

Then I became a fugitive from the French police. I went to Paris and was given the address of this photographer. This photographer gave me a set of papers that were falsified. Then I took a train to La Rochelle, on the coast south of Le Havre. There I was given an address, and the person at this address hired a boat and took me to the boat that was going to Havana.

The boat was full of refugees. Some were official refugees and others were just people who were afraid of what was going to happen in Europe in a few months. In fact, probably one hundred Jewish people came on that boat and went to Cuba or South America with the hope to come to the United States later on. There were also the remnants of the Cuban battalion that fought in Spain and a few handfuls of Spaniards. On arrival I was sent to an immigration camp for a few days for screening until the Cuban government decided to allow me to stay there.

I was only twenty-one when the war began and twenty-four when the war ended. I came to Cuba when I was twenty-four and stayed there until I was twenty-eight.

Since I had a background as an intellectual professor, although I was very young at the time, they made things easy for me and I was allowed to lecture, to teach, and to direct theater. I never thought of coming to the United States. I knew that it was almost impossible to come, although I knew a handful of friends that one way or the other came to the country. I was thinking if I could not make a living in Havana I would try to do something in Mexico.

I was active politically in Cuba, I was the head of a small group of Spanish Socialists in exile. Spanish socialism was a very old, established political party and was perhaps the best-organized political party in Spain. It had a tremendous importance in the Spanish Republic. It was not Communist inclined; in fact, it was completely different from the Communists. It was a democratic, not an authoritarian, party.

A friend of mine was invited to come to Middlebury College one summer. He came and he paid a visit to a great Spanish scholar that was teaching at Princeton, Professor Americo Castro. My specialization in Spain was Oriental Studies—I was a beginning Arabist. At that time Professor Castro was very interested in the Arabic world. He wrote me a letter saying, "If you want to come to the United

States, I could arrange to bring you for a nine-month period with a contract[."] I decided to accept and got a temporary visa.

Around August or early September 1943 I arrived in Miami. People were coming off of the plane and a loudspeaker mentioned my name and asked me to wait. I didn't know why this happened. I was on my way to Princeton, but I was detained and interrogated there for four days in relation to my friends and things that happened in the Spanish Civil War. At that time there wasn't a CIA; they were the Navy Intelligence Service or the Army Intelligence Service or the State Department. I don't know. But the questioning became so silly and so absurd that at one time after four days of asking me not to move from the hotel and to be at the disposal of the authorities, etc., I decided to forget coming to the country.

I phoned Americo Castro. I told him I had unexpected difficulties to enter the country and that I decided to go back to Havana. I will break my contract[,] I will not subject the university to anything, but I don't want to continue this type of thing.

Then he asked me to be patient and that he was going to send to Washington a colonel who was at Princeton. I didn't know it, but I was going to be used to teach army personnel Spanish to prepare officers and soldiers in language for foreign invasions. I decided to wait. Then Immigration came to me and said, "Princeton University placed a bond and you are allowed to go to the university if you want to." I stayed in Princeton teaching Spanish to our army personnel and at the same time working with Professor Castro on Oriental background.

In the middle of the program this man asked me to see somebody from the Department of War Information. I went to the New York Office of War Information and talked to the person in charge of the program for Europe. He told me that they had a file on my activities in Cuba. They knew of my democratic ideas and I could be helpful to the American war effort if I was willing to work for them.

I said, "I don't have any objection to work for democracy and for the Allies against Fascism. If what you want from me is propaganda for Spain, I would gladly accept." They told me they couldn't ask me for anything else, that this was the object of the war[,] that I would not be forced to do anything that would go against my political principles.

I went to work for the Office of War Information. I became the head of the Spanish News Desk. I was in charge of the news for Spain for eight programs every day and I became the special technical commentator of the war with a chat I gave for the Spanish underground over shortwave radio once a week. With a name that they gave me I became famous, Andres Aragon.

I was very happy doing what I was doing. I liked my job. Of course everything had to be submitted to the censors of the office before being allowed to go onto the air. I had eight daily programs of news that I prepared. I had four secretaries working for me at the time, and I had something that I wrote personally as a commentary once a week and that I delivered personally on microphones and spoke directly to Spain from New York. Then I was the official voice of the United States for Spain during that commentary of fifteen minutes or a half an hour, depending on how long it was. I commented on the policy of the American government, with the conduct of the war, what was supposed to happen after the war and to encourage people to resist Fascism, Nazism, and all those doctrines that were present in Europe.

But something happened, and what happened changed my life. I was encouraged by the authorities at the Office of War Information to ask for permanent residency in the United States. They told me that they would be happy to help me get permanent residency, not to worry about my future. I went to a lawyer to prepare my documentation which was sent to Canada to get a visa to enter the country permanently.

After doing this, April 14th of 1944 came about. That was the day that Spain celebrated the proclamation of the second Spanish Republic that was destroyed by Fascism. At that time, some people invited me to talk on radio for Spain with my own name in commemoration of this date, and I agreed to do it. An agent of the FBI came to see me and asked me to go to his office. They had an office in the Office of War Information.

I went there and he told me, "We heard that you are going to speak 14th of April for Spain in your own name and advise you not to do it." Then I replied that that was my own time, my own thing, and I didn't feel that I ought to pay any attention to this type of request. He repeated that it wasn't a wise decision on my part. I resented the thing, but anyway I went to this small radio station the appointed night.

Other people spoke that night, too. I don't remember what I said, but at the end of my speech, the man who handled the program told me, "I'm sorry, but your speech was not delivered to Spain, it was cut by order of the FBI." I felt bad about it. But that was a small thing, it was not that important and probably would not have any consequence if immediately something else hadn't happened. What happened was that Churchill in the House of Commons gave a speech. For the first time during the war he called that man Franco a "gentleman" and a "friend of England."

I received this speech over the teletype with instructions to translate it and deliver it to Spain. That was a problem of conscience for me and I decided not to do it. I went to see the head of my section and I told him, "I am not going to translate this speech. I accepted this job thinking that I would never be forced to say anything in favor of a dictator. That man is not a gentleman and I am not going to call him a gentleman."

The thing had some repercussions. I was called by the authorities. They tried to convince me and I had an altercation with the head of the European section. We had some hard words. I said, "You can dispose of my job; I don't want to work here anymore." He threw me out of his office and I left. Then I was officially expelled from the Office of War Information and I found myself in New York without a job and the thing pending from Canada and what to do.

At this time there was a man in New York who became very famous later on, the famous Spanish movie director [Luis] Buñuel. He knew about me and I knew about him and he called me and asked me what I was going to do. He offered me a position as director and writer and actor to work with him in Los Angeles. After some hassling back and forth I decided to accept.

I moved to Los Angeles. Soon I started to work. After three or four months of being here some officers from Immigration came to the door of my apartment and arrested me for illegal entry into the country. I was going to be deported. This was the first news I had that I was running this type of risk. They wanted to deport me to Spain. If I was sent back to Spain I would be shot right there because I had been writing against Franco and talking against Franco all my life.

I hired a lawyer and they gave me a kind of freedom under surveillance with a second bond I had to put to be able to continue working and doing my things. I decided to fight the case against the government. It took ten years. I also was married then. I had a child. My wife was American. I had not been authorized to leave the country or to stay in the country. If I left the country I would never be able to come back—I would be a fugitive from American Justice. If I stayed, I was not able to move from the city.

That was the period of McCarthy, pre-McCarthy, and the period of the Cold War. I saw the loyalty oaths and those things because my job in Hollywood went on for a couple of years. But then that was finished. Buñuel went to Mexico. I couldn't leave the country; I had to stay here, working here and there, giving lessons and things like that. My wife had to go to work. Immigration asked me when I was detained in 1945 if I had some money. I had some money saved. They told me, "You cannot work if you have money." Later when I didn't have a penny, they said, "Now you can start looking to find work."

I decided to come to the university, and I applied for a position here. Since I had some publications and was fairly well known, the university offered me a contract and we did not go into the details of my legal situation. I didn't mention anything, and I started to work here.

My situation was not solved. I was called by Immigration every two or three months and insulted like a common criminal, paying a lawyer all these years. That was very hard, the McCarthy period. I was called by one of the inspectors in Immigration and he told me, "The government has decided to authorize you to go to Canada to get your visa." I felt very happy with this, but before that the Un-American Activities Committee wanted to have an interview with me. I couldn't go. I called Washington. I didn't have any money to spend at that time.

Professor Americo Castro was a prominent man and very, very anti-Communist. He knew me very well, too—he was at Princeton. I asked him if he could take my place and see what these congressmen or senators wanted to find out about me. He went to Washington and was interrogated by these senators and congressmen, and my lawyer here received the deposition showing what he said about me. What my lawyer told me was, it was bad enough that this committee thought I was a dangerous Communist, but to have sent another Communist to Washington to represent me was worse. He was in danger of becoming prosecuted himself for talking in good terms about me.

After those things I went to Canada. I arrived and was received by the American consul there. What this man told me was, "You are never to get a visa from the United States. You know that you are a dangerous man, a Russian spy in my country, and my duty is to send you back to jail. Then you are going to take a plane, without any visa, without anything, and arrive in Seattle and let the authorities take care of you."

I took the plane back and arrived in Seattle. The Immigration officers in Seattle were very kind, nice people, and they were very busy. They appointed a taxi driver, a deputy of some kind, to take me to jail. No officer or policeman was there. I told this man to send a telegram to my wife in Los Angeles. I gave him ten dollars. The telegram said, "I am going to be taken to jail. I don't know for how long. Contact our lawyer." I didn't know if the taxi-man would do it or not. He did that. He sent the telegram.

This is a touch a literary touch. Since I am a writer, I like this literary touch. Someday I will probably write some of these things. This was 1955, and this country had excellent relations with Franco's Spain and the Fascist chorale or Falange [chorale of Spain] were going from city to city. I had to listen from my cell in the Seattle jail to the chorus singing Spanish songs, the chorus from the Fascist youth of Spain honoring the people in jail. There were common criminals in that jail; nobody political was there except myself, but I went through that experience of being in jail while the Fascist chorale was singing outside.

The second day or the third day I was there a man came from Washington and I was called to the warden's office. My lawyer requested that I was immediately sent to Los Angeles. They arranged some time of release based on the fact that I owned a house. The fact that I was a property owner was a decisive factor to allow me to come. They sent me here with a letter to the head of Immigration here giving me fifteen days to sell all my things. Then I arrived here, went downtown, was informed that I was still under a bond and that I would have to arrange my things. The order of deportation was standing. I decided to come to the university and for the first time explain to the chancellor what happened. I had never said anything about my situation. He didn't believe that this thing could happen in this country.

Then members of the department without exception decided to sign a letter of protest to Washington. The head of the department's sister went to college with Mrs. Johnson, the wife of the former President Lyndon Johnson, at that time the head of the senate majority. He called his sister in Texas. Ironically enough I owe my stay in this country to Lyndon Johnson. He called immigration and everybody and had the consul in Canada fired. After a few days I received a notification from Immigration to go back to the office. They told me that I was authorized to go back to Canada to pick up my visa, this time for good, in Vancouver.

I went to Canada. I went to the consulate and the American consul. The following year I became an American citizen and for the first time I was able to travel freely. I even went to Europe in 1957. My situation became legal after ten years of this type of thing.

After so many years of living in the United States I can't judge the authorities on the same level with the American people. I had excellent American friends, I worked in excellent libraries, I was able to do what I wanted to do with my life. I liked American people in general. I felt at ease here, and I think I am now convinced that the only country that I would like to live in and die in is the United States, in spite of all these experiences. If I remember these anecdotes, it is because they were dramatic, but everybody goes in life through bad experiences and bad things and I had my share, probably more than other people. I accepted and I wanted American citizenship, and I feel very comfortable being American. But it's good for other people to know that these things happen in a democracy, too, and not only under totalitarian rule. Perhaps other people may think I have a right to be bitter. I am not bitter at all.

I went back to Spain for the first time after twenty years. I saw my parents one year before they died. I went back several times for short visits. It is hard for me to understand the people.

My family stayed, my brother and sister, and it was hard for me to talk to them. I found that the psychology of the people is very much changed, the character of the people. It is not the people I knew as Spaniards, and it is no wonder. They lived through such terrible times—and human beings, they get accustomed to everything. If you are forced to live like that, it becomes a habit. To change all of a sudden, it is not easy. That country under Franco made me sick. I felt much closer to the American people than that type of life, and I would never go back to live under any type of lack of freedom, lack of dignity.

*Source*: From *First Generation: In the Words of Twentieth-Century American Immigrants*. Copyright © 1978, 1992 by June Namias. Used by permission of the University of Illinois Press.

# NICHOLAS GERROS

*Greek Horatio Alger*
(Greece; 1978)

*When Nicholas Gerros left his village in Macedonia in 1912, that area
of Greece was under the rule of the Ottoman Turks. Though he started out
poor in America, he became an owner of a thriving business. This is an oral
"essay," the result of an interview conducted by Julie Namias in 1975 in
Cambridge, Massachusetts.*

My mother died when I was nine years old. My aunt and my uncle
took care of me. I had a brother who was three or four years younger,
then still another brother when my mother died of childbirth.

My father was in the United States previously to my coming here.
He moved to Cincinnati, Ohio. When I came to the United States,
I came direct to Cincinnati. I came alone with other boys in a simi-
lar age bracket with me, from the same village—Menopilon in the
Macedonian part of Greece, Kastoria province.

The way life in the village was the men always had to go out of
their homes into other lands to make a living, come back, stay with
the family a length of time 'til the money was gone. They used to
have little farms around, that didn't produce enough to live on, so
naturally they had to go to other countries. My father had been
working in industry. They have some farming in Macedonia, but he
was in lumber.

When he came here he sent for me, sent me money and everything else.

I was at that time fourteen years old. Our village was way up in
the mountains. We didn't use anything with wheels to carry things.
We always loaded the backs of different animals. When I went to
get my passport at this Kastoria place was the first time I saw a
wagon with wheels. From there on we went south to Thessalia. We
stopped in the city by the name of Trikkala. From there we left for
Athens.

153

We were in Athens about three or four days. I was with some distant relatives, no brothers, but they were all the same age. They were all leaving Greece for the same purpose. There were about half a dozen or so of us. On the boat we stopped in Naples. We were there about a week some reason or other. It was just like a big armory, just plain buildings, not much accommodations. I remember reading all kind of writings on the wall, how bad this place was, get away from it as soon as you can. Some were in Greek and some were in Yugoslavian, all kinds of languages. Then we got into an Italian boat by the name of *Saint Georgia*. It took us two weeks from Italy. We left the village March first; we left Greece March 15; then we arrived in New York April 15. It was a little rocky. Most were a little seasick. I was a little seasick, not too much.

We got to New York, a place they call in Greek *Castn Gare*; in English it's something called Castle Island. We used to unload there. From there we go for examination, for eyes, for sickness of all kinds so it would not get into the United States. We stayed there a couple of days, I think.

The first thing shown to us was some church pamphlets written in English. We couldn't read them. Some man came along. He gave us a box containing food of some kind, a little bit of everything, and a nurse gave us the food and a Bible.

We had a ticket on us because we couldn't speak English. They look at you and tell you, you go there, or you go there. Traveling was easy because it was prearranged by the agents. We took a small boat from New York to Norfolk, Virginia. Some of us went somewhere else. I remember three or four of us was together, all young men and boys. We were waiting on the train and begun to look in the package to see what we had. Each of us had a banana to go with the rest of the food that was given him. We didn't know how to eat it. We'd never seen bananas. Finally somebody realizes that on the train and showed us.

When we went to Cincinnati, there were some people there waiting for us. They showed us how to go direct to the apartment. When we got into this apartment they treated us with ice cream. It was the first time we all had ice cream. These people before us organized a room for us. There were more than a half-dozen rooms and a big kitchen.

I stayed with my father for a while, for all the while he was there. He was working in something concerning furniture. Just before the Balkan War started, he went back to Greece.

Those years there were no Greek woman coming to the United States. Mostly all the Greeks were young, between twelve and thirty. They had to kinda stick together because none of them knew any more of the English language than they did themselves.

I remember how hard—this you can put with a line under the words because they mean so much. *The young people in America, they've got it so easy and they don't know how easy it is.* I was asked to go out to buy something. I think I was in this country for two months. It was late spring. It was still cold, and I had to go down from the second floor. There were stairs going right straight down to the door. There was a bunch of young fellows there talking to each other and having a lot of fun. I was their age, but I couldn't speak any English. I didn't want to get into any trouble with them so they're sitting down on the stairs and I tried to pass by to go do what I wanted to do. I didn't want to step on their clothes, so I was kind of careful and they realized that. One fellow, he wasn't sitting down, he was talking to a girl. I didn't know what he was saying. As far as I was concerned, any language was English to me. The only thing I could speak was Greek. I surmise now that he told me, "Let's have some fun with this fellow."

So he came to me and talked, "Blah blah." The first thing I know he gives me one upper cut and down I went.

Right in front of there was a bakery shop. This man is selling bread as well as cakes. He came out and the kids run away. He took me in. He asked me if I was hurt. Well, I looked and there was no blood so I says I wasn't hurt.

Right there and then I made up my mind. I'm going to go to school nights, learn the language, read, write, and spoken, and go to the YMCA to prepare myself to defend myself.

Here the oldest boy is supposedly boss of the rest of us living in this particular apartment. It is up to him, the rules and regulations and how to behave. The boy was about ten, twelve years older than I was. The older ones felt certain responsibility for the younger ones. They thought that they should keep us as close to them as possible, possibly as ignorant of life in the United States as possible. They thought that everything in the United States was out of proportion, was too free. They thought that I was going to school because there were girls. There *were* girls, from other countries because they moved here from Hungary, from Italy, from Austria. So when I announced it to the crowd what I was gonna do was go to school and go to YMCA, they told me, "Look, you didn't have a YMCA in the village where you come from. What do you want to go to YMCA for?"

"Exercise, take baths and meet people."

"No, you can't go."

"Can I go to night school?"

He said, "No, you can't go to night school." He said, "You don't go there for an education, you go there because girls are there."

I says, "No." I says, "I learned my lesson. I go there for an education." And I remember he tried to stop me.

He says, "You can't go. You have to be in bed at nine o'clock, the latest."

I says, "I can't be in at nine o'clock because school doesn't end until nine o'clock or quarter past. Then it takes me time to walk from there to here. The earliest I can be is nine-thirty."

He says, "I don't care what time it takes. As far as I am concerned you shouldn't go."

For the first night I went and I found the door closed. I made a lot of noise and he opened up and we had a big verbal fight and he says, "Well, I'll let you in this time, but tomorrow nine o'clock."

I couldn't get back. I came late, same thing. I was the only rebel. He told everyone not to say a word to anybody and to keep on pretending they were asleep. I knocked on the door and nothing. I knocked and knocked. So I looked around and there's an old broken up chair in the hall and I says, "There's an old broken up chair here. I'm going to pick it up and break the door down." After that he opened the door and gave me heck. Right there and then I decided to move. Some of the boys came with me and we went to another apartment.

In the meantime we were working in the shoe shop. They all made a small living in wages at that time. Like for instance, I worked from seven o'clock till six o'clock, and one hour in between for lunch. We got work. We used to take care of ourselves, no mother, no father, no uncles, no aunts, no nothing. You have to earn a living, take care of your clothing. You could eat, cook, and go to school. All this we did together, maybe six of us, but we were all over twelve then, fifteen, fourteen, and to twenty.

After a year or so I was going to school nights in a different school.

At that time, TB was the biggest killer of all the diseases, and people were scared stiff no matter if they just coughed a bit. This teacher noticed that I was sweating. She says, "You should go to a doctor." I went to this dispensary. At the end of three weeks they told me there was nothing wrong with me. In the meantime, though, I was totally scared of all this business and lots of my young fellas, they afraid to be with me.

I was determined to get well. I quit my job. I had saved some money. The salaries those years were $4.75 to $7.50 a week. Imagine what you had to figure on to eat. I also shined shoes on Sundays to make some extra money. We applied ourselves to the necessity of times.

I left those boys. I left them because first of all they didn't want me anyway because they were afraid and then because they didn't contribute anything to my life. Then I went to the farm. I figured I would get well out in the open. I was going to get well in spite of anybody. I used to take a trolley in Cincinnati, go the end of the line and get out and walk out on a farm. I remember I used to go out on both sides of Cincinnati. Cross the Ohio River from Cincinnati and you are in Kentucky. I went there just at the beginning of World War I. I stayed there on different farms until April or May the following year.

★

I had a cousin in Manchester, New Hampshire. She knew I was there and she wrote to me and she says, "Come here." She says, "The climate is better in New England. You come here and you be better off." So I came to Manchester, New Hampshire, and I got a job in one of the shoe factories.

When I lived in Manchester I used to love the men's clothing business. Even in Cincinnati I used to admire the good clothing stores and look at the way they kept their merchandise. That was my idea—sometime to have my own business. When I come to Manchester, I went to get a job in a store, part-time. They were hard to get, those jobs. I went to this place, to a German. He said, "What can you do?" He says, "Well, I don't need you today." For four or six weeks I went every day for a job. He says to me, "Why do you want a job here?"

I says, "'Cause I like your store."

He asked me more questions and he said "All right. You can work Thursday evenings and Saturdays." I think it was $1.75 for a week. Three hours on Thursday and eight hours on Saturday. Then he went up to $2.25, then he went up again. He had me sell on the floor.

In this process I met some people and they told me there were a lot of shops in Haverhill. That was 1917, 1918. I went there and I got a job in the shoe factory and was doing pretty well. I was doing finishing, pressing the shoe all around, finishing the job so it will look nice for the customer. They were all small shoe companies, there were hundreds of them. The foreman, maybe Yankee and all that, but mostly Italians, Greeks, Irish, French and all nationalities. The hours were not bad. Seven o'clock in the morning until twelve, then you go and come back at one, and then one till five. I made a lot of friends here in Haverhill. They were all in just three or four blocks around. We had a center and we felt at home. Lacking a home life, you have to be with people, naturally, and so I stayed in Haverhill. I was in the shoe shop, then I was in the life insurance business. In Haverhill I was selling to anybody. I earned quite a lot.

A couple of fellows, one was in a shoe factory and the other had a small business wasn't doing too well, and they wanted to go into the clothing business. They went in the clothing business and they found they didn't know a damn thing. In fact they couldn't even speak English very well. I had a little experience, more than they had, so they convinced me to go with them. I was making about $75 a week at the insurance and I wanted to go in the clothing business for myself, so I went with them. I had $600 to invest. I put that in there with them. Later one didn't want any part of it any more. We paid him off with $300 and we kept the store between the two of us.

The younger man, he was my age, he didn't care much for the business either. In fact he didn't know the difference between beautiful and terrible. This is my partner. I was about twenty-two, twenty-three, I told him that if he wanted to sell, to get somebody. So he finally got somebody and he sold his share to him. The new man spoke much better English. They are from one of the good families in Greece.

My dream was a store of some kind. I worked with this man for about three years and I gave him a proposition: "Either you get out of the factory and come with me," I says, "or I have to do it alone." He tried to convince me. He tried the hard way and the easy way. I told him, I says, "The only way we can do it together, we got to be within the family." In the course of talking back and forth for about two weeks, three weeks, in February I said, "Look, the time's late already for spring. We've got to get ready." He says, "All right, you buy me out." I bought him out with $6,750 for his share. From there the business grew up.

I borrowed the money from the bank and I put on a Dissolution of Partnership Sale, and I took in more money than I gave him. I went to the bank and paid 'em up. I had borrowed for five months, and I paid 'em up in five weeks. When I had the big sale on, people were coming in and out. He was across the street watching it and he felt that small, he wanted to buy the place back. Of course, I wouldn't sell.

In 1931 I had to move to another place.

When I moved it was three hundred percent better location. I was paying $150 a month rent and had two people working. The Depression did influence me and I'll tell you why. The prices went down, and I lost some money at that time, not too much. It didn't bother me too much because I was young in the business and I also was young. My future wife, she had to wait quite a few years 'cause I couldn't make up my mind. I wasn't secure enough in my business.

She was from Haverhill. She was born in Greece and came here when she was four years old. She was working for an office where they used to sell oil burners. She was the bookkeeper there. She was an orphan from her father. She came here to this country with her mother alone.

She was very, very smart and a good bookkeeper, and had a very good personality. She meets people she makes friends.

Her mother used to come quite often to the store. She got friendly with me and all that business. At that time you couldn't go out with a girl and not be engaged to her. In order to get to know her better, I had to get engaged to her. I used to go up to her office on my break quite often and talk to her. We decided to get married. I proposed to her and to her mother. This was the way it was. I got married in 1935. We had three children, all three girls. We lost the first one. That was also a girl.

The years went by and we were associated in the business. She's got a very good business head. She's very easy and she's got the gift of gab. She can really move people and their friends. Me and my wife during the World War II we tried to help with Greek relief. The poor people were suffering too much. After the war was over the people who were with the Nazis were put back in power. Why should you award the people who did wrong for the country? That's just what they were doing. The government destroyed the church, bombarded the village, my village where I was born.

In 1946 I went to Florida, St. Petersburg, around there. I was reading the newspapers. I see where a Greek prince was visiting some port in the South and they gave him a reception. I wrote a letter to the newspaper criticizing the United States, the government, especially the cities. Why do they do that when we don't believe in kings and princes? It was quite a nice letter.

Naturally I took part in supporting the leftists in Greece. I did all kinds of support. This fellow from Athens was representing the leftist newspaper in Greece. He came to New York to Boston, Boston to Haverhill. I introduced him to the newspaper in Haverhill. The city accepted him for the *Gazette* to go to work for them.

Quite a few years later they went over to my house. I don't know, FBI, CIA. They said this, "We're going to ask you a few questions regarding the security of the United States. Why you have joined this particular organization?" It was some organization to help poor people when they die so they can be buried.

"Well," I said, "I see no reason why I shouldn't support that."

They said, "But you're not a member of that."

I said, "I know it. I'm not a member." Because they just didn't know how to organize. "But I see no reason why I shouldn't do it. The United States Constitution doesn't bother me for that."

He says, "Well, you were in Florida such and such a year, such and such a month, and this is what you wrote in the paper. Why'd you do that?" And one of the men is a Greek, he asked me that question.

"I tell you," I said. "Democracy was instituted first in Greece and I'm proud of it and you should be. The United States is a democracy. We don't believe in kings or princes. Why should we give such an honor to them? My Constitution does not tell me anything like that at all." So he shut up.

We sent a lot of stuff to Greece. I had a Greek committee and we sent four tons of clothing and $6,000 in money during the war. So they called me on that. I said, "Since when does the United States forbid charity?" I wasn't afraid. "I'll do this right over again," I said. "I see nothing to stop me from doing this." They run out of questions so I say, "If you people got anything else, out with it fast because I work all day long here and I want to go out to get my supper." They never bothered me again.

*

*Whatever happened to your store?*

In 1936 we changed the name to my own name—Gerros' Mens' Shop Incorporated. I don't have the business today. I work part-time now. I was in business with the other fellow, it was $12,000 dollars for the year. When I got out of the business, it was $300,000 dollars a year. Some difference.

*To what do you attribute your success?*

Just hard work—that's all. You gotta be young. When you're young you've got to have ambition with no limit, because otherwise you are satisfied with small aims. You've got to have a challenge, feel inside of you that really you could do it without anyone else discouraging you.

Don't begin to ask too much advice from people that haven't got that problem in their hands. You've got to listen to them, but do your own decisions. Most of all, you gotta be fair with the people you do business with. Nobody can move you if you are right, and if you know you're right and if you stick to it and fight back. Nobody can move you, no matter how strong they are.

This maybe is the only thing that stopped me from being even better than I am or was, because my dreams were not big enough or long enough. I should have dreamed a bigger business, and I would have had a bigger business. I should have gone to school further when I was much younger. I should have gone to work for a big store, like Jordan's, for instance, for a little while. Go to school, to Harvard, if possible. First of all, you've got to get a goal. You have to have a dream of what you want to be. You can find it. It will take time, like everything else takes time, the sooner you dream the better.

*Many immigrants who came when you did didn't do well. Perhaps they had too much to overcome?*

No. Let me tell you something. Don't forget, everything in your life, *you decide,* nobody else decides, unless they come with a gun at your head and say, "Look, decide my way or else." Even then you got a choice, either die or do what he says. You see what I mean? But most of the time you're free to decide. Everything else we bring as alibis, that's all. They can't stop you from going on your own.

There was discrimination on account of different nationalities. They did discriminate, no doubt about it. There is a Greek organization in America called AHEPA, the American Hellenic Association. I was chairman of that, president in my city for about a year. At that time, as I told you before, there was too many Greek boys from twelve years old to thirty. Well, naturally they would be interested in girls. They couldn't speak English and they certainly didn't meet the right kind of girls anyway and they created a very ill name in the United States. With so much against 'em at that time they decided that they couldn't get justice anywhere even if they were right. Certain people began to think what should we do? They organized this AHEPA. They did that to offset those impressions that the American people had. This same thing happened with all the nationalities at that time. Naturally there were some obstacles, but listen, we have rainy days and we have sunny days and how we gonna know the difference if we didn't have them both?

You were born poor, so what? But it's all up to you. You're free to do what you want. You've got to gain it within the law. Not only political law but natural law. You've got to know the truth. This is what I say to my daughters because they expect things to be easy; they don't want to sacrifice much. We spoiled 'em. There is actually nothing in life that you cannot do if you plan it, but it takes time.

SOURCE: From *First Generation: In the Words of Twentieth-Century American Immigrants.* Copyright © 1978, 1992 by June Namias. Boston: Beacon Press. 1978. Used with permission of the University of Illinois Press.

# CARLOS BULOSAN

*My Education*
(Philippines; 1979)

*The poet Carlos Bulosan (1911–1956) arrived in the United States around 1930. He wrote his autobiography* America Is in the Heart *in 1946.*

I came to America sixteen years ago from the village where I was born in the Philippines. In reality it was only the beginning of a tortuous search for roots in a new world. I hated absentee-landlordism, not only because it had driven my family from our home and scattered us, but also because it had shattered the life and future of my generation. This system had originated in Spanish times when most of the arable lands and navigable waters were controlled by the church and powerful men in the government. It came down through our history and threatened the security of the peasantry till it became a blight in our national life.

But now that I was in America I felt a vague desire to see what I had not seen in my country. I did not know how I would approach America. I only knew that there must be a common denominator which every immigrant or native American should look for in order to understand her and be of service to her people. I felt like Columbus embarking upon a long and treacherous voyage. I felt like Icarus escaping from prison to freedom. I did not know that I was coming closer to American *reality*.

I worked for three months in an apple orchard in Sunnyside, in the state of Washington. The labor movement was under persecution and the minorities became the natural scapegoat. Toward the end I was disappointed. I had worked on a farm all my life in the Philippines, and now I was working on a farm again. I could not compromise my picture of America with the filthy bunkhouses in which we lived and the falling wooden houses in which the natives lived. This was not the America I wanted to see, but it was the first great lesson in my life.

I moved to another town and found work on a farm again. Then again I moved to another farm town. I followed the crops and the seasons, from Washington to Oregon to California, until I had worked in every town on the Pacific Coast. In the end I was sick with despair. Wherever I went I found the same horror, the same anguish and fear.

I began to ask if this was the real America—and if it was, why did I come? I was sad and confused. But I believed in the other men before me who had come and stayed to discover America. I knew they came because there was something in America which needed them and which they needed. Yet slowly I began to doubt the *promise* that was America.

If it took me almost a decade to dispel this doubt, it was because it took me that long to glimpse the *real* America. The nebulous and dynamic qualities of the dream took hold of me immensely. It became the periscope of my search for roots in America. I was driven back to history. But going back to history was actually a return to the early beginnings of America.

I had picked hops with some Indians under the towering shadow of Mt. Rainier. I had pruned apples with dispossessed Americans in the rich deltas of the Columbia River. I had cut and packed asparagus in California. I had weeded peas with Japanese in Arizona. I had picked tomatoes with Negroes in Utah. Yet I felt that I did not belong in America. My departure from the Philippines was actually the breaking of my ground, the tearing up of my roots. As I stayed longer and searched farther, this feeling of not belonging became more acute, until it distorted my early vision of America. I did not know what part of America was mine, and my awareness of not belonging made me desperate and terribly lonely.

The next two years were like a nightmare. There were sixteen million unemployed. I joined these disinherited Americans. Again I saw the rich fields and wide flat lands. I saw them from the top of a passing freight train. Sometimes I saw them from the back of a truck. I became more confused and rootless.

I was sick with despair. I was paralyzed with fear. Everywhere I went I saw that shadow of this country falling. I saw it in the anguish of girls who cried at night. I saw it in the abstract stares of unemployed workers. I saw it in the hollow eyes of children. I saw it in the abuses suffered by immigrants. I saw it in the persecution of the minorities. *I heard some men say that this was America—the dream betrayed. They told me that America was done for—dead. I fought against believing them. Yet, when I was socially strangled, I almost believed what they said about America—that she was dead.*

I do not recall how I actually started to identify myself with America. The men and women around me were just as rootless as I was in those years. I spent the next two years reading in public libraries. How well I remember those long cold nights of winter and the months of unemployment. Perhaps the gambling houses that opened only at night with one free meal for everybody—perhaps reading at the libraries in the daytime and waiting for the dark to hide my dirty clothes in the streets—perhaps all these terrible humiliations gave me the courage to fight through it all, until the months passed into years of hope and the *will* to proceed became obdurate and illumined with a sincere affinity for America. Finally, I realized that the great men who contributed something positive to the growth of America also suffered and were lonely.

I read more books, and became convinced that it was the duty of the artist to trace the origins of the disease that was festering American life. I was beginning to be aware of the dynamic social ideas that were disturbing the minds of leading artists and writers in America. I felt angry with those that fled from her. I hated the expatriates in Paris and Madrid. I studied Whitman with naive anticipations, hoping to find in him an affirmation of my growing faith in America. For a while I was inclined to believe that Whitman was the key to my search for roots. And I found that he also was terribly lonely, and he wrote of an America that would be.

I began to wonder about those who stayed in America and suffered the narrowness of the society in which they lived. I read Melville and Poe, who chose to live and work in a narrow world. I became intimate with their humiliations and defeats, their hopes and high moments of success. Then I began to hate the crass materialism of our age and the powerful chains and combines that strangled human life and made the world a horrible place to live in. Slowly, I was beginning to feel that I had found a place in America. The fight to hold onto this feeling convinced me that I was becoming a growing part of living America.

It was now toward the end of 1935, and the trade union movement was in turmoil. The old American Federation of Labor was losing power and a new union was being born. I started to write my own impressions of America. Now I was beginning to give meaning to my life. It was a discovery of America and myself. Being able to write, now, was a personal triumph and a definite identification with a living tradition. I began to recognize the forces that had driven many Americans to other countries and had made those who stayed at home homeless. Those who went away never escaped from themselves; those who stayed at home never found themselves.

I determined to find out why the artist took flight or revolted against his heritage. Then, doing organization work among agricultural workers, I fell sick with a disease caused by the years of hunger and congested living. I was forced to lie in a hospital for more than two years. Now, all that I had won seemed irrelevant to my life. Here I was dying—six years after my arrival in America. What was wrong? Was America so dislocated that she had no more place for the immigrant?

I could not believe that the resources of this country were exhausted. I almost died in the hospital. I survived death because I was determined to convince those who had lost faith in America. I knew in convincing them I would be convincing myself that America was not dead.

The Civil War in Spain was going on: it was another factor that gave coherence to the turmoil and confusion in my life. The ruthless bombings of churches and hospitals by German and Italian planes clarified some of my beliefs. I believe that this intellectual and spiritual participation in the Spanish conflict fired in me a new version of life.

It was at this period that the Congress of Industrial Organizations came to power in industry. At last its militant stand in labor disputes re-invigorated me. Some of my democratic beliefs were confirmed. I felt that I had found the mainsprings of American democracy. In this feeling I found some coherence and direction and the impulse to create became more ardent and necessary.

America's most articulate artists were stirring. They refused to follow the example of those who went into voluntary exile and those who stayed at home and were angry with America. They knew that they could truly work if they stayed near their roots and walked proudly on familiar streets. They no longer created alone. They framed a program broad enough to cover the different aspects of their needs and abilities. It was not a vow to write for art's sake.

I found a new release. I reacted to it as a sensitive artist of my generation without losing my firm belief that America was happy and alive if her artists were happy and alive. But Spain was lost and a grand dream was lost with her. The equilibrium of the world was dislocated, and the writers were greatly affected by the setback of democratic forces.

I tried in the next two years to work with the progressive forces. But some of the organizations dribbled into personal quarrels and selfish motives. There were individuals who were saturated with the false values of capitalism and the insidiousness of their bourgeois prejudices poisoned their whole thinking. I became convinced that they could not liberate America from decay. And I became doubly convinced, as Hitler seized one country after another, that their prejudices must be challenged by a stronger faith in America.

We were now moving toward the end of another decade. Writing was not sufficient. Labor demanded the active collaboration of writers. In the course of eight years I had relived the whole course of American history. I drew inspiration from my active participation in the workers' movement. The most decisive move that the writer could make was to take his stand with his workers.

I had a preliminary knowledge of American history to guide me. What could I do? I had read *Gone With the Wind*, and saw the extent of the lie that corrupted the American dream. I read Dreiser, Anderson, Lewis, and their younger contemporaries: Faulkner, Hemingway, Caldwell, Steinbeck. I had hoped to find in these writers a weapon strong enough to blast the walls that imprisoned the American soul. But they were merely describing the disease—they did not reveal any evidence that they knew how to eradicate it.

Hemingway was too preoccupied with himself, and consequently he wrote of himself and his frustrations. I was also disappointed with Faulkner. Why did he give form to decay? And Caldwell, Steinbeck—why did they write in costume? And Odets, why only middle-class disintegration? Am I not an immigrant like Louis Adamic? Perhaps I could not understand America like Richard Wright, but I felt that I would be ineffectual if I did not return to my own people. I believed that my work would be more vital and useful if I dedicated it to the cause of my own people.

It was now almost ten years since I had landed in America. But as we moved rapidly toward war with Japan, I realized how foolish it was to believe then that I could define roots in terms of places and persons. I knew, then, that I would be as rootless in the Philippines as I was in America, because roots are not physical things, but the quality of faith deeply and clearly understood and integrated in one's life. The roots I was looking for were not physical but intellectual and spiritual things. In fact, I was looking for a common faith to believe in and of which I could be a growing part.

Now I knew that I was living in the collective era. Where was I to begin? I read Marxist literature. Russia was then much in the minds of my contemporaries. In the Soviet system we seemed to have found a workable system and a common belief which bound races and peoples together for a creative purpose. I studied Russian history as I had studied American history. I tried to explain the incoherence of my life on the grounds that I was living in a decaying and capitalist society.

Then we felt that something was bound to happen in America. Socialist thinking was spreading among the workers, professionals, and intellectuals. Labor demanded immediate political action. For the first time a collective faith seemed to have appeared. To most of us it was a revelation—and a new morning in America. Here was a collective faith dynamic enough to release the creative spirit that was long thwarted in America. My personal predicaments seemed to vanish and for the first time I could feel myself growing and becoming a living part of America.

It was now the middle of 1941. The dark clouds of war were approaching our shores. Then December 7 came to awaken a decadent world. Japan offered us a powerful collective faith which was pervasive enough to sweep away our fears and doubts of America. Suddenly I began to see the dark forces that had uprooted me from my native land had driven me to a narrow corner of life in America. . . . At last the full significance of my search for roots came to me, because the war against Japan and Fascism revealed the whole meaning of the fears that had driven me as a young writer into hunger and disease and despair.

I wrote in my diary: "It is well that we in America take nourishment from a common spring. The Four Freedoms may not be realized in our times but if the war against Fascism ends, we may be sure that we have been motivated by a native force dynamic enough to give form to the creative spirit in America. Now I believe that all of us in America must be bound together by a common faith and work toward one goal."

SOURCE: *On Becoming Filipino: Selected Writings of Carlos Bulosan*. Philadelphia: Temple University Press. 1995. [Also published in May 1979 in UCLA's *Amerasia Journal*.]

# EDWIDGE DANTICAT

## *A New World Full of Strangers*
(Haiti; 1987)

*Edwidge Danticat (born in 1969) is the most famous writer of fiction to have come from Haiti. She graduated from Barnard College and earned an MFA from Brown University. Her novels and stories describe the lives and trials of Haitians and Haitian immigrants. She describes here, in an essay she wrote at eighteen, about her arrival in America. She credits this essay with helping to inspire her best-selling novel,* Breath, Eyes, Memory.

I could hear nothing over the deafening engine of the airplane, but I certainly could see their faces. They waved wildly as though this was a happy occasion. They seemed so thrilled that I was finally going off to the rich and prosperous city of New York. I was sad beyond the limits of my 12 years of life.

One of the stewardesses grabbed me from the doorway and quickly led me inside. Their waves ... their smiles ... their cheers were no more. I solemnly followed her to the seat I was to take. She flashed her smile and I was left alone for the trip.

The tears that I fought so bravely before fell uncontrollably into my lap. I was leaving my aunt, uncle, and countless cousins to embark on a mysterious trip to be with parents I barely knew and brothers I'd never met.

The stewardess woke me when the plane landed. Before I knew what was happening, she and I were filing down an endless tunnel toward what seemed like a crowd of caretakers.

First the people who made alien cards pulled me aside and snapped my picture. Then the people who handled the bags rushed me through a line to grab my suitcase. Soon, ahead of the other passengers, I was out of the airport.

Since I did not remember what my parents looked like, I was very frightened when a tall bearded man started to hug me. I was even more afraid when a chubby woman placed her arms around me and exclaimed, "At last my little girl is home!" I felt like an orphan who was being adopted against her will.

The ride home was no more comforting than the meeting with my parents. I was uncomfortably squashed between my three brothers in the back seat of the car while my parents and uncle were crowded in the front seat.

My American brothers, who had given me timid hugs before piling into the car, were now curiously staring at me. I imagined they were as anxious to know where I'd come from as I was to know where I was going.

Perhaps if they had asked me who I was, I would have explained that it was not my fault at all that I was entering their lives.

To feed and clothe our family, my parents had to desert me so early in life that now I did not even know them. The boys had probably heard about the problems in Haiti: the poverty, the oppression, the despair. I wanted to plead with them to accept me, not stare at me. But I suddenly realized that they had every right to stare. I was, after all, a stranger—even to my own family.

To avoid their glares, I turned to the car window. There must have been hundreds of thousands of lights speeding by.

Somewhere in the back of my mind, I remembered that water was somehow responsible for lighting. In Haiti, one could pay as much as ten cents for one gallon of water. I tried to imagine how many millions of gallons of water it must have taken to bathe the city in such brightness. God, I thought, this must be the richest country on the planet.

Our home was a great disappointment. It was a two-bedroom apartment on the sixth floor of a graffiti-covered building. In Haiti, homes were almost always open and spotless. In my new building, the doors were shut and dusty.

When we reached the apartment my parents lived in, I hesitated before going inside. The door looked like a cage. When my father fastened the filthy lock, I felt like I was in prison.

My parents did not wait long to enroll me in school. I could barely tell the difference between "hi" and "high" before I found myself in the car heading for Intermediate School 320. The school building had even more graffiti than the apartment building.

In Haiti, schools and churches were treated with utmost respect. Here things were obviously not the same. I wanted to run back to the car as my father and I walked by a crowd of hysterical students. In my pink cotton dress and yellow sneakers, I was sure they were laughing at me.

As we entered the building, I held my father's hand so tightly one would have thought that my life depended on it. In my school back home, I had been the best memorizer and the most articulate student. I had never given any teacher reason to hit me. Here I was sure that I would fail no matter how hard I tried.

Fortunately, there was a Haitian gentleman in the office. He had a brief talk with my father and made him sign some papers. Then the gentleman walked me to my homeroom class. As I left my father to go fight my way past the shoves of the hurried students in the halls, I felt as though I had been abandoned once again.

The Haitian gentleman introduced me to the homeroom teacher and then to one of the many Haitian girls in the class. He told me that she was one of the most respected girls in the school, mostly because of her roughness. The first day, my new friend kindly escorted me from class to class and made me sit next to her in every one.

Despite her help, I could not understand what was being said around me. As far as I was concerned, the teachers might as well have been hitting spoons against the blackboards. I understood nothing. The classes all blended into one long discouraging day. To make things worse, each time I stepped into the halls the thought of being abused by the other students scared me.

My fear was not realized until the last period when our class would eat lunch. One of the girls on the lunch line lifted my skirt up in the air and began to laugh. During her fit of laughter, she managed to spit out the word "Haitian" as though it were the filthiest and funniest word she'd ever said in her entire life.

Because my friend intervened, my humiliation that day was brief. After everyone found out that I was always with her, no one tried to touch me again.

Unfortunately, the verbal abuse did not stop. "Haitians are filthy. They have AIDS. They stink." Even when I could not understand the actual words, the hatred with which they were expressed hurt me deeply.

Now that I've grown to understand every insult, they hurt even more. In the same way that my brothers glared at me my first day in this country, people often glare at me as though searching for some sign of my nationality. If I don't fit their particular stereotype, they challenge me. They ask me whether I am sure that I am really Haitian.

Being any kind of immigrant isn't easy. Nevertheless, the view of Haitian immigrants has made us ashamed among our peers. The boat people and those few stricken with AIDS have served as profiles for all of us.

If only those who abuse us would ask, perhaps we'd explain that it is not our fault that we are intruding on their existence. To avoid brutal deaths and lead better lives, we are forced to leave our homes.

We'd plead with them to accept us and accommodate us, not make life miserable for us. Because, yes, we are strangers. Unfortunate strangers in a world full of strangers.

SOURCE: *American Me: Teens Write About the Immigrant Experience*. Edited by Marie Glancy O'Shea. New York: New Youth Connections, 2010. Originally published in September 1987 in *New Youth Connections*.

# VLADIMIR VERNIKOV

## *The ABC of a New Profession*
(Russia; 1991)

*The author, a movie editor and radio host (besides being a taxi driver), was born in 1937: "I knew for certain that I was not and never would be a taxi driver; quite the contrary, I would have been flattered if someone had mistaken me for a real cabbie. But my thoughts became confused when I asked myself whether I, who had always believed wholeheartedly that no work of any kind could be shameful, would want just then to run into somebody from the radio station or a neighbor from my building." His serial memoir,* Taxi from Hell: Confessions of a Russian Hack, *from which this excerpt is taken, was first published in New York in a Russian daily newspaper,* Novoe Russkoe Slovo *(The New Russian Word).*

In the last year of my life in Russia, waiting for an exit visa, I decided that I must get a driver's license. Of course, a license could be bought, and it cost no more than a pair of shoes, but I really did want to learn to drive an automobile. Whether my fate abroad turned out well or ill, I thought, I would undoubtedly have to drive a car. And this time even my conservative father, who usually disapproved of all my schemes, and who, like me, had never owned a car, agreed with me: "Everybody drives over there. There it's essential."

Having struggled through the mandatory six hours' study with an instructor, I received a Soviet "driver's permit." In New York my exotic certificate was exchanged for a standard license, but I had no practical experience of driving at all, since I had never once gotten behind the wheel without an instructor.

It was a little late to back out now, and, promising my wife I would take the utmost care, I showed up for work at the same Brooklyn garage that had arranged my taxi driver's papers in such a short time.

As I had been told to do, I arrived at five in the morning. In the dispatcher's office I saw "Larry"—disgustingly bloated with fat—who was assuring somebody over the phone, "Yeah, it's me, Larry!" and who waved at me to wait. It seemed to be an important conversation: the dispatcher diligently wrote down on narrow red and green forms everything that was said; evidently he was taking early orders for cabs.

From corner to corner, limping like a warped pendulum, walked a frowning alcoholic with a porous nose that resembled a piece of cinderblock. A woman of about thirty sat hunched on a backless bench. She had probably been sitting that way for a long time; one could only imagine that her browless face might be pleasant at another time, in other circumstances.

I realized it would be better not to ask these two about anything, and I sensed, with a dim foreboding, that I was entering a strange, unknown world, inhabited by some very alien people.

"D? Like in Donna?" the dispatcher asked again. "Ten also?"

The door through which I had entered a quarter of an hour before opened slightly and a disheveled head, level with the handle, poked through the crack into the office and bellowed: "Larry, is this lady going to get a cab?"

Larry's right hand went on writing, but his left slid into the desk drawer and tossed some car keys across the Plexiglas-covered desktop. The woman took them and went out. The lame man continued to pace back and forth, and the dispatcher went on writing. "F like in Frank? Ten?"

"Larry, is this gentleman going to get a cab today?"

Larry looked imploringly at the angry dwarf. "Donna—Linda?" His hand darted into the drawer. "Double?" The keys jingled. "Four?" The lame man went out.

Going up to the desk to remind Larry of my presence, I glanced at the ruled forms and saw that the dispatcher was taking down his notes on columns with headings such as AMOUNT AND TYPE OF BET, TRACK NAME, and RACE NUMBER. For the first time—a phrase I will have to use frequently from now on—I was looking at a real live bookmaker. Some kind of blue card with a photograph slid toward me across the Plexiglas. I picked it up. The photograph was mine. My name was printed next to it. And above the name glowered six bold figures, my hack number to this day.

"Don't forget the keys!" the dispatcher barked. "They'll come in handy!"

In the depths of the junk-cluttered yard stood two yellow Fords. One was brand new—forget that!—and I looked at it cautiously. The other was beat up and rusted through, and for that very reason suited me fine. No matter how I might maim this cripple, afterward I could say it had always been that way. Without further ado I made for the old car, and I was not mistaken: the key turned easily in the lock. The mangy cab was intended for me.

The engine roared. Now I had to accomplish a major acrobatic feat and turn the car toward the gates. I touched the steering wheel but it did not budge. I tried harder; no effect. The wheel would not turn to the right or the left; sweat broke out on my forehead.

"Yo, Larry!" The dwarf's head appeared alongside my car, and Larry came hurrying across the yard, wobbling and puffing.

"The wheel won't turn," I complained.

"Hey, buddy," Larry yelled, "all the cars here are like that! What's the matter, you don't get it? If the wheel jams, step on the gas. Then it'll turn."

"No, I don't get it," I said firmly. "When I have to turn the wheel, I step on the brakes, not the gas."

"But I don't have another car right now."

"Larry," the dwarf said reproachfully.

"Fine, just fine!" the dispatcher yelped. "I'm going to give him a cab with five thousand miles on the clock! But I want him to say it in front of you, Rabbit. Can I trust you with this baby?"

My mysterious defender, who for some reason was protecting my interests while appearing not to notice me, looked in my direction. I had to say something. I blushed and shook my head.

"No."

★ ★ ★

Professor Stanley Hoffman, a specialist in modern Russian history, who had been dismissed from his university post at the time of the Vietnam war and had ended up working in a hardware store, offered to give me some driving lessons free of charge.

I was a trying pupil. Stanley's long-suffering car, his only property, refused to obey me. I was afraid of my own uncertain movements, afraid of the cars that passed us, and I kept hugging the curb. However, over a weekend, the patient Stanley taught me to drive a car more or less straight, to make a turn, and even to turn around.

I felt my qualifications were increasing literally by the hour; but I still could not bring myself to reappear in front of either fat Larry or, worse, my strange friend, who—as I later learned from a talkative cab driver in a McDonald's—represented the local union at the Brooklyn garage where my debut had failed to take place. But there was no need to encounter the witnesses to my disgrace again; I was already the possessor of a blue card, a "certified" taxi driver, and taxi drivers were wanted everywhere. And so one morning, at the Freenat garage in the borough of Queens, a jumpy dispatcher named Louie shoved the keys to cab 866 at me through the window—and I ran off to look for my car!

It was getting light. Both sides of the lonely alley, which abutted the flank of the Queensboro Bridge, were lined with numbered Checkers. I went all the way around the block, which would have looked rather gloomy even in sunshine; my number was nowhere to be found. It remained to search under the bridge, where about fifty more cabs were parked, but I did not want to—it was dark out there.

Metal plates clanked underfoot. Beneath the low-slung girders of the bridge every sound echoed loudly. Hearing footsteps behind me, I looked around, stepped on a bottle, and nearly tripped. Two black men were following me along the wide alleyway! Their hair was held back by headbands, and a cigar box stuck out under each one's arm. Muggers carried revolvers in boxes like that, I had seen it in the movies.

The sinister pair was getting nearer, but I had already managed to spot cab number 866 and scuttled toward it a great deal quicker than dignity allowed.

The footsteps died away.

I squeezed into the driver's seat with difficulty; my Checker was parked between two others, both right up close. The starter squealed fearfully, I backed up, to get out from under the bridge as quickly as possible, and—got hooked on the bumper of the next car! I tried to rectify the error and hit the other cab.

A hand was thumping on the car roof above my head.

"Get out!"

I abandoned my refuge without the feeblest attempt at resistance. But the robbers did not lay a hand on me. Evidently it was the cab they wanted. The one who had knocked on the roof got into the driver's seat and in two maneuvers separated the coupled cars and stopped the Checker in the middle of the alleyway.

"Get in!"

Without looking up, I got a dollar out of my pocket.

"Put it away!"

The rear fender of my cab was pretty dented.

"Will they make me pay for this?"

"You talk too much! Get to work!"

And thus in the quiet hour before dawn on Sunday I found myself in a moving car, alone. It was July 3, my birthday, and my happiest as far back as I could remember.

How many times is a man granted the experience of happiness? How many times had *I* experienced that feeling? Well, the day I risked my life to swim across a tiny village pond, perhaps. But then that was not me. That was a consumptive boy from a deprived postwar Russia.

And I was happy again when I was teaching the haughty copper-haired receptionist from the beauty parlor on the next street to fly. I whispered to her, "Don't be afraid! Do as I do!" Copying my movements, she gracefully flapped her arms, and we soared into the air! But those were only dreams. . . . And later, many years afterward, the first time I was allowed to use the editing table, I spliced together two sequences that happened to be at hand: one, in black and white, of a plane burning in the night sky and falling to earth, and another from a different film in color, a slow panorama of a field covered with scarlet poppies. I ran the roll through the moviola and felt a sudden shiver down my spine: the two sequences joined together had produced something unexpected that neither had possessed by itself, as if a spark had flared up in the cut! What was it?

And so it was now. I drove along, not knowing where, and was happy.

In the whole of this huge city I was probably the only taxi driver who was glad there were no passengers on the streets. I wanted to be myself for a while, to get used to it all. I was even more glad when I saw that mine was the only car on the Queensboro Bridge.

Could I ever have dreamed that one day some madman would fill up his car and give it to me for an entire day so I could go tooling around? Even the good Stanley would not do that.

And now this battleship, this Checker, is mine!

I am as free as a bird. I am going where I want. Not only that: for learning to drive a car, for getting to know a thrilling and still unfamiliar city for my own pleasure, I—I! am going to be paid *money*! Do such things really happen? Can it be true?

I turned the wheel to the right, and the Checker veered toward the curb. I turned it to the left, and it straightened up again. I touched the brake, and it slowed down.

I realized that my car was sensitive and obedient. I drove more and more boldly; the speed took my breath away, the arrow on the speedometer was approaching 20. Now the main thing, I thought, was not to mix up the pedals—gas and brake!

★ ★ ★

Not a single taxi driver among the many I asked later on could recall his first passenger: who he was, where and whence he was going. I did not remember my first passenger either. But I did, of course, remember the first taxi driver who got talking with me.

Having crossed the bridge, I found myself in a still sleeping Manhattan, and, catching sight of an empty taxi outside Grand Central Station, I drew up behind it. I was longing to hobnob with my colleague, but he was sitting buried in his newspaper and, not venturing to disturb him, I began to look my Checker over.

It was roomy inside, in spite of the clear (bulletproof?) partition separating the driver from the passenger, the upper part of which slid aside. Sitting at the wheel, I could open and shut it and even flip the lock.

With the partition closed, passenger and driver could settle up using the change cup set into the Plexiglas, with a steeply sloping bottom that money could pass through, but not the barrel of a gun.

A meter with a flag was fixed to the dashboard. When a passenger got into the cab, I was supposed to push down the flag and the meter would show the initial sixty-five cents, the "drop." To the right of the meter, inserted in a special frame, my blue card shone in all its glory.

I got out of the car, admired the Checker's hypertrophied bumpers, which gave it reliable protection both front and rear, and glanced at the passenger section. I wondered if a customer sitting in the backseat could read my name and number on the card in case he wanted to complain about me. I flopped down onto the black cushion and immediately jumped as though I had been stung: the meter had clicked—sixty-five cents!

"Hot seat," said a mocking voice. The middle-aged cabman was standing next to me holding his newspaper: "Didn't they tell you?"

Sure they had, but you can't remember everything. Now, before I had earned a penny, my first sale of the day had put me in the red. Sixty-five cents to pay.

"Who the hell thought up this contraption?" I growled. "I'm not going to forget to put the meter on when a customer gets in."

"You might put it on, but someone else might not."

"And why not? "

"He'd take the money and pocket it. Cabbies are that sort of people. You've got to watch them all the time."

It was not a pleasant remark, but it had no ill effect on me, since I did not consider myself a cabbie.

"Is it true that taxi drivers make six hundred dollars a week?" I asked.

"Depends."

"Well, how much do you make, on average, for instance?"

My new acquaintance looked at me in amazement. "You think I'm a taxi driver?"

I realized I had made some kind of blunder.

"If you're going to drive a cab, you'd better learn to tell people apart!"

What did he mean?

"Don't you see the way I'm dressed?"

A grubby necktie; a crumpled black suit jacket, despite the heat. His colorless face was lined, he looked drawn.

"The owner of this cab is a friend of mine. I don't work for a garage like you. If I have any spare time, I occasionally go out for a few hours."

Our conversation was taking place at six o'clock on a Sunday morning.

"So why do you need to drive around as if you were a cabbie?"

"Good question. I meet new people, make connections, acquire information. I'm a businessman."

No matter how engrossed I was in thoughts about myself, no matter how proud of my new persona, I could still see that he was ashamed of his lot, of his yellow cab. And I felt the more sorry for him because my own position was so different. After all, I knew for certain that I was not and never would be a taxi driver; quite the contrary, I would have been flattered if someone had mistaken me for a real cabbie. But my thoughts became confused when I asked myself whether I, who had always believed wholeheartedly that no work of any kind could be shameful, would want just then to run into somebody from the radio station or a neighbor from my building. The gaunt artist from the sixteenth floor? His ugly wife? The future millionaire? Oh, no, certainly not.

We stayed outside Grand Central for a long time. Nobody came up to us; the conversation petered out. Pondering how to accommodate my beliefs to my present situation, I concluded that driving a cab was no worse than any other kind of job, but if it was still demeaning, wasn't it because a taxi driver is offered and accepts tips—a lackey's wages? And with this thought I drove away.

★ ★ ★

I still see no passersby on the streets, and the cars around me are only yellow, only taxis. All of them empty, without passengers. And all of them hurrying somewhere—where?

How stupid, I think. As far as I can tell, a taxi driver should go fast when he's carrying a customer; but if he doesn't have one he should go slowly, so as not to let a chance slip by. In fact, wouldn't the most sensible thing be to stop and wait? Whoever needs a taxi will see my Checker himself.

I stopped on a corner and began to wait. Five minutes. Ten. The cabs rushed by on and on. And not alongside the sidewalk, but right down the middle of the avenue.

Suddenly I noticed a strange figure: a girl in an evening gown. It was an absurd sight—the city flooded with sunlight, and she in a long dress drooping from its slender straps, tangled hair and bleary eyes.

The girl could barely walk; she was swaying. But she was headed toward me. For some reason, however, when she neared the curb, only a few steps from my Checker, she raised her arm. And instantly a cab, speeding down the middle of the road, shuddered like a wounded bird stumbling in flight and veered sharply in our direction. Indignant that some smart guy was taking "my" fare away from me, I honked the horn, but the yellow predator's door slammed smugly and in the place where the party girl had been teetering a second before, a bluish-gray cloud was already evaporating. I decided that in her hungover state the customer had simply not noticed my cab was empty.

I had thought it all through: the money I would take from customers, the money I would not. Only one detail was missing—where was I going to get those customers?

How long had it been since I rejoiced that the streets were empty? A dead Sunday in July.

Don't worry, I kept telling myself encouragingly, my fares will me. But it seemed my fares had not woken up yet. Maybe they had left New York altogether? What would they be doing on a weekend in the stuffy city? The Checker had already gotten hot in the sun; the air inside was thick and sticky.

Everything conspired against me that first day. The next customer, who appeared on the corner where I lay in wait for my quarry, deceived me just as the tipsy maiden had. He did not wobble; he was not drunk. He could see me perfectly well, but for some reason he stopped a *moving* cab. I realized—instinctively rather than intellectually—that in order to get a fare, I had to *keep moving*.

At the end of the block that my Checker was meandering along, a passerby raised his hand. He was on my side, my "territory," but a cab racing down the center lane darted swiftly toward him—and he was gone.

A little way down the street a couple stopped at the curb. Instantly, two cabs headed toward them and nearly collided. But the couple waved the importunate ones away with all four hands, as if to say, We don't need a taxi! And both cabs departed empty.

Quite close by, fifty yards from me, a youth ran out from a door yelling "Taxi! Taxi!" But I did not get him either. Another cab hurtled across my path from the other side of the street; I barely managed to brake in time.

Now it became clear to me where the empty taxis were hurrying; they were trying to overtake each other. It was a real race. The cabbie won the race got the prize—the fare. But I could not take part in this contest. I stood no chance of winning. I tried to wait it out, to let the contestants pass, but to no avail—the yellow cars streamed past in an uninterrupted flow.

I decided to look for another thoroughfare with fewer cabs, and found one right away. It was Fifth Avenue, all shining with shop windows. But the stores were still closed, and I drove from Central Park to Forty-second Street without seeing a single pedestrian. Only some homeless people were sleeping here and there on the sidewalks, and one morose policeman strolled up and down, guarding the Aeroflot office from Jewish activists. However, the time was not exactly wasted: I was learning to drive a car. After all, had my father not said, "Everyone drives over there"? And here I was at last, like everyone else, driving too.

SOURCE: Vladimir Vernikov. *Taxi from Hell: Confessions of a Russian Hack.* New York: Soho Press. 1991. Translated from the Russian by Tamara Glenny.

# DYMPNA UGWU-OJU

*Raising Delia*
(Nigeria; 1995)

*The author, from the Igbo community in Nigeria, teaches English and Jour-
nalism in Fresno, California. "Raising Delia" is the introduction to her
memoir.*

About a year ago, I walked in on my husband berating our daughter
for wrestling on the living-room floor with her brothers. His voice
showed both his anger and disappointment that eleven-year-old Delia had neglected some chores assigned her.

"But, Dad, how come the boys don't have to do anything around
here?" Delia asked, her voice devoid of the whininess that usually
marked her complaints.

"Because they're boys, and you're a girl, and it's time you learned
that."

"Well, being a girl doesn't make me different from the boys, right,
Mom?" Delia dragged me into a conversation I was desperately trying to avoid.

"Not really, Delia," I responded, my noncommittal answer rein-
forcing neither my husband's nor my daughter's position, the vague-
ness reflecting my long-standing confusion and ambivalence about
how to raise my daughter.

Later that day, my husband accused me of misleading Delia. "How
can you tell her there's no difference between being a boy and a girl?
Was that what your own mother taught you?"

"This is California, not Nigeria. She's an American child," I argued, not for the first time that month. "We'll be doing her a lot of
damage if we insist on teaching her that her femaleness is all she's
about. We have to stress that girl or not, she's as able as anyone else
to accomplish whatever she wants." My voice sounded convincing,
surprising even me; did I really say that gender was irrelevant? Wow!
What would my mother say about that?

"Whatever you say," my husband snapped before retreating, clearly angry with me, too. "But you'll only have yourself to blame if she doesn't turn out right."

"Turn out right?" I fought an urge to yell. "She will turn out right, you wait and see!"

But I've said that many times, more to myself than to anyone else. Like my husband, and probably more than he, I worry constantly about what will become of my daughter, my Ibo-American child.

I wonder what my legacy, if any, to her will be. How can I be a good mother to a child whose world, scope, and experience are totally different from mine? Sometimes I am so consumed with my helplessness over the matter that I cannot think of anything else for days. I can't help but compare Delia's life to mine at that age, as well as comparing her mother (me) to my mother (Mama), whose constant admonition, "Remember, you're only a woman," was the refrain of my early life.

Inevitably, I arrive at the conclusion that my daughter is short-changed by my lack of a fully articulated vision for her. I would readily admit that I constantly vacillate between attempting to mold Delia by the rigid standards of Ibo womanhood, relying mostly on my experiences with own my mother, on one hand, and on the other hand instilling in her my Americanism, pushing her to assert herself and excel in everything. While I burst with pride when she receives awards for academic accomplishments, I cannot quell that inner voice, my mother's, which warns, "These things are not really important for a girl; they'll take her nowhere." When Delia won the presidency of her school's student body this past year, I experienced my greatest confusion yet. "My daughter, the president," I congratulated her, even as I saw Mama's index finger wagging, and heard her say, "Remember, first and foremost, she's a girl. She's only a girl."

So I try to provide my daughter with the tools of Ibo woman-hood, to mold Delia into the sort of woman her grandmother would be proud of—the sort of woman I was raised to be. But even with those simple traditional tasks, my indecisiveness gets the better of me. I teach Delia how to cook, but by using cookbooks, not in the "real-women-cook-by-instinct" approach my mother insisted on with me. I tell Delia I prefer that she wear only dresses, but when she emerges from fitting rooms holding only the pants and shorts from the stack of clothing I sent in with her, I buy her the pants and shorts. I caution her to remember to speak softly, but I pretend not to hear her boisterous voice.

Two years ago, in an attempt to break away from the trappings of my Ibo-ness and my mother's pressures, I presented Delia the blue-print for her adult life. I told my daughter that right after she graduates from college, she's to proceed directly into medical school, do a residency in neurosurgery, and establish her own medical practice; then, and only then, she can begin to contemplate marriage. "And, yes," I told her, "strictly in that order."

Delia asked, "But what if I meet a man that I want to marry while I'm in college or medical school?"

"Both of you will have to wait."

"But Mom! I'll be at least thirty-five years old by the time I'm done," she reminded me. Her voice was suddenly the voice of my mother: "She'll be way past her prime by then; a marriageable girl must be married or at least spoken for before she turns twenty."

"You'll still be able to have children," I said, asserting myself, raising my voice to drown out my mother's and my daughter's protests.

Ironically, Mama and Delia often sound identical, although they argue from the opposite ends of the spectrum. Neither experiences any doubts about her place in life; Mama is as traditional as Delia is modern. I'm the one caught in the cross-fire of two divergent cultures.

Minutes later, I began to worry about things my mother would consider important. Whom will Delia marry? Will she let me guide her to a professional Ibo man (even though she neither understands nor speaks Ibo) from a good family, as my mother did for me? Should I follow my mother's advice and send Delia home (to Nigeria) more often, so she'll be adept in the culture and noticed as one who'll be on the market in the near future? Only my ambivalence remains constant in my approach to motherhood as far as Delia is concerned. For my two sons, Chuka and Ubi, on the other hand, there is no ambivalence, no confusion. I am the mother that my mother was to her own sons, geographical and language differences notwithstanding. I've experienced no difficulties in raising male children; I nurture them and teach them exactly what my mother taught my brothers, "Go out there and do the best that you can." I'm confident that I teach them well, and I have no doubt that they'll succeed, whether in the American or in the Ibo context.

Why does raising Delia create such a difficulty? Because I sense that my success or failure as an individual ultimately rests on what becomes of my only daughter. Because each day, each activity, each decision concerning her is a tug-of-war between the old and the new, between my Ibo and American selves, between my mother and me. Because where and when I was growing up, children, especially daughters, accepted their parents' authority completely, without question or resentment. Therein lies my conflict, one that I'm sure is shared by millions of immigrant women who, like me, are raising American-born daughters. We are having to deal with situations that our mothers could not have anticipated.

Sometimes I envy my mother her straight uncomplicated life. As much as she complained about "today's children" when she raised us, she had no cross-cultural confusions. Her sense of tradition remained intact and unthreatened by Western influence, as mine has become. With only two years of formal education, her frame of reference was limited by her culture: her own mother, aunts, cousins, the church, all spoke in unison when it came to the essence of womanhood. Mama had no ambivalence about her place and she taught her daughters all she knew about life—Ibo womanhood, marriage, children, death. None of what she learned contradicted anything else that she learned: that the essence of womanhood is marriage and children and a good woman knows her place and never leaves it.

That is what I grew up with, and to a great extent, still live with.

But, unlike my mother, I continued my education beyond grade school and acquired most of that education in America, in the classrooms and on the streets, from television and books. I know enough not to continue to believe that God intended women to be inferior to men, but I'm so used to living with that understanding that it would be a struggle to do otherwise.

I am my mother in more ways than not. Despite my American education and liberalism, when I was ready to marry I allowed my family to choose a groom who came closest to pre-determined criteria. I let them negotiate and accept a bride price on my head. But I'm as American in my career pursuits as I'm Ibo in my relationship with my husband. While I manage to reconcile the two parts of my life for myself and embody them efficiently, I cannot seem to do the same for Delia. Instead, when I view them in the context of my daughter, those two parts seem to be on a collision course.

Today, I watch Delia racing her brothers on their bikes. She does not cede any ground to them, but actually finishes a hair's breadth ahead of the boys. My urge to cheer her gets caught in my throat as I imagine my mother shaking her head, saying, "That girl needs to be taught that men don't go for aggressive women."

"I finished first," Chuka claims.

"No, I did!" Obi asserts.

The boys argue, and I fully expect Delia to interject and claim her rightful prize, but she gets on her bike and rides away slowly. I catch up with her and ask why.

My Ibo-American daughter explains, "Mom, if it's that important to them, let them believe they won."

I look up and see Mama's face. It's not smiling, because Delia raced and beat her brothers, but it's not frowning either, because Delia let them have their place. I whisper to my mother, "She'll turn out right; your granddaughter will be all right."

SOURCE: Dympna Ugwu-Oju. "Raising Delia." *What Will My Mother Say: A Tribal African Girl Comes of Age in America*. Chicago: Bonus Books. 1995.

# ALEKSANDAR HEMON

*Door to Door*
(Yugoslavia/Bosnia; 2001)

*Aleksandar Hemon (born in 1964) is a novelist and short story writer who lives in Chicago.*

By the time I graduated from my high school in Sarajevo, in 1983, my favorite movie of all time was *Apocalypse Now*, and I was convinced that Robert Altman was a genius. I loved the Talking Heads and Television, and CBGB was to me what the Vatican is to a devout Catholic. I fantasized about starting a band whose first album cover would be designed by Andy Warhol. I imitated Holden Caulfield's diction (in translation), and I manipulated my unwitting father into buying me a Charles Bukowski book for my seventeenth birthday.

By 1990, when I graduated from college, my sister and I could perform chunks of dialogue from *His Girl Friday*. I'd get angry at people who didn't recognize the genius of Brian de Palma. I could recite Public Enemy's angry invectives, and was up to my ears in the New York noise scene, particularly Sonic Youth and the Swans. I read the American short-story anthologies that were available in translation, and it was not uncommon for me to spend a boozy night extolling the brilliance of Raymond Carver. I wrote an essay on Bret Easton Ellis and corporate capitalism, and, though I hadn't read Barth's essay, held firmly to the belief that I was living in the age of the literature of exhaustion.

I came to the United States for the first time in the winter of 1992, as a participant in a cultural-exchange program, and I traveled all over the country, showing off my familiarity with the local culture to befuddled professors, writers, and filmmakers, many of whom had no idea where Sarajevo was. By the time I reached Chicago, at the end of my trip, the war in Bosnia had begun, my honeymoon with America was over, and I had to find a job. I was not going back home.

Nothing in my experience had taught me how to get a job in the United States. It took me a few weeks to learn that (a) rambling on about the short story to restaurant managers and temp-agency employees does not get you hired; and (b) when they say, "We'll call you," they don't really mean it. Eventually, I found work as a canvasser for Greenpeace. I knew of the organization, but I had never heard of canvassing—it was an activity that had not existed in the former Yugoslavia. I was worried about the idea of knocking on people's doors and asking for money. I imagined decent Americans swinging baseball bats at my knees to express their dismay at being bothered in this way by a foreigner. By the end of the first day, I was ready to write my own contribution to the literature of exhaustion.

But, in the end, I canvassed for Greenpeace for two and a half years. I traversed the suburbs of Chicago, learning to assess a household's annual income by the look of its lawn and the makes of the family vehicles. I steeled myself to questions about Bosnia and Yugoslavia, and their nonexistent relation to the nonexistent Czechoslovakia; I managed to grin through lectures on the spirituality of *Star Trek*, and to confirm, calmly, that, yes, I had been exposed to television back home. I talked to a Christian fundamentalist in Wheaton who kept interrupting my discourse to call out "Amen" and finally confided that his daughter had left home for some "weird" California cult. I smiled at a young man in La Grange who implored me to understand how broke he was because he had just bought a Porsche. In Blue Island I drank lemonade at the home of a soft-spoken Catholic priest and his young, gorgeous boyfriend, who was bored and tipsy. I sought shelter with people in Glencoe, who had a beautiful Alphonse Mucha print on the wall, after their neighbor had shown me his gun—and his willingness to use it. In a far-western suburb, I discussed helmet laws with a herd of potbellied, balding bikers, some of them Vietnam veterans who believed they had fought for the freedom to spill their brains on the highways of America. I saw my African-American colleagues repeatedly stopped by the police in the very white North Shore.

After a while, my view of American culture changed. I began to understand the meaning of the Talking Heads' songs, the anarchic pretentiousness of Altman's movies, the vapidity of the De Palma oeuvre, the rage of Public Enemy, and the magnitude of America's defeat in Vietnam. I saw Campbell's soup being eaten straight from the can on a porch in Elk Grove Village. I peered into the morose houses of Carver's people. I got an idea why literature might have been exhausted.

Toward the end of my canvassing career, a woman in Schaumburg opened her door with a welcoming smile, which quickly transmogrified into a suspicious smirk. "I thought you were someone else," she said, disappointed. "I am someone else," I said. And I was.

SOURCE: Aleksandar Hemon. "Door to Door." *The New Yorker*. October 15, 2001.

# MELA TANNENBAUM

## *A Musician's Journey*
(Ukraine; 2002)

*When Mela Tannenbaum left Ukraine, she was a mother of adult children and a soloist with the Kiev Philharmonic.*

I was born in a small town called Chernovtsy. It belongs to the Ukraine now, but earlier it was part of Romania. In another time, as Czernowitz, it belonged to Poland and later to the Austro-Hungarian Empire. So it had a very special culture. Most of the people in this town could speak three languages and were highly educated. Aside from that, Chernovtsy was one of those Jewish towns that had its own Jewish professor, Jewish shoemaker, Jewish doctor, and even Jewish alcoholic. So I was raised in this very special environment, where I spent my childhood and part of my adult life. I studied at a music school in Chernovtsy. It was a very good school.

All of my former schoolmates now work as professional musicians in different parts of the world—some in Russia, some in Tel Aviv, and some in New York. The cultural differences between my native town and the rest of the Soviet Union were so immense that when I moved to Kiev to study in the conservatory in 1964, it was no less dramatic than my immigration to America. For instance, going to a concert was always a big event at Chernovtsy. People would prepare way in advance, thinking of what they would wear, how they would look. In Kiev, you could easily attend a concert wearing slippers; or a T-shirt; it was a much more casual event.

It's not easy to explain why I decided to leave Kiev. We used to say it was because we were Jews. In truth, it was the Chernobyl disaster that completely turned our lives upside down. My children became sick after the explosion of the nuclear reactor in 1986. I thought we'd lose them. My eldest son was twenty-seven at the time, my daughter twenty-five, and my youngest son was ten. After the catastrophe in Chernobyl, the general mood in Kiev was one of doom. People really felt hopeless. At first we expected measures to be taken to improve our living conditions, such as new apartments or raises in salary. But nothing happened. The authorities didn't spend a cent on social benefits. So we lost all hope of better living conditions. My family lived in a tiny apartment, and I had no room to practice. I wanted very much to leave, but that wasn't so easy.

I was a soloist with the Kiev Philharmonic. I went on wonderful tours and played with the best orchestras in the country. At a certain point, I made a deal with myself: that I'd never regret anything, even if I happened never again to play the violin. In the Soviet Union, musicians were always a privileged caste. The belief was that if you're an engineer, you were trained to become an engineer; but if you're a musician, you were born to be one.

Yet, after Chernobyl, we decided to leave the country. I left with my husband and children. Four days before our departure, I gave my last performance with the Kiev Philharmonic. So I had these fresh memories of the audience's applause. They all knew me and loved me. From the time I was a child, I remember being always surrounded by people, wherever I'd go. Part of it was language: I knew and loved my language, the Russian language, I could express myself with precision, express the slightest shade of meaning in this language. And now I was going to a country whose language I didn't know at all. I couldn't ask for a piece of bread in English. I knew German very well. I could have gone to Germany, like a lot of our friends from Chernovtsy. In Germany we would receive passports right away. They don't call Jewish immigrants "Jews" in Germany, they call them "German citizens who practice Judaism." I loathed those words the first time I heard them. Anyway, I couldn't seriously think of going to Germany.

We took a train from Kiev to Vienna. It was a peculiar experience. Imagine it: you throw your luggage, your suitcases, through the window into the train, and next to you in the compartment is a family of ten people, only three of whom are men. Two women are pregnant, and one of the men, the youngest, drinks nonstop. The oldest tries to carry the suitcases, but he's ninety-two years old so everybody shouts at him to leave the suitcases alone. But there is nobody else to carry those suitcases because the third man has no legs. So, all this: tossing the suitcases, children who are always ill on the road, overcrowded trains, kids looking for their parents. When we finally arrived in Vienna, we stood in this long line on the platform with the other immigrants, absolutely faceless, because what matters to a Soviet person is his passport, not himself. So, we were waiting on this platform, with my son lying ill on the trunks, and suddenly we saw a crowd coming out from the nearby opera house.

The show had just ended. We saw all these dressed-up people, talking, and not laughing. Austrians don't laugh, they cackle, they roar. And I began to cry: it was actually the first time that I cried in my adult life. I had this piercing feeling that I'd never again play the violin, never again be on stage. But I knew I had made my choice.

We went to Italy. It happened that we spent five-and-a-half months in Italy. We had wanted to go to New York, but New York was overcrowded with immigrants at the time, so we had to wait in Italy. We spoke Italian relatively well. We lived in a house in the mountains, near Florence, with nine other immigrant families. There were all kinds of people: a shoemaker, musicians, engineers. There is one observation I made about Russian emigrants. When they had to write their resumes, describing the positions they held back in Russia, somehow they all turned into "supervisors." If someone was a shoemaker, he was a "supervisor-shoemaker." If he was a doctor, he was a supervisor-doctor. I remember my first English teacher in America once asking her students, "Why have things turned out so badly in Russia?" And I replied, using whatever bad English I had at the time: "Because all the supervisors have left."

Our Italian friends tried to talk us into staying in Italy. One of them owned a photo shop. He often visited us and heard me play. There was a man who belonged to Italian high society. The man owned an enormous estate, as well as coffee plantations in Brazil. He had graduated from the conservatory in Rome and considered himself an artist. He was a painter and a hunter. Anyway, he invited us to his home for dinner one evening. I'll never forget his mansion—all that land, a huge lake with white swans. He greeted us wearing tall leather boots and a hunter's hat with a feather—an artistic look. Two tables were set up: one was for his wife, the woman who had introduced us, some other couple, and my husband; the second table was for himself and me. There were two servants to take care of us. The women were all wrapped in white sheets, like tunics. After dinner, he took a brush and began to paint these sheets, their dresses. I felt as if I were in a Fellini movie, only this was much more ridiculous. After he finished painting the dresses, he told me, "Well, now, we can play some music." He sat at the piano. I took my violin. I thought

I'd choke with laughter, but I had to accompany him. The women in painted dresses were sitting at his feet.

Eventually, we arrived in New York and settled in Brooklyn. We had friends living in Brooklyn, and they found us an apartment. Compared to our tiny apartment in Kiev, it seemed like paradise. Two of my cousins were born here, both doctors. Their father was the only one in the family who had emigrated to America before the Revolution. After he had immigrated, one of his sisters wrote him about how hard life in Russia was at the time. What she really meant, but couldn't spell out, was the threat of pogroms that was spreading. Her letter may have been a cry for help. But he hadn't understood and wrote back, "Don't think that life in America is easy, it's not." Five months later she was killed, buried alive with her five small sons. And he bore a burden of guilt throughout his entire life. "If at any time someone from Russia tells you that life in Russia is hard," he told his sons, "don't respond that it's hard here, too. Because what they mean by 'hard' is an entirely different thing."

My cousins are wonderful people and they did their best to help us. I don't think they understood precisely what we were going through. Many Soviet people, when they come to America, are very needy. So I think they were scared a bit. But now, they're the ones who keep calling us; inviting us over, asking why we don't call them. Now they eagerly follow my tours with the orchestra.

From the beginning, I decided that I'd never be on welfare. I realized that if I said to myself, even just once, "Come on, relax, there's nothing bad about it," there would be no way out. I often recalled this Russian folktale about two frogs who fell into a milk jar. One of them gave up immediately, saying, "There is nothing I can do," and she drowned. The other started moving around, trying to get out, until she whipped the milk into butter. I wanted to be like this other frog. I couldn't whip the butter yet, and I may never do it, but at least I'm trying.

I remember my first job in America. I was supposed to hand out flyers on the bridge, above the Battery Tunnel. My English wasn't great at the time. I was supposed to pass out flyers to truck drivers. But I had never driven a car in my life. I couldn't tell a truck from a cab. My supervisor, an Indian guy, obviously didn't trust me very much. He stood next to me on this bridge, watching what I did. One time, a small car stopped next to me. It was so small that even I was able to notice it wasn't a truck. The driver asked me, "Can I have this paper?" And I said, "No, this is only for the truck drivers." He reached into his pocket. During the training session, we had all been warned that if somebody didn't want a flyer, we should never insist, because he could draw a pistol and shoot. So, when I saw that driver reaching for something in his pocket, I felt funny. But what he took out was a quarter. He handed it to me and said, "Lady, I'm giving you a good-citizen price. Take it and give me the paper." So I took the twenty-five cents and gave him the flyer.

When I turned around, I saw the Indian guy laughing so hard he had to hold his stomach. Then he asked me, in this quiet, almost intimate voice: "Are you Jewish?" "How do you know?" I answered. "Only a Jewish person can sell something that nobody wants to take for free," he said, adding: "If you could sell this piece of paper, you will never be without a job."

That's another thing I came to realize: if you do something professionally, you've got to be paid for it. Otherwise, people don't take you seriously. In my first year here, I didn't understand it. I remember one day walking down the street in Brooklyn, carrying my instrument. A man approached and introduced himself as the director of a school orchestra. He asked me to play for the school but said he couldn't pay me: the school had no money and was trying to raise funds for its music program. I agreed. My husband and I gave a concert. The principal of the school was there, along with some people from the Board of Education. After the concert, they kept thanking and hugging me. A year later, an old friend told me that he had gotten a call from that school. They were looking for professional musicians who lived in Brooklyn. About a year earlier, they told him, two people had come to play in their school, and the concert helped them to raise money for the music program. But now that they could pay, they wanted professionals, not people from the street.

That taught us a good lesson. In Russia we had gotten used to barter: you don't pay the doctor for treating you and he doesn't pay you for playing the violin. Or a neighbor asks you to give music lessons to her son, and you refuse the money; so she brings you a box of chocolates instead. But here it's different: if you don't accept money, then people will think you're not a professional musician. The more money you take, the better they think that you play.

I never stopped practicing. And then I met a woman, an organist. She suggested that we ask the Chamber Music Society to arrange a concert for us. They asked us for a tape, a professional recording. The recording was very expensive, fifty dollars for an hour of work. For me, at the time, it was a lot of money. But we agreed and decided to share the cost. We found a sound engineer who had a studio, a Russian who had lived here for seventeen years. I'll be grateful to him for the rest of my life—and my future life, too. Everything good that happened to me in the next five years, I owe to him. We had arranged to make the recording in a small church in Queens.

My friend was playing the organ; I was playing viola d'amore. We had hoped to finish recording in an hour, playing nonstop, so that it wouldn't cost more than fifty dollars. As soon as we began to play, he stopped us and asked for my name. "You don't have to pay me anything, Mela," he said. "I'll pay you, just to hear you play." So we made the recording and sent it to the manager of the Chamber Music Society. Of course, he never even listened to the tape.

But I was lucky. It happened that this sound engineer, Misha Liberman, was listening to the tape in his studio when he had a visit from the orchestra conductor that I'm working with now. The conductor heard the tape and asked who it was. Misha told him about me. The conductor said, "I would like to meet this woman." And we met. Because I played the viola d'amore on the tape, he was convinced I was a violist. "I'm very impressed with your playing," he said. "Would you play just a few notes for me?" And I did. After I had finished, he asked me to play with his orchestra in two weeks. It was the Philharmonia Virtuosi, one of the finest chamber orchestras in New York. I hadn't told him I could play the violin.

I gave solo concerts, playing both viola and viola d'amore. But one day—the way it happens in Hollywood—the concertmaster became sick, and there was nobody to play first violin. "It's too bad you don't play the violin," the conductor said. And I replied, "Of course I play the violin." He was so surprised that I'd kept it a secret for two years. But I couldn't tell him any sooner. Competition was so intense among the musicians, and I felt I was, well, too strong for them. I couldn't just say, "Here I am, and I can play violin and viola and viola d'amore." They would have killed me. You have to respect the rules, especially if you're in another country. Anyway, it has worked out well. I've been playing with the Philharmonia Virtuosi for five years now.

What I learned in this country is that one has to work hard in order to achieve something. Another thing I learned is that so much is left to chance—as Americans put it, "Being in the right place at the right time." Because the competition is so tough, being good at something is not always good enough.

I travel a lot now, touring with the orchestra. We've been to the most remote parts of the world. What we've seen in these past five years is enough to last a couple of lives. So I don't have any regrets. Still, I miss Russia terribly. I miss the snow especially. But I have a house in Canada now. I went to Canada two years ago and found this house on an island. Suddenly, there was everything I remembered so well from my childhood—only here it wasn't scary. I decided it was time to stop being frightened. There is always a place for snow in your life. It doesn't have to be in Russia.

SOURCE: *Red Blues: Voices from the Last Wave of Russian Immigrants*, edited by Dennis Shasha and Marina Shron. Used with permission by Lynne Rienner Publishers, Inc.

# FIROOZEH DUMAS

*Funny in Farsi: The "F Word"*
(Iran; 2003)

*Born in 1965, Firoozeh Dumas (her married name), is the daughter of an Iranian engineer who brought his family to the United States for two years in the early 1970s. The family emigrated for good when she was nine. Her memoir,* Funny in Farsi: A Memoir of Growing Up Iranian in America, *is a collection of touching and comical essays about her family's experiences as immigrants.*

My cousin's name, Farbod, means "Greatness." When he moved to America, all the kids called him "Farthead." My brother Farshid ("He Who Enlightens") became "Fartshit." The name of my friend Neggar means "Beloved," although it can be more accurately translated as "She Whose Name Almost Incites Riots." Her brother Arash ("Giver") initially couldn't understand why every time he'd say his name, people would laugh and ask him if he itched.

All of us immigrants knew that moving to America would be fraught with challenges, but none of us thought that our names would be such an obstacle. How could our parents have ever imagined that someday we would end up in a country where monosyllabic names reign supreme, a land where "William" is shortened to "Bill," where "Susan" becomes "Sue," and "Richard" somehow evolves into "Dick"? America is a great country, but nobody without a mask and a cape has a $z$ in his name. And have Americans ever realized the great scope of the guttural sounds they're missing? Okay, so it has to do with linguistic roots, but I do believe this would be a richer country if all Americans could do a little tongue aerobics and learn to pronounce the "kh," a sound more commonly associated in this culture with phlegm, or "gh," the sound usually made by actors in the final moments of a choking scene. It's like adding a few new spices to the kitchen pantry. Move over, cinnamon and nutmeg, make way for cardamom and sumac.

Exotic analogies aside, having a foreign name in this land of Joes and Marys is a pain in the spice cabinet. When I was twelve, I decided to simplify my life by adding an American middle name. This decision serves as proof that sometimes simplifying one's life in the short run only complicates it in the long run.

My name, Firoozeh, chosen by my mother, means "Turquoise" in Farsi. In America, it means "Unpronounceable" or "I'm Not Going to Talk to You Because I Cannot Possibly Learn Your Name and I Just Don't Want to Have to Ask You Again and Again Because You'll Think I'm Dumb or You Might Get Upset or Something." My father, incidentally, had wanted to name me Sara. I do wish he had won that argument.

To strengthen my decision to add an American name, I had just finished fifth grade in Whittier, where all the kids incessantly called me "Ferocious." That summer, my family moved to Newport Beach, where I looked forward to starting a new life. I wanted to be a kid with a name that didn't draw so much attention, a name that didn't come with a built-in inquisition as to when and why I had moved to America and how was it that I spoke English without an accent and was I planning on going back and what did I think of America?

My last name didn't help any. I can't mention my maiden name, because:

"Dad, I'm writing a memoir."

"Great! Just don't mention our name."

Suffice it to say that, with eight letters, including a z, and four syllables, my last name is as difficult and foreign as my first. My first and last name together generally served the same person as a high brick wall. There was one exception to this rule. In Berkeley, and only in Berkeley, my name drew people like flies to baklava. These were usually people named Amaryllis or Chrysanthemum, types who vacationed in Costa Rica and to whom lentils described a type of burger. These folks were probably not the pride of Poughkeepsie, but they were refreshingly nonjudgmental.

When I announced to my family that I wanted to add an American name, they reacted with their usual laughter. Never one to let mockery or good judgment stand in my way, I proceeded to ask for suggestions. My father suggested "Fifi." Had I had a special affinity for French poodles or been considering a career in prostitution, I would've gone with that one. My mom suggested "Farah," a name easier than "Firoozeh" yet still Iranian. Her reasoning made sense, except that Farrah Fawcett was at the height of her popularity and I didn't want to be associated with somebody whose poster hung in every postpubescent boy's bedroom. We couldn't think of any American names beginning with *F*, so we moved on to *J*, the first letter of our last name. I don't know why we limited ourselves to names beginning with my initials, but it made sense at that moment, perhaps by the logic employed moments before bungee jumping. I finally chose the name "Julie" mainly for its simplicity. My brothers, Farid and Farshid, thought that adding an American name was totally stupid. They later became Fred and Sean.

That same afternoon, our doorbell rang. It was our new next-door neighbor, a friendly girl my age named Julie. She asked me my name and after a moment of hesitation, I introduced myself as Julie. "What a coincidence!" she said. I didn't mention that I had been Julie for only half an hour.

Thus I started sixth grade with my new, easy name and life became infinitely simpler. People actually remembered my name, which was an entirely refreshing new sensation. All was well until the Iranian Revolution, when I found myself with a new set of problems. Because I spoke English without an accent and was known as Julie, people assumed I was American. This meant that I was often privy to their real feelings about those "damn I-raynians." It was like having those X-ray glasses that let you see people undressed, except that what I was seeing was far uglier than people's underwear. It dawned on me that these people would have probably never invited me to their house had they known me as Firoozeh. I felt like a fake.

When I went to college, I eventually went back to using my real name. All was well until I graduated and started looking for a job. Even though I had graduated with honors from UC-Berkeley, I couldn't get a single interview. I was guilty of being a humanities major, but I began to suspect that there was more to my problems. After three months of rejections, I added "Julie" to my resume. Call it coincidence, but the job offers started coming in. Perhaps it's the same kind of coincidence that keeps African Americans from getting cabs in New York.

Once I got married, my name became Julie Dumas. I went from having an identifiably "ethnic" name to having ancestors who wore clogs. My family and non-American friends continued calling me Firoozeh, while my coworkers and American friends called me Julie.

My life became one big knot, especially when friends who knew me as Julie met friends who knew me as Firoozeh. I felt like those characters in soap operas who have an evil twin. The two, of course, can never be in the same room, since they're played by the same person, a struggling actress who wears a wig to play one of the twins and dreams of moving on to bigger and better roles. I couldn't blame my mess on a screenwriter; it was my own doing.

I decided to untangle the knot once and for all by going back to my real name. By then, I was a stay-at-home mom, so I really didn't care whether people remembered my name or gave me job interviews. Besides, most of the people I dealt with were in diapers and were in no position to judge. I was also living in Silicon Valley, an area filled with people named Rajeev, Avishai, and Insook.

Every once in a while, though, somebody comes up with a new permutation and I am once again reminded that I am an immigrant with a foreign name. I recently went to have blood drawn for a physical exam. The waiting room for blood work at our local medical clinic is in the basement of the building, and no matter how early one arrives for an appointment, forty coughing wheezing people have gotten there first. Apart from reading *Golf Digest* and *Popular Mechanics*, there isn't much to do except guess the number of contagious diseases represented in the windowless room. Every ten minutes, a name is called and everyone looks to see which cough matches that name. As I waited patiently, the receptionist called out, "Fritzy! Fritzy!" Everyone looked around, but no one stood up. Usually, if I'm waiting to be called by someone who doesn't know me, I will respond to just about any name starting with an *F*. Having been called Froozy, Frizzy, Fiorucci, and Frooz and just plain "Uhhhh . . . ," I am highly accommodating. I did not, however, respond to "Fritzy" because there is, as far as I know, no *t* in my name. The receptionist tried again, "Fritzy, Fritzy DumbAss." As I stood up to this most linguistically original version of my name, I could feel all eyes upon me. The room was momentarily silent as all of these sick people sat united in a moment of gratitude for their own names.

Despite a few exceptions, I have found that Americans are now far more willing to learn new names, just as they're far more willing to try new ethnic foods. Of course, some people just don't like to learn. One mom at my children's school adamantly refused to learn my "impossible" name and instead settled on calling me "F Word." She was recently transferred to New York where, from what I've heard, she might meet an immigrant or two and, who knows, she just might have to make some room in her spice cabinet.

# JUNOT DÍAZ

*Homecoming with Turtle*
(Dominican Republic; 2004)

*Junot Díaz (born in 1968) is a professor at the Massachusetts Institute of Technology. He came with his mother and siblings to New Jersey in 1974 to join his father, who had moved to New York to find work. Díaz is the author of* Drown *(1996), a book of short fiction; his novel* The Brief Wondrous Life of Oscar Wao *(2008) won the Pulitzer Prize. This essay tells the story of his "homecoming" to the Dominican Republic amid a bad fight with a girlfriend.*

That summer! Eleven years ago, and I still remember every bit of it. Me and the girlfriend had decided to spend our vacation in Santo Domingo, a big milestone for me, one of the biggest, really: my first time "home" in nearly twenty years. (Blame it on certain "irregularities" in paperwork, blame it on my threadbare finances, blame it on me.) The trip was to accomplish many things. It would end my exile—what Salman Rushdie has famously called one's dreams of glorious return; it would plug me back into that island world, which I'd almost forgotten, closing a circle that had opened with my family's immigration to New Jersey, when I was six years old; and it would improve my Spanish. As in Tom Waits's song "Step Right Up," this trip would be and would fix everything.

Maybe if I hadn't had such high expectations everything would have turned out better. Who knows? What I can say is that the bad luck started early. Two weeks before the departure date, my novia found out that I'd cheated on her a couple of months earlier. Apparently, my ex-sucia had heard about our planned trip from a mutual friend and decided in a fit of vengeance, jealousy, justice, cruelty, transparency (please pick one) to give us an early bon-voyage gift: an "anonymous" letter to my novia that revealed my infidelities in excruciating detail (where do women get these memories?). I won't describe the lío me and the novia got into over that letter, or the crusade I had to launch to keep her from dumping me and the trip altogether. In brief, I begged and promised and wheedled, and two weeks later we were touching down on the island of Hispaniola. What do I remember? Holding hands awkwardly while everybody else clapped and the fields outside La Capital burned. How did I feel? All I will say is that if you fused the instant when heartbreak occurs to the instant when one falls in love and shot that concoction straight into your brain stem you might have a sense of what it felt like for me to be back "home."

As for me and the novia, our first week wasn't too bad. In one of those weird details that you just couldn't make up, before leaving the States we had volunteered to spend a week in the Dominican Republic helping a group of American dentists who were on a good-will mission. We would be translating for them and handing them elevators and forceps and generally making ourselves useful. Even with the advantage of hindsight, I can't figure out why I thought this was a good way to kick off a homecoming, but that's just how we thought back then. We were young. We had ideals.

Our group of five dentists and five assistants treated roughly fourteen hundred kids from some of the poorest barrios in the city of La Romana (which is, ironically, the sugar capital of the D.R.). We weren't practicing the kind of dentistry that First Worlders with insurance are accustomed to, either; this was no-joke Third World care. No time or materials for fillings. If a tooth had a cavity, it would be numbed and pulled, and that was that. Nothing else we can do, our chief explained. That week, I learned more about bombed-out sixes, elevators, and cowhorns than a layperson should ever have to know. Of our group, only me and the novia could be said to speak any Spanish. We worked triage, calming the kids, translating for everybody, and still we had it easy, compared with the dentists. These guys were animals; they worked so hard you would have thought they were in a competition, but by the thousandth patient even their hands started to fail. On the last day, our chief, an immensely compassionate Chinese-American with the forearms of a major-league shortstop, was confronted with one extraction he just couldn't finish. He tried everything to coax that kid's stubborn molar out of its socket, and finally he had to call over another dentist, and together they pulled out a long bloody scimitar of a six. During the ordeal the twelve-year-old patient never complained. ¿Te duele? we asked every couple of minutes, but he would shake his head fiercely, as though the question annoyed him.

Tu eres fuerte, I said, and that might have been the first sentence I had conjugated correctly all week.

No, he said, shaking his beautiful head, no soy.

Of course, we fought, me and the novia—I mean, the needs of the pueblo aside, I had just been bagged fucking some other girl—but it was nothing too outrageous. For one thing, we were too busy wrenching teeth. It wasn't until the mission was over and the dentists had packed their bags and we had headed out into the rest of the island that our real troubles began.

I don't know what I was thinking. Traveling the Third World is challenging enough as it is, but try it with a girlfriend who is only just realizing how badly she's been hurt and a boyfriend who is so worried that he no longer "fits in" at "home" that every little incident and interaction is sifted for rejection, for approval—a boyfriend who is so worried about his busted-up Spanish that he fucks up even more than normal. What I wanted more than anything was to be recognized as the long-lost son I was, but that wasn't going to happen. Not after nearly twenty years. Nobody believed I was Dominican! You? one cabdriver said incredulously, and then turned and laughed. That's doubtful. Instead of being welcomed with open arms, I was overcharged for everything and called un americano. I put us on all the wrong buses. If there was money to lose, I lost it; if there was a bus to catch, I made us miss it, and through some twist of bad luck all my relatives were in the States for the summer. The one relative we did manage to locate, a great-aunt, had been feuding with my moms since 1951, when Mami had accidentally broken her only vase, and my arrival signalled a new stage in the age-old conflict: each morning, she blithely served me and the novia sandwiches completely covered in fire ants.

Now that we didn't have the dentists to hold us back, we basically went off the deep end. We fought about everything: where to eat, what town we should visit, how to pronounce certain words in Spanish. We fought our way across the country: from La Capital to San Cristóbal to Santiago to Puerto Plata and back. It was miserable. If one of us wasn't storming off down the road with a backpack, the other one was trying to hitch a ride to the airport with strangers. Our craziness culminated one night in a hotel in Puerto Plata when the novia woke up and cried out, There's someone in the room! If you've never heard those words being shouted into your dreams, then yours has been a blessed life. I woke in a terrible fright and there he was—the intruder we'd all been waiting for.

It's at a crossroads like this that you really learn something about yourself. There was someone in the room with us, and I could have done any number of things. I could have frozen, I could have screamed for help, I could have fled, but instead I did what my military father had beaten into us during his weekend toughening-up exercises: no matter what the situation, always attack. So I attacked. I threw myself with a roar at the intruder.

It wasn't a person, of course. The intruder was a sea-turtle shell that had been cured and waxed and mounted on the wall. For the sake of national honor, I can say that I acquitted myself well in the battle. I smashed my head clean through the shell, struck the concrete wall, and bounced back to the floor. But instead of staying down I went back at him again, and only then did I realize I was punching décor.

That was the end. A couple of days later, we returned home, defeated, she to New Jersey, me to upstate New York. There was no miracle reconciliation. For a couple of lousy months, the relationship dragged on to its inevitable conclusion, like the heat death of a universe, until finally, having had enough of me, she found herself a new man who she claimed spent more money on her than I did. You're cheap, she asserted, even though I'd used a travel grant and all my savings to pay for our trip. She broke my heart, that girl did, which was a fair trade, considering that I'd broken hers first. But in the end none of it mattered. Even though a dead turtle had kicked my ass, even though my girlfriend had dumped me and a family member had tried to poison me with fire ants, even though I was not granted a glorious return by my homeland, I wasn't entirely crushed. Turned out I wasn't all that easy to crumb; before the year was out, I was back in the D.R., trying again. I kept going back, too. I had committed myself to the lucha, much as I had committed myself to that fight with the damned turtle.

These days, I get around Santo Domingo pretty easily (Los Tres Brazos? La Pintura? Katanga? Capotillo? No sweat), and most people will at least concede that I have some Dominican in me. My Spanish has improved to the point where I can hold forth on any subject—animal, vegetable, mineral—with only one major fuckup per sentence. I'm sure if you'd shown me that future during those last days of my trip with the novia I would have laughed at you. But even in the midst of the rubble there were signs; even on that last day, at the airport, I was still trying to pick my stupid self off the floor. My head was throbbing from the tortual beat-down, and my nose felt as if it had only recently been reattached. (When I got home, my roommate blurted out, without so much as a hello, Fool, what the hell happened to you?) I was beat, truly beat, and, just in case I hadn't got the point, there was nothing cold to drink at the airport. But that didn't stop me from engaging in the debates that were going on all around me regarding the recent election and Santo Domingo's eternal President Balaguer—blind, deaf, and dumb but still jodiendo el pueblo. A present that the United States gave our country after its last military occupation, in 1965—God bless them all! Just before our flight was called, I was asked by a group of locals what I thought of Balaguer. I went into fulmination mode, and said he was a murderer, an election thief, an apologist of genocide, and, of course, a U.S. stooge of the Hosni Mubarak variety.

See, the newspaper seller announced triumphantly. Even the gringo knows.

SOURCE: First published in *The New Yorker* and reprinted by permission of Junot Díaz and Aragi Inc.

# ROSE CASTILLO GUILBAULT

from *Farmworker's Daughter: Growing Up Mexican in America*
(Mexico; 2005)

*The author was born in 1952. This excerpt consists of two chapters ("Leaving the Desert" and "King City") from her memoir.*

We left the desert at dawn. Pink rays of light streaked the steel gray horizon. The air felt cool and still. By mid-morning, heat would drip from the sun, a molten ball in the sky. But at 6 a.m. when we crossed the border from Nogales, Sonora, into Nogales, Arizona, the air smelled sweet and warm like the breath of a waking baby. My mother's friend drove us across the border to the Nogales Greyhound bus depot. He left us standing near a handful of other early-bird travelers. We stood apart. My mother silhouetted against the dung-colored building looked glamorous in her freshly permed hair, stylish polka-dot short-sleeved dress, and black pumps. I wore a cotton pastel dress, white socks, and white Mary Janes. Our finery was new, purchased in the American department store La Vie de Paris in Nogales, Arizona. I loved shopping there. It was clean and cool. I never tired of hearing the piped-in music playing "The Poor People of Paris," which was played over and over. So much so that customers made up silly lyrics, *"Pobre gente de Paris, les cortaron la nariz."* (Poor people of Paris, they cut off their noses.)

My mother pushed me forward, urging me into the dark, cave-like interior of the bus. I climbed the steep steps and stumbled down the wide aisle. She impatiently scooted me into our seats. I yawned and rubbed my eyes. They felt as grainy as the sandy air of a desert morning. I snuggled into what felt like the plushest seat I'd ever sat upon—nothing like the train seats we rode on our frequent visits to see Tia Julia and her family in Vicam.

My mother sat ramrod straight, alert and tense. Outside my window the sky had lost its pink blush and the horizon shimmered with undulating waves of heat. I turned to my mother. She did not notice me, so intense was her stare at the driver who stood casually talking to a passenger in the aisle. I knew he was speaking English, a language neither she nor I spoke or understood. She had not noticed that morning had broken through the dawn. I wanted her to say something about it, as she did about every weather change. The Yaqui Indian servants of her childhood had taught her how to observe nature.

*"Ay, mira, hija,"* she would say, "The moon has a cloud around it. That means rain."

Or, "See the horizon? It's red and glaring. That means tomorrow will be another hot day."

I waited for her to speak, to tell me about the day's weather, about how it would be in California. But when her nervous eyes finally focused on me it was to scold gently. "You should go to sleep now. We have a long way to go."

The driver sat behind the large wheel, and the long bus lurched forward. Soon we were rolling down a smooth road. I shivered from the air conditioner's chilly draft. My mother crossed herself and silently prayed.

After the prayer she sighed deeply. I must have looked concerned because she offered a small, quick smile and put her arm around my shoulder, rubbing me with her hand. Her warmth relaxed my body.

I was too sleepy to watch the moving landscape through the window. The motion made my eyes close involuntarily and I let my head sink into my mother's chest. I inhaled her familiar scent. It was reassuring and secure. She smelled like the desert.

Had I been older I might have shared her anxiety. I might have questioned the wisdom of a newly divorced, uneducated woman with a five-year-old child leaving her family and country in search of a better life. To be such a willing immigrant a person must have great optimism and little to lose. But my mother was leaving behind a great many things. Her family roots ran deep, to the sixteenth century when her Spanish ancestors settled in Batacosa, at the foot of the Sierra Madre. Siblings, aunts, uncles, cousins remained. No other family members lived in the United States, nor did they aspire to. Only our hostess, Rafaela, lived there and she was too distant on the family tree (having married a second or third cousin) to count as real family. It was on the thin thread of her invitation and encouragement to start a new life with her in California that my mother staked our fixture.

As a teenager I once asked my mother why she had left since she always talked about the greatness of Mexico. Maybe she had given up too much to come here, I suggested. She thoughtfully considered what I knew to be an impudent comment, and I immediately felt guilty. She shook her head sadly and looked into space, as if her gaze could travel back in time and pinpoint the precise moment she had made that momentous decision. Her eyes filled with tears—a given whenever she spoke of her life in Mexico or of her deceased mother.

"There was nothing to lose. There was nothing for you and me."

The day we crossed the border into a new country, a new world, my mother was not filled with optimism or the courage that comes from certainty. What I saw in my mother's rigid body and intense eyes was pure fear. Was she reexamining her decision? Whatever her concerns, they kept her tight-lipped and mute, squelching her usual talkative and extroverted personality. I would see this transformation at other times in my life—once on a road trip when the fog was so thick we could not see the road for miles ahead, and another time driving through the curvy, narrow roads of the Rumorosa mountain pass outside Tijuana during a snowstorm.

It was late afternoon when the bus approached the Salinas Valley through country roads. Miles and miles of green hills and valleys surrounded fields planted with a patchwork quilt of crops. White-faced brown cows dotted the hills. We passed towns so small the name was lost in the blink of an eye. Then there were no more towns, only vast fields watered by whirling sprinklers. In the afternoon sun, the water's mist cast hundreds of rainbows. I pressed my nose against the bus window and saw tractors driven by dusty men, dogs running alongside farm trucks, and an occasional child standing by a lonely mailbox, waving energetically as we passed.

"*Ya llegamos, Mami?*" (Are we there yet, Mommy?)

My mother peered over my head, outside the window. "Yes, I think we're almost there."

"It's nice. California looks nice."

My mother nodded and smiled. There was a glimmer in her eyes.

★ ★ ★

We emerged from the bus at the King City depot in late afternoon. The depot was inside a hotel called the El Camino Real, and I guess the "depot" part was the small café attached to it. Then again, it might have been just the bench outside with the Greyhound sign hanging directly overhead. In any case, Rafaela was not there to meet us. We wandered inside the café to wait and order coffee for my mother and

Coca-Cola for me. A couple of leather-faced men sat smoking filter-less cigarettes and drinking inky coffee. They wore jeans and scuffed boots, and stained cowboy hats laid next to their seats.

"American cowboys!" I thought excitedly. Now there really was no doubt we were in the United States!

But even American cowboys couldn't hold my attention long that day. Everything seemed so different—the dark paneled walls, the curious smells, and the inviting room just beyond the doorway. I asked my mother if I could look through the door that led to the hotel sitting area. She seemed tense and nodded absently.

Walking in was like stepping into the frame of a Western movie: worn brown leather couches and chairs were strewn throughout a large, bright room, and murals depicting rodeo scenes graced entire walls. There were huge, ferocious bucking bulls and bowlegged cowboys dressed in leather chaps and tall hats, lassos swirling over their heads, with snorting, rearing horses. Another area featured smoldering iron brands poised in the hands of skinny cowboys aiming toward the backsides of complacent-looking cows.

"There you are!" Rafaela's high-pitched voice broke through my revelry. The tap-tap of her high heels echoed through the empty room as she walked briskly toward us. I noticed her figure-hugging flowered dress and new hairstyle. Red locks were piled high up on her head and not hanging loosely like last time we saw her. My mother followed her, laughing, her face relaxed.

"I'm late because I have so much to do at work! My God, I can barely handle so much work! My waitress quit today!" Her hands fluttered in front of her and I noticed her nails were still long and very red.

"Don't worry, Rafaela. I'll be happy to help out while I'm here," my mother soothed her.

"Oh, what a godsend you are, Maria Luisa! But you've come to change your life and I'm going to help you. You'll see." She winked at my mother and they both giggled. I didn't think what she had said was funny. I figured it was one of those grown-up inside jokes they never wanted to explain if you asked.

Driving to Rafaela's house, King City revealed itself like a penny arcade film. Pastel-hued houses with green lawns and borders of color-coordinated flowers flew by replaced in the next frame by wide streets lined with mulberry trees and sprawling sycamores, followed by a sidewalk scene of blond-headed children balancing ice-cream cones on two-wheeled bicycles. I rolled down my car window and was rewarded with the sweet fragrance of newly cut grass. It smelled fresh and clean, so different from the dusty aroma of the desert. I gulped air, trying to absorb its essence into my pores before the scent faded in the breeze.

Rafaela's house was a white clapboard bungalow surrounded by pretty flowers she called "daisies." I decided these daisies were the prettiest flowers with the nicest name I'd ever known. Inside, the house was very small, just a bedroom, bathroom, and kitchenette. From the window we could see a bigger house with a large yard surrounding it. Rafaela's daughter lived there with her husband. The house belonged to Rafaela too, but she said her daughter was going to start a family and needed more space than she did.

"It's just more to clean. Besides, I spend so much time at work. I just come here to sleep some nights."

"Don't worry, Rafaela, we won't be in your way. We'll help you out," my mother assured her.

The next day we started a pattern that remained during our stay with Rafaela. We'd leave early in the morning to her restaurant/bar, where we'd spend all day. Lunch was pretty slow, most of the customers came for drinks, some for dinner. Early on Rafaela would take advantage of the afternoon doldrums to take us calling on her relatives in town. There were Mike and Estela, Mila and Manuel, and Luz and Leopoldo. They were all from the Sonora and all interrelated. They seemed very old to me and very dull. Mike and Estela already had grandchildren. Mila and Manuel would have if they'd had children of their own. Only Luz and Leo were still raising a family, four daughters and one son. Their youngest daughter was only four years older than I. Theirs was the liveliest house, the one I liked visiting the best even though the older girls intimidated me.

My mother was pleased to find *gente decente* so far away in this small town in the middle of California's Salinas Valley. She noted that they all owned their homes. Owning a home was my mother's greatest dream.

"There's much to like about King City," she sighed one night as we lay together in Rafaela's guest bed, drifting off to sleep.

* * *

Rafaela was proud of her restaurant. It was the only place in town that served Mexican food.

In reality the place was no more than a hole in the wall, more bar than restaurant. A screen divided the bar stools from the handful of tables covered with brightly flowered oilcloth. It drew a steady stream of customers: Mexican farmworkers nostalgic for home cooking and American ranchers who liked drinking the beer more than eating the food.

My mother called the American customers "los caboys." They were coarse, blunt-talking farmers, ranchers, or ranch hands. And they liked flirting with her.

Rafaela noticed. Her gimlet eyes never missed anything.

"That's what you need to do, Maria Luisa," she said decisively one night as they smoked their last cigarette before bedtime. "You must marry an American. It's your best chance for a good life here."

My mother looked down. "But I can't even understand what they're saying to me."

"You'll learn English. Look, all the Mexican men here are braceros. There's no future for someone like you with one."

My mother tried to take Rafaela's advice. We had quickly learned that Rafaela expected everyone to do as she told them. The cook didn't and left soon after another waitress.

My mother's increased time in the restaurant provided more time for her conversations with the customers, who were definitely interested in her. But it was Rafaela's final word that gave approval as to who my mother would go on a date with and who she had to turn down.

"He's got a nice car and house. No, he's lazy and drinks too much. Well, he's divorced but so what, so are you."

My mother had no problem being asked out on dates. The complication was that she always brought me along. That was the way it was done in Mexico. We soon found out why it was not done in the United States.

Mr. Brown had a nice, new four-door sedan and seemed to indulge her requirement that I come on their first date. I sat in the back and stared at his half-dollar-sized bald spot. That's about all I remember of the first time. Soon more dates followed.

"Do you like Mr. Brown?" she asked me.

"I guess so," I shrugged.'

Her face fell.

"He's nice. He brings me candy bars sometimes," I quickly added. I didn't want to hurt my mother's feelings if she really liked Mr.

Brown, and I wasn't certain what I thought about him. Sometimes I felt he was nice to me just to please my mother. But who could be sure about anything? Between his broken Spanish and my mother's barely existent English, nobody understood anybody anyway.

It was not long before things became clear. It started like any other date. Mr. Brown came in his cream-colored sedan to pick up my mother at Rafaela's house. When she opened the door Mr. Brown grinned and pinned a corsage to her dress. She blushed with pleasure. I stepped out behind the door, grinning and ready to go with my coat over my arm.

His small eyes narrowed at me but he turned to my mother and half-whispered in his halting Spanish, "We're going to be a little late tonight. After dinner I thought we'd go for a ride. It'll be tiring for the little girl."

"It's okay, she'll be fine with us," my mother smiled reassuringly.

"I'm sure Rafaela can take care of her tonight, Maria," Mr. Brown persisted.

But my mother had already started out the door with me in tow. Mr. Brown didn't realize that my mother never left me in anybody's care. We had never been separated since I was born.

Mr. Brown took a deep breath and briskly walked toward us.

It was a fine night. We had a lovely dinner and afterward Mr. Brown insisted on going for that little ride in the country. My mother looked uncomfortable.

"I think it's late . . ." she started to say.

"No, no, Maria. I told you it was part of our evening. That's why I suggested *la nina* stay home tonight."

My mother forced a tight smile.

We drove onto a country lane. The road was very dark; only the car lights could be seen. In the front seat Mr. Brown reached over and pulled my mother to him. She demurred. Then he tried to kiss her, as if I couldn't see just because it was dark and I was in the back seat. She pushed him away, which caused the car to swerve. I sensed her fear and reached up and turned on the overhead light.

"Turn that off," scolded Mr. Brown. But I didn't know how.

He swung around, feeling the buttons until he turned the light off.

Once again in the darkness he tried to grab my mother. This time she cried an audible "No!" and once again I jumped up and turned on the light.

Mr. Brown's face was red, contorted with anger.

"You brat," he breathed between clenched teeth, swatting the air around me. I shrank away, digging my back into the seat as far as I could, more amazed than scared.

Suddenly my mother's voice demanded loudly and clearly, "Go home now. Home now, Bill."

Mr. Brown was remorseful the next day and came by the restaurant to patch things up with my mother. She would have none of him.

"He would punish her by hitting her," I heard her say to Rafaela. "I could never give her that kind of father."

SOURCE: *Farmworker's Daughter: Growing Up Mexican in America* by Rose Castillo Guilbault, published by Heyday Books. Permission through Copyright Clearance Center.

# ORUBBA ALMANSOURI

*University of Kitchen*
(Yemen; 2009)

*Almansouri was a sixteen-year-old high school student in New York City when she wrote this essay, first published in a magazine for and about public school students,* New Youth Connections. *She went on to attend the City College of New York.*

"We're halfway through the summer. Are we going to New York or what?" I asked my older sister Yasmin. She had come to visit us at our house back in my country, Yemen. We were in the room we'd shared until she got married and moved away.

"Do you really want to go?" she replied, opening the Kit Kat bar she had in her hand.

"Yes and no," I answered as I lay down on my bed. "I want to stay here for you and all our extended family, but I also want to see Dad and New York City."

"What's the rush, then? It's not like you're going to school when you get there," she said.

In my family, most men believe that the best place for a woman is in the house and the best job for us women is to cook, clean and raise a family. Many girls in my family—including Yasmin—stop going to school before high school, and none have gone to college. Girls live with their families until they are 15 or a little older, then it's time to say goodbye to being single and hello to marriage.

My religion (Islam) is not against girls being educated. In fact our Prophet Mohammed, may peace be upon him, said that we should seek education even if we have to go to China for it. The problem isn't my culture either, since many Yemeni girls are educated and have jobs. Where my family's tradition came from, I don't know. But so far, no one has broken it.

I never imagined my destiny would be any different. In my country I was an excellent student and teachers loved me. In 7th grade, I

216

was first in my class. They put my name in big letters on a piece of paper and hung it up in the main hallway. I felt so proud of myself.

I didn't mind leaving school at any time, though, because I knew the path girls in my family followed and I didn't expect anything else. When we came to the United States the first time (when I was five—we stayed for a few years), my older sisters were teenagers and they didn't get a chance to go to school, even though they really wanted to go and learn English. So when I was 14 years old and I heard that we were moving back to the U.S., I figured I wouldn't be going to school anymore.

Then we got to New York, and my dad announced he was planning to enroll my sister Lebeya and me in school. I was surprised. From what I used to see on TV, American high schools were another planet compared to schools in Yemen. I wasn't used to going to school with boys, or talking to them. In fact, I was a little worried: I'd heard that many Yemeni students who go to American high schools start to do what the other kids are doing, like having relationships and even drinking, neither of which is allowed by my religion. I'd expected my dad would want to keep my sister and me away from this environment. (My mom wants us to be educated, as she never had the chance to be, but like most Yemeni women she follows her husband's decisions.)

But my dad was determined. When my oldest sisters didn't go to school in New York, that affected their lives and his. They couldn't go out alone because they didn't understand English and couldn't communicate. My dad had to translate for them at doctors' appointments. When we moved to New York, he said putting my sister and me in school would help us become independent so we could help ourselves when necessary.

For my part, I decided that since I had the chance to go to school, I would definitely take it. Today my sisters are both married and have children sweet as honey, but they still wish they had gone to school here and learned to speak English. I saw from my sisters' experience that education was the best thing for me, and I felt that going to school might be fun and a way to get out of the house. I had no idea what it would become to me.

While we were getting records and report cards sent from Yemen to New York so my sister and I could enroll here, the men in my extended family started telling my dad that we would get ourselves into trouble and hurt the family's reputation. They thought that high school in America would Americanize us, causing us to drop the traditions we'd been learning our entire lives and pick up others.

One day my dad was on the phone with one of my cousins and I heard some of my dad's replies. (It's not my fault he thought that I was sleeping when I wasn't.) They went like this:

"They are my daughters and I have raised them right. I know what is good for them."

"It's none of your business."

"I don't care what they say, I have listened to you guys once and I won't make that mistake again."

After I heard that, I was saying to myself, "Way to go, Dad!" I saw my father as someone who is ready to make a change and someone who really cares about his daughters' education; I saw him in a way that made me feel proud to be the daughter of Ali Almansouri. I knew that my dad had put all his trust in us and this made me want to be on my best behavior.

My first day at Brooklyn International High School was scary because I was starting 9th grade at the end of September and I was the new girl. I felt lonely at first, but luckily my English was OK from living here as a kid. By second period I'd talked to two Hispanic girls and we became friends. My teachers were so nice to me; they helped me when I needed help and they always asked me how I was doing. I began to love school once again. I worked hard and got excellent grades. My classmates started telling me, "You're so smart."

I don't believe that I'm as smart as they say, but I do believe that I am clever. Because I did well, ideas of actually graduating started coming into my head. My love for school grew, especially when I learned new things, went on trips or met new friends.

"You know that I will be the first girl from our family to actually go to college," I said one day to my sisters and a group of other girls, while we were sitting together talking.

"Yeah, and you'll go to the University of Kitchen," my younger cousin said.

"And earn your cooking degree," my sister added.

Then they all started laughing, including me. "You'll see when I become the first Almansouri girl to go to college and break the 'girls don't go to college' rule," I said. "You'll see what I will do."

The truth is, though, that there is always a question mark over my future. In spite of the things I overheard my dad say on the phone, his decisions about my future are not all made yet. My dad doesn't really follow up on my schoolwork, and when opportunities come up—like leadership programs, after-school activities or writing for New Youth Connections—it's not easily that he lets me participate.

I think that even though he put me in school, sometimes he still thinks the way other men in my family do. This worries me, because it makes me think he may not allow me to finish the path that he let me start. However, if I give him a great speech about why he should let me do some extracurricular thing, and if I'm persistent, he usually gives in. I think that when I put it in his head that I can benefit a lot from these things, he sees it, and that gives me hope for the future.

My being allowed to finish high school and go to college depends on two people: Dad and me. I will never disobey him because he is everything to me. My basic hope is that we don't go back to Yemen before I graduate from high school. Then, if my dad lets me, I'd prefer to put off marriage until I am settled in college.

What will actually happen, I don't know. My dad hasn't told me what he's thinking. Even though I hate not knowing what's going to be next, in another way I don't want the topic to come up yet. I'm afraid of the answer I'll get, in case it's a "no." Anyway, as they say, you have to walk up the ladder step by step or you'll fall down.

When I'm feeling hopeful, I think my dad will let me go to college. I want to attend a good one like Columbia University, major in English or journalism and also study biology. I see my future as a finishing line with red and white stripes, and I see myself crossing the line, then getting my prize—in other words, working in a career and feeling true power and independence. I also want to feel useful to the world and to people around me. I want to learn more and be an educated person.

Sometimes, though, I feel that everything I do is for no reason and that I will never be able to go to college or even finish high school. I worry that if I do graduate from high school, my dad will say, "I already let you finish high school and we don't have women who go to college in this family." I worry about the pressure that will be on him if he does let me go to college. Our family made such a big deal about us going to high school, I can't imagine what they would say about college.

When I hear things like, "Look—girls your age are getting married and soon it will be your turn," those comments are like rockets landing in my ears. I find a place to be alone and think to myself, "All this hard work, these top grades, these compliments, for what? For me to remember when I'm seasoning the soup. Why did they put me in the race when I had no interest in participating? They put the idea in my head, made me like it and actually work toward something—all so that when I reach the finish line they'll tell me I can't cross it."

I imagine watching others cross the line without me, and hunt myself down for all the time I spent dreaming of things I want to accomplish. "Maybe it's not time, Orubba," I think. "Maybe the girl that will break your family's record hasn't been born yet."

With that I cry myself to sleep. Sometimes I even have nightmares about not finishing high school. A lot of people think that it's no big deal; I'll get married and my husband will give me everything I need. But that's not enough for me because I want my life to have different flavors and taste them all, not just repeat the same flavor over and over every day. I also want to feel that I'm prepared if something happens to my husband. How will I feed my children? I want to have a weapon in my hand and education is one weapon that never hurts anyone, but actually helps.

In Yemen, I always thought that going to college was a good thing for girls, but I didn't feel envious of the girls from other families who could go. Since I came to the U.S., though, I have been thinking more about my future and I want more out of life. Because I see college as a possibility for me, but not a sure thing, today I feel envious toward Yemeni girls who know they can go to college.

Sometimes I get mad that my family keeps on pushing boys to go to college, even though most of them don't have any interest, while some of us girls are ready to work for it and never get a chance. Other times, I tell myself that whatever education I end up with is better than nothing. I'm even a little afraid of going to college in case I fail. I'm torn between two things, but the tear is not straight down the middle. I'm happy that my obsession with success is greater than my worries.

Now I'm a junior, my grades are still excellent, and my desire to live my dream is greater than ever. I agree with some of my family's traditions, like girls not going out alone and not sleeping at anyone's house outside the family. But the education issue is too much. If they give all us girls a chance and support us, we can help our family reach higher than ever before. If I go to college, I'll open a path and be a role model for future generations of girls in the family, teaching them not to give up.